For Wilhelm F.H. Nicolaisen

Contents

[Color illustrations follow page 144]

A craft, a house, a food, that comes from one's hands or heart, one's shared experience with other people in a community, one's learned ideas and symbols, visibly connects persons and groups to society and to the reality around them. That interconnection is material culture. Material culture is made up of tangible things crafted, shaped, altered, and used across time and across space. It is inherently personal and social, mental and physical. It is art, architecture, food, clothing, and furnishing. But more so, it is the weave of these objects in the everyday lives of individuals and communities. It is the migration and settlement, custom and practice, production and consumption that is American history and culture. It is the gestures and processes that extend ideas and feelings into three-dimensional form.

—Simon J. Bronner, *American Material Culture and Folklife*

Preface

My subject is the material life of Americans. I am concerned with their bonds to the things around them—houses, art, food—and the ways those things are produced and consumed. Often they are so immediate, so worldly, that they escape the analysis reserved for literature, yet their very worldliness connects them directly to the society we live in. My approach to the subject is to describe things in action, to analyze them as parts of cultural scenes where actors can be identified. In events such as the building of a brick house on Main Street where frame once predominated or the preparation of a soup not found on grocery shelves, I find parables with broader meaning. Central to the moral is the often uneasy relation of a dominant electronic mass society with its sense of handwrought folk tradition.

The title of this book speaks the theme of objects having physical and intellectual consequences. "Grasping," basic to material life, is literally a physical action of touching an object, and figuratively it is an intellectual action of perceiving an underlying idea and comprehending application. "Things" has its levels of meanings, too. It can refer to specific items and it can extend to a general reference to our surroundings. "Grasping Things" brings out the active physical and intellectual, specific and general, meanings that Americans bring to their objects.

I rely on the evidence of history and culture. I trace changes in the relation of folk and mass society in the last century when Americans became particularly aware of their transformation to a mass society. Against this historical background, I examine small scenes, slices of life, where the symbolic power of folk material culture to a larger society can be made apparent. The scenes cover personal worlds within American society, worlds framed by family, friends, and community. As organizations in relation to a larger whole, those worlds have their politics framed by history and culture. It is not a politics of who gets what but a cultural politics of what is made and what is made of it.

I look at the things of tradition because they commonly force reactions from people that tell of cultural values. Invoking the past in the present, calling on local intimacy in a broad commercial world, and usually summoning the touch of handwork in a visual, electronic culture, folk material culture takes on a presence in contemporary life that draws out commentaries on the continuities and changes in society. Behind the commentaries is the question of how such things fit our views. It is a question also of cultural politics.

The scenes I analyze are mostly from Indiana and Pennsylvania, where I have lived and studied between 1977 and 1985. I also bring in fieldwork I completed during that time from Mississippi, Michigan, and New York. Much of this fieldwork was in isolated or lower-class settings, but I also found expressions of middle-class culture and episodes from American community history which have either not been adequately interpreted or have not been given proper attention in American studies. I devote analysis to these events and settings because they deserve more cultural comment than they have been given, and to the relations among the people, things, and places I encountered because I want to make analysis more integrative in material culture and folklore than it has been. Taken together, my interpretations are meant as contributions to American cultural criticism, especially as the interpretations deal with American attitudes toward modernism and materialism.

Although some of the places I have been may not be familiar to you and the names I mention do not make headlines, the lessons from them should come close to home. The places are real, as are the lives described, but some names are not. "Cal," "Anna," and some supporting actors had asked that their real names not be used, and I complied with that request. Their stories remain intact, with an emphasis, as in the other episodes of the book, on their actions and the way things figured in cultural scenes. The scenes show houses, furniture, crafts, art, food, clothing, and books, in towns and cities, galleries and streets. The chapters in which they are found name actions that surround such things: grasping, entering, making, and consuming.

In chapter 1, I give a background in the physical and intellectual foundations of human encounters with objects. I bring out the priority of touch and sight, the sensory basis of material life, in American culture. I discuss objects as extensions of ourselves and as mediators of social relations. I review the premises of folk studies and use them to establish my behavioral analysis of people and their things.

Having established my terms and premises in chapter 1, I move in the rest of the book to different cultural scenes. Each chapter works from a historical problem to a contemporary issue. Although I have a sequence of chapters in mind, it is possible for readers familiar with the background in chapter 1, or eager for my scenes, to review the first chapter later and start with the second chapter.

In chapter 2, I give examples of things people enter and allow to enclose them—houses and rooms. Beginning with Thoreau's familiar rustic cabin and proceeding to the less familiar news of Samuel Harris's imposing brick house on Main Street Indiana in the mid-nineteenth century, I move to the late nineteenth-century urban movements in housing and manners that helped bring a middle-class standard to the places we commonly enter. As examples, I explore suburban housing and the middle-class movement back to the city in the 1980s. Working from Main Street to suburbia, the chapter concludes with Penn Street, where a housepainter called Cal takes center stage.

In chapter 3, I discuss the revealing actions of using our hands to make things, especially as those things relate to makers within traditional communities. I begin with a family's tombstone carving in southern Indiana, move to the painting of an Old Order Mennonite woman, and conclude with the sacred work of a rural woodcarver and an urban mural painter who spark discussion of the symbolism of contemporary religious art. I trace the role of handwork in mass society and I point especially to the climactic connection of the late nineteenth century with the orchestrated rise of mechanized society.

In chapter 4, I tackle the thorny issue of consumption. Consumption, like grasping, has more than one meaning. The first meaning is eating, then comes buying goods and services, and then being absorbed by something. In the chapter I analyze an example of food consumption—turtle soup eating—which has absorbed a rural region, then I provide an example of goods consumption—"folk art" collecting and display—which has absorbed an urban commercial region. This last discussion provides a climax to the book, for it especially demonstrates the relation of subject and object and the conflicts that can arise over things. The chapter also moves toward an ending for a future beginning, since society is quickly becoming more familiar with consumption than with production.

This book is itself a work of material culture, and I extend my gratitude to those who made its production possible. Granting acknowledgments is a chance to deny possessiveness, and I do so freely, while retaining responsibility for my work. The Rockefeller Foundation from 1978 to 1981 helped fund the fieldwork for the Indiana material. A National Endowment for the Humanities fellowship at the Henry Francis du Pont Winterthur Museum in 1984 gave me the opportunity to work on the manuscript in earnest. Kenneth Ames, Barbara Ward, Robert St. George, Elizabeth Cromley, Joseph Ernst, John McIntyre, Ian Quimby, Catherine Hutchins, Neville Thompson, and Patricia Mercer gave me valued encouragement while I was there.

I am grateful to the persons in this book who allowed me to be part of their cultural scenes. In some of my Indiana fieldwork I had companions I want to acknowledge, notably Lil Blemker, Carol Blemker, Warren Roberts, Kathleen Mundell, Elizabeth Mosby Adler, Wendy Shay, and Susan Johnson. In Harrisburg, I was blessed with the friendship and intelligence of Deborah Bowman, Frederick Richmond, Pam deWall, Henry Koretzky, Sean Downey, Jess Dalton, Harry Spector, Beebe Frazer, Karen Healy, Kate Jacoski, and Shalom Staub. My mother can be credited for sincerely caring about my progress on the book, my sister for forcing me away from it once in a while.

Acknowledgment is due to organizations that encouraged me to develop my ideas into lectures and papers which fed into this book. I appreciate the courtesy of the American Folklife Center at the Library of Congress; the University of California at Los Angeles, Center for the Study of Comparative Folklore and Mythology; the Museum of American Folk Art, New York Council on the Humanities; the University of Pennsylvania Folklore and Folklife Department; the Pennsylvania State University Geography Department; the University of Kansas American Studies and Anthropology Departments; the California Folklore Society; and the Pioneer America Society. Portions of chapter 3 are a revision of my article "Investigating Identity and Expression in Folk Art," which appeared in *Winterthur Portfolio,* © 1981 by the Henry Francis du Pont Winterthur Museum, and are reprinted by permission of the publisher.

The staff at the Pennsylvania State University Capitol Campus gave me help and good humor while completing the work, especially photographer Darrell Peterson and secretary Kathy Ritter. Archivist Iris Wood ably worked on the index. I was fortunate to have at Capitol Campus bright students and attentive faculty to give me tough questions. I want to acknowledge professors John Patterson, Sue Samuelson, Irwin Richman, Priscilla Ord, Janet Theophano, William Mahar, and Michael Barton in Humanities; William Henk, Herbert Hunter, James Rooney, Edward Beck, John Teske, Stanley Miller, and James Hudson in Behavioral Sciences; Robert Bresler and Carol Nechemias in Public Policy; Charles Townley, Carolyn Miller, and Ruth Runion in the Library; assistants John Drexler and Juanita Singletary, and graphic artist Shirley Marquet. I would be remiss if I didn't add faculty in political science and history at the State University of New York and Indiana University who gave of their knowledge freely: H.L. Nieburg, Louis Gawthrop, Langdon Wright, Richard Dalfiume, Robert Gunderson, and George Juergens.

Many patient ears in my profession were willing to hear me out and give me their opinions while I wrote this book. My gratitude extends to Warren Roberts, Thomas Schlereth, John Vlach, Beverly Brannan, William McNeil, Elliott Oring, Henry Glassie, Louis C. Jones, Robert Smith, Eugene Metcalf, Yvonne Milspaw, Ronald L. Baker, William Wilson, William Ferris, C. Kurt Dewhurst, Stephen Stern, Marsha MacDowell, John Hasse, and Michael Owen Jones. To this list must be added Richard M. Dorson, who to my regret did not live to see this work completed.

My dedication to Wilhelm Nicolaisen merits explanation. It was his folklore class in my first semester of college that awakened me to a new world of study. What made him really special, however, was the beacon his personality provided for so many young souls. In the many years since then, his teaching and friendship have been my most enduring. My dedication recognizes his inspiration. He is the most deserving recipient I know of "distinguished professor," a title he now bears but which I knew him by long ago.

I finish this preface realizing that I am writing in the very region where two centuries ago, James, the American Farmer of J. Hector St. John Crèvecoeur's classic *Letters from an American Farmer*, asked, "What then is the American, this new man?" His answer, like mine, took in, as he said, this new man's "material difference." Crèvecoeur's subtitle, "Describing Certain Provincial Situations, Manners, and Customs, Not Generally Known; and Conveying Some Idea of the Late and Present Interior Circumstances of the British Colonies in North America," could easily be mine. The book you hold is my "Letters from an American Farmer," now equipped with camera and computer.

1

Grasping Things

TO EXPRESS THEMSELVES people respond quickly with words, but the objects they grasp have more lasting things to say. The object derives power from its fixity. More stable than speech, the object attracts inspection by many senses, especially those of touch and sight. Differences appear in the priority of senses in modern mass society and many older folk societies. Folklorist Alan Dundes made the claim that in modern American culture, vision comes first. He pointed out that in everyday speech, "vision" stands for "understanding." "I see what you mean," "eyewitness," "eye-opener," "insight," and "the mind's eye" are phrases equating sight with proof. In short, "Seeing is believing."[1]

The proverb used to continue with "but feeling's the truth." Despite the common dropping of the second part in modern usage, people in modern culture still rely on touch, for "believing" is not convincing. Sight has become dominant, but it gives surface evidence. It is not objective. Someone may claim that you were "seeing things" or witnessed an "optical illusion." If that claim is true, you are liable to be accused of being "out of touch with reality." Sure facts are tangible, gripping, clinching, and hard. Together, sight and touch provide the basis for grasping things, which is at the foundation of material life. Like mass and folk, touch and sight are not exclusive, although one may dominate and have a function different from the other.

We argue with, and against, words, but find it hard to deny the evidence of tangible things. Setting the pace in 1662 for this attitude, the august Royal Society of London declared its scientific intention of finding "not the Artifice of Words, but a bare knowledge of things." Recall the origin of the phrase "doubting Thomas." According to the Bible, Thomas doubted Jesus Christ's resurrection until he had tactual proof. Until he could put his finger into the print of the nails, he declared, and thrust his hand into Jesus's side, he would not believe. Analogously, "hands-on experience" today is highly valued. Apollo

10's close sighting of the moon failed to satisfy the American public; Neil Armstrong in Apollo 11 captured the imagination of the American public with his walk on the moon. The media glorified his grasp of a terrain at which we could formerly only peer. The rocks Armstrong brought back held a special fascination for the public because they could be touched, literally apprehended firsthand.

The special experience is one that "touches us deeply." Americans may occasionally "follow their nose," but they are chastised for being "as stupid as to be led by the nose." Typically, sight identifies, touch verifies. The sense of touch is connected to the body's largest organ—the skin. Its enclosure of the body and offering of sensitive three-dimensionality make us relate its properties to feelings of wholeness in tangible objects.

Erasmus Darwin in *Zoonomia* (1794) laid down the foundation for the importance of touch. He wrote, "The first ideas we become acquainted with, are those of the sense of touch; for the foetus must experience some varieties of agitation, and exert some muscular action, in the womb; and may with great probability be supposed thus to gain some ideas of its own figure, of that of the uterus, and of the tenacity of the fluid that surrounds it. . . . We acquire our tangible ideas of objects either by the simple pressure of this organ of touch against a solid body, or by moving our organ of touch along the surface of it." To this physiology was later added the psychological impact of "the mind of the skin." Sigmund Freud, for example, regarded the first tactile reactions of sucking by the child as influential in its later sexual development, since sexual activities restore many infantile tactile behaviors.[2]

As children, we learn by grasping things. Psychologists Harriet Rheingold and Carol Eckerman point out that "the infant comes in contact with an increasing number and variety of objects. Through touching them he learns their shapes, dimensions, slopes, edges, and textures. He also fingers, grasps, pushes, and pulls, and thus learns the material variables of heaviness, mass, and rigidity, as well as the changes in visual and auditory stimuli that some objects provide." As children move from place to place, room to room, they learn the position of objects in relation to others. The child "learns the invariant nature of many sources of stimulation. In a word, he learns the properties of the physical world, including the principles of object constancy and the conservation of matter."[3]

Anthropologists looking at cultural development early on saw the connection of the hand, immediately associated with touch, and cultural forms. In 1892, Frank Hamilton Cushing made a case for the importance of "hand-usage" in aboriginal cultures. Counting sys-

Sign for a craft outlet, Lancaster, Pennsylvania

tems, he observed, are commonly based on 10 fingers; one brushes them to confirm a count. In Zuñi, he found temples and ceremonies modeled after the hand. He concluded that "the hand of man has been so intimately associated with the mind of man that it has moulded intangible thoughts no less than the tangible products of his brain."[4]

Ashley Montagu writing in 1971 expanded the investigation of touch's influence into modern culture. He argued that "the impersonal child-rearing practices which have long been the mode in the United States, with the early severance of the mother-child tie, and the separation of mothers and children by the interposition of bottles, blankets, clothes, carriages, cribs, and other physical objects, will produce individuals who are able to lead lonely, isolated lives in the crowded urban world with its materialistic values and its addiction to things." After all, he argues, "Awareness of self is largely a matter of tactile experience."[5] The accusation of "materialism" can also be explained by noting that in a society where sight becomes more important, more objects are needed to fill the view. Based on touch, a person's built environment would be defined more by his reach.

In a culture like America's where social taboos exist against open displays of affection, objects often become symbolic substitutes for tactile experiences. Montagu gives the example of children who approach their mothers for affection with play objects. For adults, pets and worrybeads serve this function. On a particularly materialistic landscape, that of Route 30 in Lancaster, Pennsylvania, a strip many term a "tourist trap" of countless souvenir stands, the Amish folk society is marketed to "sightseers" as a touch-oriented world. One stark reminder is a commercial sign whose mass-produced letters announce, "Handmade Gifts for a Touch of Warmth."

Signs point to the materialistic landscape, itself a terrain of signs. The rise of signs shows the transition from a localistic, touch-oriented society to a visual mass society. The transition was a slow one, but given impetus by rapid settlement of new areas of the country and replacement of agricultural communities by industrial towns. Americans relied more on sight as they moved around more aided by advances in transportation. As they left their small towns by rail and later car, they became strangers to one another. They needed signs, visual signs, to let them know where they were and who the people they met were. Street signs and clothing helped direct behavior, where before, knowing the tradition of place and person had. More built things arose to replace the intangible information of tradition. More than leaving tradition-bound enclaves, the speed by which people moved around meant that they needed an efficient way to absorb more information. Tradition could not support it all. Reliance on visual markers, supported by writing or illustration, came to dominate the landscape.

In America's pre-industrial past, people identified themselves by what they produced. Surnames still retain the productive identities of "Baker," "Wright," and "Smith." Today, geared toward consumption, Americans accumulate and arrange tangible things to show their "identity" through taste. Mihalyi Csikszentmihalyi and Eugene Rochberg-Halton in their book *The Meaning of Things* (1981) present their findings from a quantitative study of objects in modern households and of attitudes people hold toward those objects. They conclude that "men and women make order in their selves (i.e., 'retrieve their identity') by first creating and then interacting with the material world. The nature of that transaction will determine to a great extent, the kind of person that emerges. Thus the things that surround us are inseparable from who we are."[6]

Many modern synthetic fabrics lack a hand-controlled feel. They feel unreal. In a store you ask to "see" goods, although what you mean is that you want to have them in hand. You feel their weight and texture. The cotton industry has to appeal in advertisements to the naturalness of cotton: "You know you're wearing it." The increasing emphasis in the last two centuries on appearance as a strategy for social mobility, coupled with the "freeing-of-hands" goals of technology, has heightened our visual reliance. Microfilm often edges out solid books; video games simulate tactile participation; computer screens replace the closeness of hand, pen, and paper. Reflecting on the tactile values of a visual medium like painting, anthropologist Alfred Kroeber wrote, "All children, and many adults, want to handle a new sight. . . . But what is seen and touched is always made part of ourselves more intensely and more meaningfully than what is only seen. And so in art representation the representative picture we *only* see but cannot, in imagination, touch, does not carry the same attraction and concentration of interest as the one we can, imaginatively, handle and touch as well as see clearly."[7]

Touch takes on importance, too, because its association with the hands implies the grip of possession. In conversation, "wanting to see something" is weaker than "wanting to get my hands on something." To give concreteness to security, we are told, "You're in good hands." Employers ask that a degree be "in hand." The relation of touch to the self is extended into the object owned. As one proverb states, "touch my property, touch my life." Touching objects is commonly proprietary, and hence a potential source of social conflict as well as embrace.

The separation of our bodies into right and left sides leads to different associations extending from right and left hands. The right, in general, is considered superior, as in the phrases "right-hand man" as opposed to "left-handed compliment." At the same time, the social and personal roles of touch are represented by the left hand's use to protect the self, while the right extends out. In Zuñi, Cushing found that in rituals the right hand was called the "taker" and the left hand was the "holder." In boxing, one hand jabs while the other defends.

Objects, made by human hands, and having been extended properties of human bodies, bring human design and personality outward. Cars take names; guitars have necks; chairs have feet; clocks have faces. Cars, guitars, and planes have "bodies." The word "object" has its origin in bodily action. It comes from the root for "to throw" and takes its meaning from the sense of objects being thrown before the mind. The mind catches the object to comprehend it. The object, being removed from the center of emotion, gives the adjective "objective." The truthful connotation of objects is again related to touch, as Cushing pointed out: "Man attained to both the perception and formal ascertainment of truth first through the *use* of and then through the *using* of his hands."[8]

Having made a case for the cultural consequences of sensing things, let me suggest related concepts for the study of material life. The first refers to the touchstone. The touchstone is a hard black stone used to test the presence and quality of gold and silver. In a

The last wooden chain carved by Ollie Schuch (Darrell Peterson)

figurative sense, the touchstone is a standard by which to express the reality of valued experience, as in the proverb, "Adversity is the touchstone of friendship."

I began thinking about touchstones of "grasping things" while studying elderly woodcarvers in southern Indiana.[9] Their favorite item was a wooden chain made by carving freely dangling links from a solid block of wood. The wooden chain poses a technical problem for viewers of the chain. The carver challenges the viewer to comprehend a seemingly illogical construction. "Bet you don't know how I did this," the carver playfully asks. To find out how he did, the viewer takes the object into his hands to figure out the trick. For these men, mostly retired furniture factory workers, the carving gives them a chance to show their real skills. When the viewer touches the object in his hands, the carver has him in his way of thinking. He is using his hands, examining the workmanship, grasping the rural-craftsman values that went into the making of the object. The repertoires of the carvers differed, but they shared the making of this humble chain. The chain's traditionality, and the social symbolism associated with making and showing it, made the chain the touchstone for them of their abilities and values.

Ollie Schuch was a carver facing death. His stroke left him unable to write, barely able to speak. He gave me his last chains. One was portly and proud, the other smaller and less aged. They told of his life and his relationship to me. They would endure after he was gone. He was handing them down to me, telling me to close my fingers over them. Words could not express the way he felt, as the saying goes, but objects could. This is not to belittle the value of expressive words in prose, poetry, and song. But objects are the means through which people commonly enlarge upon their experiences, or express what cannot be articulated in words. Limited by their muteness, objects speak through the lives that experience them. At the same time, muteness draws us closer to objects to sense their meaning.

For the chain carvers, making a product in wood that normally would be made of industrial iron was a reaction to the modern technological era. To them, the era removed an object's manual means of production from the consumer. It made them feel more dependent on others. It made them feel more distant from nature. The carvers were commonly industrial workers who had come from an artisan background. "Machinery ruined us," one carver told me. "No one does much work by hand anymore." Manual work, and its artisan shop setting, suggested to them a more egalitarian system based on teamwork and toil, rather than on formal education and social status. It relied on face-to-face communication rather than bureaucracy with unseen management. Their objects were not "beyond" them. They were in their reach, in their control.

Advertising for service and technological corporations compensates for the carvers' feelings that might be held by others. "Reach out and touch someone" describes long-distance telephoning. A television network claims that it "got the touch." A large insurance company uses "Good hands people." An auto manufacturing company shows workers pridefully handling the final product. To be sure, industrial workers can feel proud of products to which they contributed in a small way, but routinization, mechanization, impersonality, and close supervision continue to be complaints of workers in service, industry, and technology fields. "Thus," historian Susan Hirsch points out, "new conditions—affluence and automation—have encouraged workers to continue to seek independence, mastery, and the realization of their values primarily off the job in the family and leisure." And on the job, "desk jobbers" make little personal environments in their offices to differentiate themselves, and satirical memos and humorous cartoons, a form of folk material culture, pass hand to hand.[10]

The use of hands and the production of objects have had class associations in American culture. Our bodies provide a model for division of upper and lower, and our hands show us that equally appearing objects can still be divided into an upper and a lower hand. Manual labor, "those hired hands," often is used to describe the work of lower classes, and upper classes are pictured with the resources to pay the most attention to labor-saving devices, books, and visual arts. The "white collar job" is typically a desk job where one manages, rather than produces, barks orders rather than implements them. Csikszentmihalyi and Rochberg-Halton found considerable difference between things picked as "special objects" by upper middle-class and those picked by lower middle-class respondents. Of the upper class, 37 percent mentioned visual art, compared to 14 percent for the lower class; yet only 5 percent of the upper class mentioned plants, whereas 23 percent of the lower class mentioned them. Other differences exist for stereos (28 for upper, 16 for lower) and clocks (3 for upper, 13 for lower) as special objects. The surroundings of the lower class stressed stronger, natural textures and called for more active participation. The upper class tended to favor a more passive heard and seen environment.

Handmade objects and the skills to make them have not disappeared. A constant demand can still be heard for them, especially to provide special gifts and to lend an atmosphere of authenticity. Children's development still relies on them. When I surveyed two hundred college students in Vermont, Mississippi, and Pennsylvania about their childhood playthings, every one listed an object they had made alone or with others. A national survey in 1978 reported that 62 percent of nine-year-olds and 65 percent of thirteen-year-olds had "built something out of wood," although the jobs they took at seventeen most likely involved "service" (40 percent).[11] Among adults today, quilting, pottery, gardening, and breadbaking enjoy popularity, usually as leisure pursuits. As hand skills they stand in contrast to the work most people do. They are tactile behaviors offering intense involvement. The handmade object more than ever draws attention, symbolic and social, to itself. It raises questions of its purpose. It is commonly celebrated for the control it gives its maker and the compassion it conveys to the user.

Handmade objects are expressions of reality and escapes from it. Aging furniture factory worker George Blume buried his wife in 1959. He faced loneliness and grief. He used carving to reduce his anxieties. "If you sit there and don't do nothing," he remarked, "you go thinking about that stuff that troubles you. There's a lot of things that'll drive you nuts. When I started to whittle out them things, by gosh, I put my mind all on there. That'd take the worrying away from me." He took plain wood and made exciting carvings. He reshaped objects. He reshaped himself.

George Blume's barn

Distress raises familiar tactual responses. In uncomfortable situations people wring their hands or nervously ply objects. Productive experiences like chain carving are not unique. American mothers, for instance, analogously make crib quilts and knit infant socks to tactually signify preparation for giving birth. People periodically "try their hand" at preparing particular foods, such as bread, for the enjoyment of transforming loose raw materials into a unified whole. One friend of mine really enjoys the kneading and pounding. "Gets out your tensions," she reports. Touch is an adjustment to new surroundings. People "break a new place in" by making their first meal there, having sex, or adding their decorative touches. People put their hands together to reinforce meaning in prayer and they tautly cross their fingers to deliver a wish. Incidentally, they often close their eyes when doing so. Such behaviors remind us that, indeed, we are objects unto ourselves.

Folklorists refer to "contagious magic," the belief that things in contact with a person have special meanings and can be used to effect powerful changes. Fingernail cuttings, for instance, are favorite magical items. But taboos on touch in modern culture are conveyed in popular childhood games like "cooties tag." One avoids the touch of a marked "it." A form of ritual dirt passed by touch, the cootie is treated like a disease or insect. Responding technologically, children make contraptions such as a "cootie catcher" to remove the cootie should one be touched. Or children apply visual marks on their bodies to ward off the touch.[12]

Although hand skills and the production of objects suggest that manual dexterity is common, it involves risks. One faces risks of rejection, of failure, when touch or objects are extended, for they are, by definition, personal. You draw attention to yourself. An appliance is handed to you and you stand behind a mass. Simply creating is a demonstration of difference; the "creative individual" is a special category.

The details of creating are less familiar today than the created result. Like death, production is more removed from view and as a result is more mysterious. Indeed, legends arise to question the mystery. Word gets around of worms put into mass-produced hamburgers or rats passing for instant fried chicken. According to legend, a highly prized secret recipe for Red Velvet Cake supposedly served at the Waldorf Astoria is nothing more than a matter of red food coloring.[13]

The emphasis on consumption has encouraged the speed by which things are made turned into ready products. The evening news reports the Gross National Product to measure how well we're working.

Yet, showing again the distancing of process from product, historian Samuel Eliot Morison expressed the popular opinion of the GNP as that mysterious sum computed by anonymous statisticians which politicians watch as they once did the stock market. Geared to visual outcome rather than tactile process, quantity, critics complain, has overshadowed quality.[14]

Museums house the quality objects. The objects are there for their historical associations. Henry Ford, ever the industrialist, nonetheless recognized "the history of our people as written into things their hands made and used," for "by looking at things people used and that show the way they lived, a better and truer impression can be gained than can be gained in a month of reading."[15] Most museums strengthen the value of their objects by prohibiting us from touching them. The objects remain something of a mystery. Museums tend to choose objects because they are unusual—extremely rare, large, small, or intricate.

Museum objects draw attention, too, because they have a connection to a notable event, place, or person. Such prejudices come typically from a visual orientation. The touch-oriented world, reproduced in some natural history "discovery rooms" and "living history" or "folk" museums, is oriented toward a more direct experience of everyday life's flow. Montagu comments, "The touch-oriented world is more immediate and friendly than the sight-oriented world. In the sight-oriented world space is friendly, but also often horribly empty or filled with dangerous and unpredictable, unsteadying objects." The touch-oriented world tends to call for human action and social participation, and stresses immediate human interplay with the environment. Such is the basis of worries about the passivity and alienation of a modern generation content to sit back and watch.[16]

What gives people in everyday life their recognition of, and comfort with, objects? I have suggested the touchstone as a measure of value. The figurative meanings of *proximity, resistance,* and *benchmark* further describe our use of objects. Students, for instance, predicate their use of "lucky pens" during examinations on a feeling of mental comfort and wish fulfillment that the object physically bestows. Why? Basing their feelings on the pen's previous "proximity" to a place where students felt comfortable or did well, they judge their abilities to perform on the physical "resistance" of the objects to their hand and therefore their mind. The precedent is converted to a tangible measure, a "benchmark" for action. The benchmark makes one take notice of the resistance of the pen. Similarly, people often report that they are disconcerted by controls on gadgets that rely on the closeness of heat from a finger. They prefer the security of resistant push buttons. With the lucky pen and the push button, they feel the comfort of a material force resisting the push and stimulating the skin. It gives a sense of control.

The ubiquity of benchmark objects signifies the human need for material means of capturing experience, especially for tense moments in the life span. Wedding bands placed strategically on sensual hands give such a reference. Bronzed baby shoes, graduation tassels, saved birthday ribbons, retirement plaques, and gravestones have an emotional presence beyond the physical presence. "Souvenirs," preoccupations of Americans on the move, take their name from "memory," and further show the propensity for objects to "call to mind." "Memorials," larger and more imposing, are often merely shapes—obelisks and spires serving as resistant marks on the landscape—converting fleeting moments and lives into things to remember.

I asked sixty students at Penn State's campus in Middletown to name landmarks they recalled from their drives to school. Similar sets of landmarks appeared in their answers. The students mentioned a large barn apparently out of place next to the highway, Three-Mile Island's nuclear towers jutting out of the Susquehanna River, a white-domed Oddfellows home that lies next to campus. The students passed thousands of objects but only a few stuck in mind, not just because of their size but because of the feeling of imbalance or resistance that existed or the proximity of objects to the one they had foremost in their mind. To be sure, people learn about their environments through what others tell them, but they also have to discover their surroundings by themselves. Objects are tangible references people use to outline the routes and experiences they know and knew, the worlds they try to cope with, and those they imagine.

Reliance on proximity can be explained by recalling that people associate objects, like persons, with other prominent objects around them. This helps people define a center by establishing borders, usually on either side, which guide movement to the center. Doing so is a basic way of constructing malleable categories as part of a system of navigation—social and physical—and thus of judging experience. Social psychologist George Herbert Mead adds, "In our perceptual space an individual finds the center of the system within himself, and the coordinates extend up and down, to right and left and before and behind him. They are organically given in his bilateral symmetry and his maintenance of his erect position over a distant object in the line of vision."[17] We judge the compatibility within, and the distinctiveness of, a category by the feeling of resistance the border places on the center. We notice the contrast. We "picture" objects in our heads as they will appear or have appeared in our experience.

Resistance is physical and intellectual, and in between, culture comes in. Objects or sights that resist expectations of consistency stimulate the mind and heighten the senses. Carved chains—being wood but simulating iron, being natural but artificial, being connected but unattached—challenge our usual associations, a reason to take them into our hands. The barn by the highway and the towers in the river juxtapose clashing shapes and ideas. The mind seeks clarity, perhaps an explanation of irregularity, which culture helps define.

Creativity offers resistance, normally to the ordinary, and thus in decoration, improvisation, and design draws the mind's eye. Having a category of creativity assumes that standards exist by which relative terms such as *ordinary, traditional, improvisational,* and *extraordinary* are measured. Standards imply a socially accepted principle, often in a local setting where they are applied informally, or more formally where they are subject to the dominance of a large social order. Since the nineteenth century, America has increasingly been characterized by the formal standards of its middle class. What scholars call *formal, popular, mass,* or *national* is typically a reflection of middle-class norms. Indeed, few Americans are willing to admit they are lower or higher class. Middle is where to be, perhaps because of the historical passion of Americans for centeredness. Today, mainstreaming is the goal for what we categorically call handicapped groups. Hats go off to the middle of the road, the midway, the elastic middle American. But it seems that no matter where Americans lie on the scale, they are aspiring upward.[18]

CBS News, reporting the 1984 Democratic National Convention, labeled San Francisco a "one-class, three-piece-suit city," a place where the counterculture became the over-the-counter culture. The relation of a covering object to class was clear. But if Americans insist on avoiding class, they still bemoan being part of a disenfranchised community, a hard-pressed working force, a discriminated minority, a subordinate group, or a neglected segment of the population. No longer a "salad of groups," America imagines itself as various separated chips in an encompassing mainstream batter. It is an image influenced by the dominance of marketing and media demographics of taste, rather than the older isolable categories of ethnicity and region. It is a consumer image.[19] Richard Parker in *The Myth of the Middle Class* notes that in 1972 according to the official definition, about 13 percent of the population was poor, yet the lower middle class was a distinct group suffering from material and cultural deprivation. He writes, "Only the upper middle class and the rich, who comprise about 50 per cent of the population, enjoy the affluence that is often erroneously attributed to most of the nation."[20] By 1983, the number of Americans officially below the poverty line had risen to over 35 million. The rhetoric used to avoid class exhibits a heightened American double-talk. A public face of uniformity is put forward while stratification is felt privately.

Combining anthropological, sociological, and historical perspectives, scholarship since the 1960s has approached more of the social realities of the American experience. One contributor to this scholarship, Michael Zuckerman, comments, "Relinquishing ethnocentric assumptions of the pervasive primacy of middle-class culture, historians suddenly find a multitude of other worlds. Investigators of early America discover landlessness and economic marginality that dwarfs the yeoman prosperity they had been schooled to suppose. They discover cities teeming with paupers, not just in stagnant Boston but also in booming Philadelphia. They discover artisans who preferred a sufficiency to any more vaulting ambition, farmers who preferred to remain subservient even after they were entitled to their independence." The discovery of these worlds, however, was limited by their study "in isolation, disconnected from the larger social order."[21]

My purpose, too, is to approach the social realities of the American experience, but since I want to connect the other worlds to the larger social order, I have integrated the study of middle-class culture with other groupings. The other worlds become more apparent when objects are taken into account, since the other worlds are more likely to leave objects than books to describe their experience. Objects serve to convey more of the intimate and everyday. The objects, too, give added dimensions to the words we have to study.

"Process" is often invoked in this orientation. Its importance may indeed stem from realizing that the explanation of products in the processes that made them is more distant in our economy. Putting process in a study requires direct observation and interview, even participation sometimes, and for this reason I engage in fieldwork. Henry Glassie notes that "any process, from making a mudpie to a nuclear submarine, might be described, but the folklorist's interest is drawn to processes over which people have control."[22] Seeking processes of control means looking for individual and communal contributions to culture, often through some form of creation, manipulation, or use.

To get at the symbolic dimensions of material life, I ask questions of makers and their specialties, of different processes of production, and of the consumers of their products. To this view in the present, I add history to get at precedent, to get at the movements that provide influence. In my study I divide events of living into scenes where people are individuals, and those where they form groups by the very act of having things in common. The events and things carry meanings which commonly do not come out in conversation. Where the events cannot be recorded, the things—whether houses, stories, or crafts—are ciphers for social relations. Variables of place, time, and class, have to be considered of course, and although my sample is from America, I have to take into account behavior not necessarily American but rather fundamentally human, or part of Western tradition.

The scenes I describe cut across the domains of the folklorist, anthropologist, and cultural historian. To some, little difference exists among them. They share concerns with everyday life and place, and influential expressions and patterns of culture. I largely call upon folk studies, however, for its distinctive, useful tools. It is attractive because it probes the emergence of tradition. Its literature has brought to light creative responses to social surroundings. It has long covered those other worlds historians are discovering and those that close-to-home anthropologists have recently explored. Let me review some premises of folk studies and how they may be expanded so as to allow for the interdisciplinary behavioral inquiry I have proposed.

Folklorists commonly use the term *folk* as an adjective to describe things learned informally, by tradition, rather than formally, by schools and commercial media. Typically, textbooks describe informal learning as processes of word of mouth, demonstration and imitation, and custom. I will expand on that idea. Word of mouth is readily apparent. When someone orally passes on a story or proverb and it is attached historically to a group, folklorists are wont to call the item a folk item. The folk item, like a story, will invite repetition and variation. The formal item, like a novel, is more fixed in time. When a carver makes a wooden chain based on the techniques or forms he has seen previously, or when a child learns to cook a dish common to his or her heritage by watching a parent do it, folklorists talk of tradition passing by repeated demonstration and imitation.

Some confusion may exist in characterizing tradition because two levels are commonly applied—mass and local. Folk custom, for instance, is typically associated with local groups of family, church, and neighborhood, although folklorists also name national customs. Often the formality of the custom is a guide. Custom can be subdivided into "unconsciously enacted patterns" and "consciously invoked codes." By unconsciously enacted patterns I mean regularities in our conduct that are outside of our awareness, yet that constitute instances of tradition. Alan Dundes has made such an argument for the primacy of the number three in American mass culture. "The third time's a charm," he points out, and he finds the pattern pervasive in formal cultural products such as the acronyms of professional organizations (AAA, AMA, ABA) and the division of government into executive, legislative, and judicial branches.[23]

Americans also have a mass tendency toward upward incrementalism. This pattern is regularly invoked when we one-up someone, raise the stakes, take one step at a time, climb to the top, or work our way up. People don't just exercise, they "build their bodies up." Wars don't erupt, the action escalates. Although scholars of public administration argue that a "rational and comprehensive" way for policy to be implemented is by large-leap investment of resources into a project, American political leadership normally appropriates in "increasing incremental" steps.[24]

Let me mention one more "unconsciously enacted pattern." People regularly display oppositions in pairs. We talk significantly of "on the one hand . . . and then on the other," pro and con, for and against, front and back, left and right, before and after, old and new, right and wrong, good and bad, pre and post. As children we act out one-to-one oppositions on the teeter-totter or see-saw and when we meet face to face. The favor for linearly balanced pairs is especially evident in sports. One side squares off against the other; football and basketball have two equal halves. We have a two-party political system; one is in power while the other is the "opposition." I claim that the prevalence of this pattern has to do with our referring to our own bodily shape: the presence of two equal arms and hands. The favor in modern Western culture for the form *aba,* called bilateral symmetry, a special case of oppositions, can be related to that culture's preoccupation with directing attention to the human body by indirect visual symbols. Many of our taboos and references refer to the body, and bilateral symmetry serves to project the body in dress, architecture, and art.[25]

An extension of this idea of linear oppositions is found in the basic rectangular form for much of American design. The rectangle is shaped by the opposition of vertical and horizontal lines. The first space most infants know is the rectangular crib, and their rooms are normally rectangular. Referring to Western museum design, Edward Alexander noted the pervasive "tyranny of the rectangular room." But this extends to other, more intimate spaces. Every folk house-type in America is based on the rectangle. The same cannot be said for other cultures, which favor round and elliptical designs in housing and cosmology.[26] In America, we don't expect paintings or arguments to be circular and we don't expect our rooms to be so. Whether a bed or a coffin, a rectangle frames our bodies from birth to grave.

Worth noting is that design books of the late nineteenth and early twentieth centuries, the time when such aesthetics were becoming firmly entrenched in society, held up the rectangular "Greek Oblong" as the model of good form. At a time when Americans were concerned with establishing a stable, new civilization to rival that of the Greeks, the sharp lines and symbolic images of the Greeks became more appealing. The rectangle was not the only symptom of this. Classical names in America and Greek revival architecture flourished. At issue here again is the creative response to social conditions and its effect on the shape of tradition.

Recall that the host of novel commercial buildings shaped like the product sold from the building, such as hot dogs, screamed novelty because their cylindrical forms stood in sharp contrast to the rectangular buildings around them (and the round barn never did catch on). The religious fervor that Americans show for sports spectacles is heightened by the imposing elliptical shape of stadiums (even though fields are commonly rectangular). The addition of domes helps gives them a sacred status akin to shrines. In folk belief the circle is generally a supernatural or unusual sign. UFOs are generically called saucers. Motioning circles around your ears is a gesture of craziness.

In contrast to circularity, straightness connotes regularity, conformity. Lest one be thrown a curve, go crooked, or get bent, Americans draw sharp lines when making divisions among people. The countryside, being a romantic landscape for a past ethos, brings to mind rolling hills and curving paths. The dominant urban landscape brings to mind the linear grid. Curves in design have not been replaced, but increasingly in the last two centuries straight lines have been how order has been arranged. Taking their meaning from our bodies, straight lines show a rising emphasis of human control, upward orientation, and centeredness exhibited in our erectness. If political rhetoric is evidence, then "posturing" and "showing backbone" are signs of life in the body politic. Erectness and its projection in upward, straight lines are, more to the point, symbols of human control over and elevation above nature, at least in our minds, as our technology advances. I came across a house in Mechanicsburg, Pennsylvania, that illustrates changes in our design of tradition. In the 1980s it barely attracted notice. Faced with aluminum siding, its blank facade, straight lines, and verticality seemed natural to the streetscape. Although in step with the twentieth century, the siding covered over a nineteenth-century building of log. The rough-hewn lines, natural color, and human scale were natural for another time. When the aluminum siding was removed from the first floor, the confusion of material traditions attracted inspections. It provided resistance to viewers.

By "consciously invoked codes" I mean those customs in a mass

A log house with aluminum siding, Mechanicsburg, Pennsylvania

society which are often learned by overtly stated rules. Written laws give us the dates of our holidays. Reasons for scheduling them at convenient times—for example, to create the coveted three-day weekend for a nation which governs its work by time rather than by task—reveal sentiments of a larger social order. For middle-class society, the etiquette book, essential for late nineteenth-century urban life, provided elaborate codes for behaving in a variety of public scenes. Often etiquette advisers used folk traditions of unconsciously enacted patterns to prepare the more formal and more encompassing written codes. I see in them a model of the channeling of folk culture into mass society, for the lines between formal and informal became blurred in a mass cultural system. Yet alternatives persisted in local traditions, although they were often identified apart, labeled *ethnic* and *regional* in combination with *folk*. The alternatives held attention because they appeared more intense, more intimate, than mass traditions.

Some folklore is recognized historically—fairy tales, carved chains, and proverbs—even though the circumstances surrounding their creation may not be traditional. Other materials, often contemporary, are less apparent as folklore—urban legends, birthday celebrations, and home decorations. My effort here is to approach folk material culture especially as it comes up against formal learning and the "official" standards that emerge. I am less concerned with adding to the inventory of folk props than with uncovering the behavior that marks American cultural scenes. One of those behaviors is the naming of culture. For while I have steeped *folk* in informal learning for the purposes of description, others attach meaning to things and persons "low on the scale" or "lost in time" by using the term *folk*. In common discourse, use of the resistant term *folk* encapsulates attitudes toward others—others apart from modernity and power.

Given the ideational basis of culture, cultural products commonly express ideology as well as utility. Such products are political because they draw power from a person, community, or larger order. Products become ethical when as cultural expressions they raise conflicting social meanings. Such was the controversy over what some called nonstandard English and others defended as a cultural product, black English. Such was the controversy at the Vega plant in Lordstown, Ohio, where workers informally devised their own teamwork system of production which conflicted with the formal system of individual stations.[27]

Production and consumption of things like words and cars are tied to social lives. Bringing together the ideological implications of this statement is Aristotle's term *praxis*. He used it to refer to activities that mark one's political and ethical life. For cultural study, praxis is activity resulting in the production, and I would add consumption, of an object, but one where the doing, the processes involved and the conditions present, rather than solely the end, is paramount. Marshall Sahlins elaborates that praxis is "on the one hand, the historically given means and relations of production; on the other, the experience men have of themselves and the objects of their existence in the course of productively transforming the world through a given instrumental mode." Drawing on American pragmatism and Western Marxism, philosophies contemplating the influence of material conditions, attention to praxis serves to amend humanistic scholarship normally preoccupied with end-products and apparently unconcerned with political consequences.[28] Much revision has been made of Marx's ideas for this humanistic study, but essential, as philosopher Richard Bernstein points out, is "understanding of the ways in which men *are* what they *do,* of how their social *praxis* shapes and is shaped by the complex web of historical institutions and practices within which they function and work."[29]

Accordingly, anthropologist Mary Douglas opened the activity of consumption to cultural account in *The World of Goods* (1979). Her argument is that "the very idea of consumption itself has to be set back into the social process, not merely looked upon as a result or objective of work. Consumption has to be recognized as an integral part of the same social system that accounts for the drive to work, itself a part of the social need to relate to other people, and to have mediating materials for relating to them." In America, for example, consumption is most notable at Christmas. The allowed number of "shopping days till Christmas" steadily grows. Portly gift-bearing figures like Santa Claus suggest the good life of consumption. Adding to the distinctive mythology for a mass society, Santa's craft workshop is in the distant North Pole. Production and delivery of Santa's goods are shrouded in mystery; mythical laboring elves accomplish tasks. Stockings are stuffed; streets are filled with decoration; people are bundled up. No, I am not the Grinch that steals Christmas. My point is that Christmas takes on social importance in a mobile culture like America's because it is commonly a rare occasion to have the family together. The common quantitative listing of commercial gifts—practical for men, luxurious for women—has made Christmas a ritual affirmation of consumption and social roles in the primary structure of family. To be sure, handmade goods in American mass culture are most evident at Christmas time. They reinforce the communal intimacy, the unusual "spirit" in the most material of seasons.[30]

Consumption is like production because it involves individual choices and socioeconomic influences. But production becomes harder to define as tasks become more separated. As Glassie comments, "Delegating accumulation and marketing can leave individuals with a sense of the end product's being their own work. But when manufacture is broken into separate jobs done by separate people, the maker's control is abandoned to the design, and the product, the latest Ford automobile, is more the designer's than the maker's; it seems more the product of circumstance than of culture."[31] The objective in a study of praxis is to seek things that connect makers and users in an intimate communal setting, and producers and consumers in a more formal market system. Interpretation draws on symbols found in doing and considers their unforeseen social effects.

Analysis of material culture simply as behavior would be misleadingly mechanical. Culture would merely be the packaging. You've experienced the approach in which the house is studied as a practical machine, or basketmaking as a technical procedure in which natural materials are turned to a useful product. But when unifying and conflicting social effects, taking in the often-unforeseen political and ethical meanings of productive and consumptive activity, become involved, then behavior becomes cultural. Then it is praxis.

With this must be emphasized the role of mind. It is a problem of language that we have separate categories for thought and action, body and mind. Although influential, categories of thought and mind give analysts trouble because they cannot be grasped. They are necessarily abstract. Pragmatic philosopher George Herbert Mead suggests therefore that we grasp mind through behavior. "Even the most recondite intellectual processes," he writes, "come back to the things we do; and, of course, for an intelligent human being his thinking is the most important part of what he does and the larger part of that thinking is a process of the analysis of situations, finding out just what it is that ought to be attacked, what has to be avoided."[32] Yet people don't normally think about, or articulate, the fact that the things they do fit into patterns of threes, upward incrementalism, or linear oppositions. They are what comes naturally. The analyst makes the natural and abstract artificial and concrete. Appropriately, analysts take on the label of *intellectuals*. The label serves to indicate some removal from praxis, although even intellectuals divide into productive and unproductive scholars.

I step away from specific scenes in this book to judge tendencies that can be tied to broader cultural movements. Because my analysis is itself praxis, it is subject to consideration as "relative theoretical accounts, respectively appropriate to specific cultural universes or historical epochs."[33] That caveat leads me to claim interpretations rather than laws. They are intended to provide object lessons from various lives and surroundings, of modes of making and using, and indeed of ways of acting and thinking.

2

Entering Things

"WHO DOES NOT REMEMBER the interest with which, when young, he looked at shelving rocks, or any approach to a cave?" Henry David Thoreau asked in 1854, reporting his experience in *Walden*. He had come to the woods to reflect on the things that a man can build and use to gain nature's blessing. In the childhood of life, he mused, as in history, one entered caves: "From the cave we have advanced to roofs of palm leaves, of bark and boughs, of linen woven and stretched, of grass and straw, of boards and shingles, of stones, and tiles." "Expansive" and more "advanced," "modern" materials nonetheless lacked beauty, he said, and they held an ominous power to sway a shelter's inhabitants. "But lo! men have become the tools of their tools. The man who independently plucked the fruits when he was hungry is become a farmer; and he who stood under a tree for shelter, a housekeeper. We now no longer camp as for a night, but have settled down on earth and forgotten heaven."

Thoreau felt the shelter in his native Concord, Massachusetts, to have been removed from nature and tradition and placed instead in the "superfluous" realm of fashion. When artificial and imposing, shelter became houses. Yet, "most men appear never to have considered what a house is, and are actually though needlessly poor all their lives because they think that they must have such a one as their neighbors have." Houses to Thoreau were seats for their inhabitants, seats to humbly view nature and celestial bodies.

Houses are unique artifacts because they are things we enter and allow to enclose us. We imagine that we manage and shape our immediate environment, although we are less aware of how the larger built environment and the spaces in which we live and sit influence us. Humans hide behind the house's walls and build private symbols through furniture, layout, and decoration, but the house's face can stand starkly exposed to the community. The house is a community of relations inside and out. In shape, material, and design, the house is

Reconstruction of Thoreau's house at Walden Pond (Thoreau Lyceum)

an expandable, manipulable skin announcing status being grasped at and values being held. Thoreau's observation still holds truth: "At last, we know not what it is to live in the open air, and our lives are domestic in more senses than we think."

Drawing on "country" tradition, Thoreau built his timber-frame house at Walden in white pine, all the while considering "what foundation a door, a window, a cellar, a garret, have in the nature of man." Working from the foundation, Thoreau found that the house is man, his body and senses, working in relation to his social and natural environment. "Much it concerns a man, forsooth, how a few sticks are slanted over him or under him, and what colors are daubed upon his box. It would signify somewhat, if, in any earnest sense, *he* slanted them and daubed it." Thoreau's box ended up being a "tight shingled and plastered house, ten feet wide by fifteen long, and eight-feet posts, with a garret and a closet, a large window on each side, two trap-doors, one door at the end, and a brick fireplace opposite."

Thoreau was proud of his accomplishment, completed mostly with the aid of a borrowed axe. It took care of his physical needs at, he emphasized, low cost. It also brought him a spiritual pleasure by being a work of toiling hands working under nature's gaze. His house was out in the country, a site "some might have thought too far from the village, but to my eyes the village was too far from it." Yet more and more in the 1850s, country people were villagers and were becoming townspeople. Thoreau's house lacked community. Noble in intention, the house nonetheless had no viewers using it as a social touchstone. Most American builders of Thoreau's time raised houses that reflected and encouraged social and economic changes associated with the corporate reshaping of communities.

One example is Samuel Boyd Harris of Monroe County, Indiana. He was distinguished enough to be included in county histories, although he is not more widely known. Nonetheless, this farmer, blacksmith, builder, businessman, and journalist had a leading role reenacted in many nineteenth-century communities—building a house that fixed the gaze of viewers, a house that bridged old and new, village and town, communal and corporate.

Harris's family line followed the route of many others settling Indiana in the 1850s. Harrises traveled to Virginia from Scotland around 1740, moved to Kentucky in the 1780s, and came to south-central Indiana in 1829. The rolling Indiana landscape hid its scattered farms. Woods and streams held sway. Farmers, independent, mostly in community with their land and family rather than municipality, nonetheless informally relied upon communal-aid relationships with one another. Owen County, transversed by the west fork of the White River, two counties in from the Illinois line, became the site for the farm and log house of the Harris family. Samuel's father Thomas added to the family farming income with shoemaking and harnessmaking.

Born in 1823, Samuel worked on his father's Owen County farm until he reached sixteen. As a child, Samuel was sent with the farm goods to market. He would pass through the villages of Mt. Tabor and Ellettsville in Monroe County, where Hezekiah Wampler, "the flatboat king," as he was known, transported goods to New Orleans. The Jeffersonville Turnpike, running to the Ohio River, carried goods and ideas through Indiana and Kentucky from points south and east.

From age sixteen to nineteen Harris was an apprentice blacksmith, after which he set up his own shop on his father's farm. During that time, log and frame marked the landscape. Excitement was raised in Owen County when Philip Hart, an original settler of the county, replaced his log house with one composed of locally fired bricks. Later,

Samuel Harris

the use of brick in the county flourished: "Clays for the manufacture of brick and tile are found all over the county. Our facilities for the manufacture of fire brick, pottery, drain tile, and the best brick are unlimited, and ought to be utilized." So said Charles Blanchard in his history of Morgan, Monroe, and Brown counties published in 1884.

Although brick was known in America as a construction material in settlements as early as Jamestown, timber-frame and log construction dominated American building. The clearing of woods created open fields and raw materials for a technical manipulation perceived as working from nature, rather than against it. This was important, for moral importance often attached to the "natural" humble shape and appearance of worldly goods. Brick caused excite-

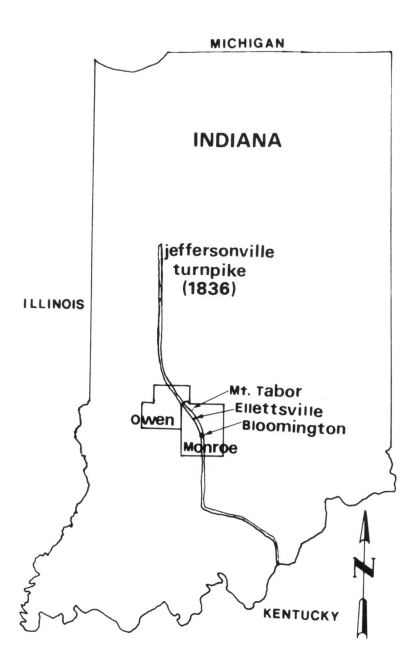

The Harris House, Ellettsville, Indiana

ment because its straight lines, harsh color, and rectangular rigidity clashed with the curving lines of the countryside and the rustic hues of log and frame. Brick put man more clearly above nature. It suggested the grids of secular urban spaces and orderliness of industry. It announced a heightening of technical designs and human control.

Samuel Harris married in 1846 and moved to his own farm on Mt. Tabor outside of Ellettsville. Ellettsville was founded in 1816, but it was not until 1837 that a Main Street was laid out. In 1849 Samuel moved to town. With the move came the construction of his brick house, the first in town. It too created excitement. It symbolized the permanence of the community and the goal of commercial success. Its imposing, balanced front and neat rows of bricks suggested order and expansion. Harris, too, was expanding. After moving to Ellettsville he operated a general goods store, a woolen mill, a grist mill, a saw mill, and a newspaper. He was active in the order of the Freemasons, the Republican Party, and the Universalist Church.

Samuel Harris lived in his brick house on Main Street until his death in 1904. He was absent for only two years, 1867 and 1868, when he went to Coles County, Illinois, to establish a grist and saw mill. Of Samuel's six children, four reached adulthood: Mary, John, William, and Perry. Samuel's son John inherited the house in 1905, but sold it in 1915 to his brother William. William boarded the fireplaces and added indoor plumbing, stoves, and electricity. After William died in 1939, his son William, Jr., occupied the house. Only in 1964 would someone outside the Harris family own the house.

The Harris House was built before the industrial revolution made its full impact on Indiana. Yet the house became witness to changes quickly moving west. William Harris said of his parents: "Their memories runneth back to the period our country was a wilderness. They have seen the windowless log schoolhouse displaced by conveniently arranged school buildings; the reap hook supplanted by the self-binder; the wooden breaking plow give place to a perfect breaking plow; the hum of the tiresome spinning wheel taken up and carried along by the methods showing wonderful ingenuity; in fact they have lived through a period of social and mechanical revolution."[1] The Harris House was old-fashioned in design. In contrast to the look of the Harris House, the Italianate style, championed by eastern taste-makers such as Andrew Jackson Downing and Alexander Jackson Davis, was sweeping the country in the 1850s. Yet in size, material, and position, the Harris House was new and remained a symbol for the community through the nineteenth century.

Businessman and farmer, man of the soil and town, Samuel lived several paradoxes caused by social and economic changes. His son described his father's ambivalence toward the private and public life. Publicly he was the new businessman bringing industry and prosperity to Ellettsville, but privately he was Thoreau's man in the woods. Samuel insisted on making candles at home, even after coal oil lamps, and later electricity, had arrived in Indiana. Samuel's wife continued to make the family's clothing by hand after sewing machines and factories came in. At the same time, local legend had it that Harris hid silver, attained after his business prospered, in the House's fireplace during the Civil War.

Samuel Harris built a brick kiln on the site of the house on Main Street, and carried clay to it from Jack's Defeat Creek nearby. Samuel and his brothers James, William, Thomas, and Oliver worked on the house. They laid the bricks with five courses of stretchers alternating with one course of headers throughout the exterior of the house. This ratio of stretchers to headers was common in southern Indiana in the nineteenth century, but was overtaken after 1850 by the configuration of seven courses of stretchers to one of headers as the most popular bond. The house was the mark of Harris's increased economic attainment and family expansion, yet its I-house shape—two rooms wide, one room deep, and two stories high—matched the predominant tradition of the surrounding built landscape.

The Harris House measures forty four feet by four inches across the front; the front facade measures eighteen feet to the roofline. There are two floors, each containing one room on either side of a central hallway. The plan of the house looks like an *L* because of a kitchen section protruding from the back of the house. The west side of the building, which includes the kitchen, measures thirty five feet and six inches. The height from the ground to the gable is twenty three feet. The house has two interior end chimneys. The exterior walls are one foot thick; the interior supporting walls are ten inches thick. The rooms of the house are eight feet and seven inches from floor to ceiling. The first floor ceiling has openings covered with metal grilles that allow heat from the fireplaces downstairs to reach the second floor. The rooms vary slightly: the west room measures sixteen feet wide, whereas the east is fourteen feet. The downstairs west room served as a dining room while the east was a parlor. The upstairs has one bedroom on either side of the stairwell. Also between the bedrooms, but in front of the stair, is a room that was used as a small study.

The study and the hallway were innovations for housing in the area. The hallway would previously have been considered wasted space, not serving pragmatic functions such as cooking, washing, and sleeping. Houses such as the double-pen house, usually built of timber, had rooms directly entering the front rooms, often a kitchen or a combination eating and entertaining area. Increased social and economic mobility, as sociologist Erving Goffman has suggested, led to more concern for public presentation of status and connection. As a result, private areas were needed to prepare for public presentations and to provide a balance of space.[2] Appropriately, the hallway forced a social function. It ushered traffic into a neutral zone, allowing for a transition made necessary by the increased distance between public and private presentations. Additionally, it allowed for distancing between social classes. In town, where consciousness of public presentation and class differences grew, the private moved back and passages were erected to control the flow between rooms. A portico in front of the hallway emphasized the new social role of the hallway. The kitchen moved back; the parlor moved forward. The entrance became the house's social sentry box.

Houses also showed the increased power of the book in the nineteenth century. As the middle class increased its leisure reading, the need for privacy of study grew and was met by setting aside space for study, appropriately on the more private second floor, right above the hallway. The study, too, was emphasized by an outside portico topped with a classical pediment. The study may have acquired popularity in a period of social transition, because, as geographer Yi-Fu Tuan points out, "Within a book-lined room, social customs and rules of proper behavior would no longer seem to apply not only because the occupant was alone but also because no physical action existed other than the silent turning of the pages of a book. And yet it was here that worlds opened up and it may well be here that individuals found the leisure and security to question moral beliefs and values, those of other cultures as well as their own."[3]

In shape, the Harris House built up from the folk foundation of the double-pen house common in the countryside. The Harris House took the shape of a double-pen house on top of another double-pen separated by new social space and adornment. Folklorist Henry Glassie traced the double-pen to English forms introduced into the Tidewater Region of Virginia and spreading west along the route of migration.[4] Among the most common folk types, the double-pen is distinguished by its rectangular plan and opposed front and rear doors. The I-house, being a two-over-two form, is the grammatically traditional extension of the double-pen. In the Upland South the I-house marks middle-class expansion in the nineteenth century. Few single-story folk houses were in brick. The option of brick usually came with the move upward to the I. Surveying Kentucky folk architecture, William Lynwood Montell and Michael Lynn Morse located log and frame double-pens throughout the region, and reported that the central-hallway I-house with a two-story portico is most common in "the better farming areas of Kentucky."[5] In a detailed study of middle Virginia folk housing, Glassie found a preponderance of timber and log construction, and a few I-houses in brick, which shows the "Anglo-American fondness for technological complication and conceptual simplification. Brick construction expressed a desire to control nature completely."[6]

Close similarities exist in the dimensions of Indiana and Virginia brick I-houses. In her survey of western Virginia, Grace Heffelfinger found widths ranging from twenty eight to fifty feet and depths from seventeen and twenty five feet.[7] I surveyed brick I-houses in Monroe County and found widths from thirty to forty seven feet and depths from eighteen to forty six feet (see table, page 34). In middle Virginia, Glassie found comparable I-houses to be the most frequently appearing traditional type.

Differences do exist between Indiana brick construction and precedents in Virginia from which Harris and his neighbors came. Hoosier

10 feet

The Harris House: front and side

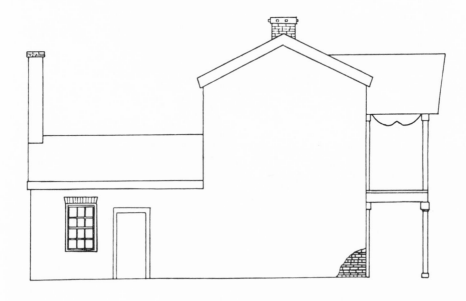

10 feet

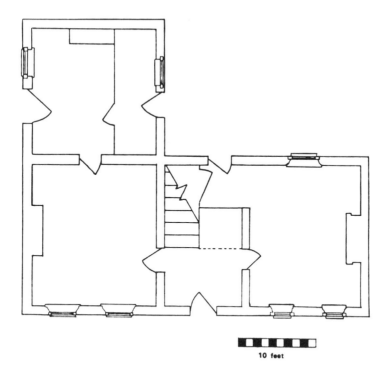

The Harris House: first floor (above) and second floor (below)

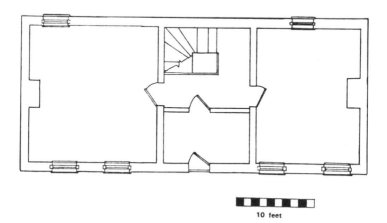

Characteristics of Brick Houses in Monroe County, Indiana

House Name	Type	Date	Location	Bond	Front Measurement				Depth (Side)	Front Doors		
					Total	Left	Hall	Right		L	C	R
Harris	I	1853	Ellettsville	5:1	44'4"	16'	9'	14'	35'6"			1
Unionville	I	1850	New Unionville	F	35'9"	17'4"	NF	17'4"	42'2"		1	1
West South	I	1863	Bloomington	5:1	31'6"	19'	10'	NF	18'			1
Bynum	I	1870	Bloomington	7:1	30'9"	NF	10'	19'6"	35'7"		1	
East Fourth	I	1850	Bloomington	5:1	38'6"	15'6"	6'6"	15'6"	21'4"	1		
Floyd	I	1861	Kirby	F	39'	18'	8'	18'	46'	1		
Sluss	I	1858	Kirby	5:1	47'	18'	10'	18'	18'	1		
Porter	I	1861	Kirby	7:1	43'	17'	8'	17'	31'	1		
Mean Measurements					38'8"	17'3"	8'9"	17'	30'11"			

L = left.   C = center.   R = right.   NF = no feature.   F = Flemish.   I = I = house.

The Harris House: ventilation tunnels

brick houses lacked molded brick cornices and instead had wooden dentil cornices often accompanied by Greek Revival embellishments. Representing carryovers of classical traditions in architecture, especially prevalent from New York State west to northern Indiana from 1820 to 1850, Greek Revival embellishments show some mixing of regional traditions, another trend witnessed by the Harris House.

Many of the double-pen structures outside of town were raised off the ground, in the manner of much southern folk housing, to counteract the damp southern Indiana soil. Harris's brick house called for different techniques. Harris built ventilation tunnels transecting the foundation on all sides of the house. The openings give the illusion of extending beyond the house because of the placement of a small wall two bricks high on three sides and the exterior house wall for the fourth side. Among the first examples of brick buildings in Indiana, those constructed at New Harmony have ventilation tunnels. The Harmonists used tunnels to cool cellars, whereas Harris used them to keep the ground beneath his house cool and dry so as to prevent damage to the wood floor, which rested at ground level on top of a shallow stone foundation. Although other examples of brick houses in

The Harris House: tongue-and-groove boards

the Upland South and Middle Atlantic regions contain ventilation passages in the foundations, the distinguishing characteristic of the ventilation system of the Harris house is its placement below the foundation. Its effectiveness became evident when owners of the house in the 1970s, desiring a closed, insulated house, sealed the tunnels. As a result, parts of the floor became damp and rotted. In addition, the common location of the chimneys in the interior ends marked a compromise of southern exterior and northern interior chimney placement.

Many features of the Harris House are common to preindustrial houses. The floor boards are joined by tongue-and-groove joints. An original closet located under the staircase on the first floor is closed by a "goosebill" latch, also known as a thumblatch. Such hardware loosely secured other doors of the house, according to the description by William Harris of a robbery incident: "Door locks were not too dependable, they being nothing more than the old-time 'goosebill' thrown forward over the door latch. On the night in question, two such doorlocks gave way to a housebreaker."[8] The joined doors were handmade and had two panels. The windows were mortised and tenoned in the style of timber-frame construction. The roof shows details usually found on timber-frame houses. Joists run from the front to the back of the house. There being no attic floor, the lathes and plaster of the ceilings of the second-floor rooms show in its place. The joists are attached to plates on the front and back of the house and girts on the gable ends. The rafters are butted at the gable, without a ridge pole, and reinforced by collar beams. Such descriptions often serve architectural, rather than cultural, interest. But culturally, they point out the symbolic ambivalence of the house in relation to its community: its boasting of brick and its quiet retention of frame, its display of public adornment and creation of private space, its covering of innovation over a core of tradition.

Main Street in Ellettsville still displays the architectural codes of Harris's day. On the northern end of the street stands an early frame double-pen house with a central passage. Shortly after its construction, the kitchen was moved into a lean-to addition and a front porch was built. The result is the extension of public space forward and private space back. The Harris House marks the center of Main Street. Almost directly across is a frame I-house with a kitchen ell adjoining the main rooms. Behind the house is a house with the same floor-plan and porticos with the same pediment and cornice decoration as the Harris House. The portico on the other house has double pillars on each floor, compared with single pillars on the Harris House, and it has an elaborate wooden balustrade enclosing the second floor portico. Similar I-houses and double-pen buildings, predominantly timber-framed, occur in the rest of south-central Indiana, but a concentration of traditional brick structures appears in the urban Bloomington area, seven miles south of Ellettsville.

The Harris House was less a symbol of the community as the twentieth century wore on. A state highway came through Ellettsville two blocks west of Main Street, thus moving the center of the town and placing the town's focus on the automobile. The appearance of the Harris House, now off the beaten track, became less important and it became neglected. Shabby and aged, the house was home to lower-class residents. The town still had some industry, but it was becoming more of a bedroom community for Bloomington. "Modern" developments with veneer brick fronts and prefabricated shells increasingly took the place of older I-houses. Romantic, rustic log buildings rediscovered beneath added rooms and modern weatherboarding now caused excitement in town. When the American bicentennial sparked community interest in Ellettsville's roots, town leaders brought in a log house from outside of town and placed it between Main Street and the highway. The Harris House met its doom, a victim of fire, when the decade of the 1980s was two days old. It was also a victim of its losing touch with the currents of life around and inside it. The brick skeleton managed to stay erect, but the house's heart was gone.

When it was raised, the Harris House was a benchmark for a social organization geared toward the business of town life. More busi-

The Harris House: portico

Vine Street I-house: portico

East Fourth I-house, Bloomington, Indiana

West Sixth I-house, Bloomington, Indiana

Unionville I-house, New Unionville, Indiana

Mt. Tabor I-house, Ellettsville, Indiana

nesses, more books, and more buildings came to influence, and were influenced by, the ordered public facade symbolized by the Harris House. The suburban houses that came to dominate the town appeared "new," but they had their roots in transforming cultural patterns of the nineteenth century.

What happened? It was not that every worker suddenly embraced machines, but that the heightened pace of industrialization and urbanization, and increased literacy nurtured influential ways of thinking. The new streetscapes influenced the future shape of tradition. Samuel Harris's control of his product from start to finish was replaced by a division of labor, opening up the way for middlemen to offer services. The design of work became more linear and individualized, as men in a row worked at their specific tasks rather than working together at common skills. Uniformity across time and space was necessary to make the new system work. Time, measurements, and tools became standardized nationally in the late nineteenth century. Leaders assumed that production and consumption were infinitely expandable. The quickening beat for a working public became more regular, controlled by time rather than the task at hand. The demand for standardization and a more forward-moving, linear way of thinking materialized in a rising favor for straight lines and rectangles in popular nineteenth-century design.[9]

Increased literacy fostered what anthropologist Jack Goody calls "tabular thinking." Writing arranged recall in linear rows. Writing also ordered information in downward lists and allowed for cross-cutting classes, which formed rectilinear tables. Tables affirmed the importance of making information visible. The leveling regularity of the table suggested sharper dichotomies and concrete standards, and, Goody argues, regularly repeated models for action (just look at the justified margins on these pages as an example).[10] It was easier to make local "unconsciously enacted patterns" into mass "overtly stated rules." Differences between public and private, work and play, science and magic, men and women could be made clear in plain black and white. Literacy did not replace oral tradition, however. Word of mouth still thrived to provide the localism and face-to-face contact that formal writing lacked. But oral tradition was intellectually relegated to the realm of the private, the family, the informal gathering, and the countryside.

New cities in a literate age emphasized rectilinear grids. More formal correspondences emerged, such as between lettered streets and numbered avenues. The urbanization of America also established cities as the dominant mass centers for regional provinces. By 1890, most of those cities destined to achieve even moderate size had appeared. By 1910, 228 had a population of 25,000 or more, and cities with over 100,000 composed a larger percentage of the total population than had all urban places in 1860.[11] The urban landscape brought heightened social tensions as different classes, races, and nationalities were closer than before. Cities also brought into mind the whirl of "traffic" as a central metaphor for social navigation.

Those who read appeared modern and urban. Books became important to the middle class for directing the traffic of modern life, because the rectangular order of books suggested the power of formal artifacts. The book stresses individuality; it is read alone. It stresses uniformity; it repeats. It creates a shared culture of those who read it. The audience of periodicals, newspapers, and books became a middle-class one. Reading appeared more attractive because it was illustrated as part of a life of leisure. The person at leisure, the person holding a symbol of order, did not worry about the whirl of traffic nearby. Books were commonly found in the home. They were connected symbolically to the enclosure of homes, because one opened, entered, and shut them. Book consumption ballooned in the 1850s.

Literacy and leisure, from *Social Culture* by Maud C. Cooke (1896)

FIFTH AVENUE, NEW YORK, SUNDAY AFTERNOON.

"Politeness in Public Places," from *Our Manners at Home and Abroad* (1883)

Harper's Magazine in December 1857 reported that "every book of every publisher was in the twenty-sixth thousand, and the unparalleled demand was increasing at an unprecedented rate." It noted that the demand was coming not from the upper class but from the rising middle-class "American home."

A nineteenth-century book that influenced the way the middle class entered as well as the design of the thing it entered was the etiquette book. I want to dwell on this book here and its connection to the shape of mass culture, particularly the suburban house, to point out a prominent example of how the channeling of folk culture into a mass society created new forms of design, of economy, and of polity. I want to show how the themes of the books were materialized in modern homes and set the backdrop for conflicts in the later back-to-the-city movement.

The etiquette or manner book was an "adviser." It was a written code of social behavior that flourished especially between the Civil War and World War II. From 1830 to 1860, fewer than seventy manner books were published, but that many were published in the 1870s alone, and over three hundred new titles came out to 1917. No single

OUR MANNERS

AT

HOME AND ABROAD:

A COMPLETE MANUAL

ON THE

MANNERS, CUSTOMS, AND SOCIAL FORMS OF THE BEST AMERICAN SOCIETY,

INCLUDING

Specimen Letters, Invitations, Acceptances, and Regrets.

COMPILED FROM THE LEADING AND MOST RELI-ABLE MODERN AUTHORITIES.

HARRISBURG:

PENNSYLVANIA PUBLISHING COMPANY.

Title page: *Our Manners at Home and Abroad*

manner book or publisher dominated. Hundreds of manner books vied for a corner of the market. Many were sold as parts of sets of books on "culture," which included guides to games and morals. Others were given as premiums by soap companies and soft-drink bottlers. Most were sold separately and reissued in new versions to report the latest trends. The books typically sold by title rather than author. The impression was of a generally held knowledge rather than of the opinions of an individual. Indeed, advisers freely cribbed from other books. Before the Civil War, country religion dominated the entitled code of manners, but from the 1870s on, an urban secular tone predominated. Jacob Abbott's quarter-million selling *The Young Christian* (1832) gave way to the model of Mary Elizabeth Sherwood's *Manners and Social Usage* (1887) and Maud C. Cooke's successful *Social Culture* (1896). Morals appeared to be shaped more by external than by internal forces, by worldly rather than by heavenly influences. Whereas the early ones tended to give a running sermon on proper behavior, the later books subdivided etiquette into leisure situations, such as receiving guests, dining at home, and walking on the street. Later books were also more specialized, like society's roles. Separate titles covered conversation, dress, and decoration.

Although no one manner book dominated after the Civil War, each sold well, estimated in the tens of thousands apiece. The books stressed matters of family and home and the need for more rigid rules out in public, that is, in the street or at business. They connected values to material surroundings. Reshaping one's home, dress, and table altered character. The books reached out to new entrepreneurial wealth, the middle class, who did not have the advantage of training in deportment given to those of inherited wealth.[12] The market for the books was high between 1890 and 1914, dipped between 1915 and 1921, and then picked up with the million-sellers of Emily Post and Lillian Eichler in the mid-1920s. The later etiquette books were a different breed, however. A few dominated. They were encyclopedic rather than narrative. They were references to consult occasionally, rather than formulas for living. They celebrated an extraordinary author.

The books were sure things in a vague city. The city represented technological order and progress, yet it also suggested confusion and squalor. It was a place of excitement and refinement, yet it also appeared decadent and immoral. The city was where "better society" could be found, yet also where painted women and confidence men ran amuck.[13] The books proposed that the better society and its order should obviously predominate.

Were bourgeois urban dwellers most in possession of manners or

"Etiquette," from *Our Manners at Home and Abroad*

"Free from the Restraints of Society," from *Social Culture*

most in need of them? Or were they just most concerned with them? Yi-Fu Tuan points out that "whereas a courtier in the seventeenth century might still feel free to urinate in any convenient nook of a sprawling palace, a century later such acts would be deemed quite intolerable; and still later, incontinence and other evidence of gross bodily behavior would be judged moral failings, not merely breaches of etiquette. The bourgeois house typically reflected this growing tendency to hide people's biological nature."[14] Manners and houses became domesticated; manner books and house decorating guides became guides to tame culture.

What to hide and what to show became more pressing concerns in the city, for new urban dwellers faced strangers more than they ever had before. Social status was not clear, since one did not know where the person was "from." Material appearances increasingly served to communicate status. Since, in a world of strangers, one traveled more in silence than in the familiarity of the country, one relied on visual cues for whom to address and how. What were those visual cues? In the privacy of the study, Victorians checked with books on how to act and dress in public. As "the most complete work on this subject ever issued" announced, one would be aware of *Social Culture: or, Our Manners, Conversation and Dress; Containing Rules of Etiquette for All Occasions, Including Calls, Invitations, Parties, Weddings, Receptions, Dinners and Teas, Etiquette of the Street, Public Places, Etc., Etc.; Forming a Complete Hand-Book of Deportment; The Art of Dressing Well, Conversation, Courtship, Etiquette for Children, Letter Writing, Artistic Home and Interior Decorations, Etc.* "In short," the book proclaimed, "this work is a treasury of rules and information on every subject of Social Etiquette, Self-Culture and Home Life."

Taking a historical interest in how the ancestors had misbehaved, manner books announced the advancement of the age and the lead of "better society," the upper classes. The books primarily constituted manuals for, as one declared, *Manners, Customs, and Social Forms of the Best American Society.* The important question in this and other works was "How shall the less fortunate in birth and social position acquire the knowledge so necessary to the society with which they mingle?" Indeed, the book stated, "Few are willing to admit ignorance of the requirements of good society, and not all have had those advantages of birth, education, and association which render good manners second nature to the possessor."[15] The books were benchmarks, then, for an upwardly aspiring bourgeoisie in a time of more social mobility. The manner books called upon "the wisdom and experience of those who have wielded no little influence in shaping the customs of the American people, thus making them independent of the English forms so long imitated by our forefathers, and adapting them to the requirements of our nation, where neither birth nor fortune, but education and gentility of manner, determine one's position in the social ranks."[16]

Historian Arthur Schlesinger understood the continued popularity of manner books primarily as "the need many earnest souls felt for a steadying hand in a period of bewildering flux in social conventions."[17] At a time of increasingly varied and complex urban settings, social actors became progressively aware of the shifting panoply of appropriate behavior. By structuring conduct, the manner books clarified social divisions. In a society appearing more fluid, the books offered concreteness. Materially and socially, they offered the "order" of print in an urban world apparently run by the doctrine of laissez-faire."

Sarah Josepha Hale, the influential editor of *Godey's Ladies Book*, made the appeal: "Order, if not Heaven's first law, is the law through which human beings gain their most useful knowledge of nature."[18] Whose laws? Experts had to be sought, and the manner books provided them. In doing so, manner books marked the rise of a new middle-class basis for the economy, a service relationship between a professional agent and a client. The manner adviser acted as a cultural agent for a client who sought improvement. The adviser navigated the client through a world the adviser knew better. The adviser had a specialized knowledge of past manners which could explain rapid changes occurring in society and could dictate the latest trends. "At any given moment," Schlesinger asserts, "the code of behavior was like a palimpsest, showing traces of older writings under the new. Oncoming generations, insisting on innovations suitable for their times, commonly took for granted certain inherited axioms of conduct."[19]

To make their cultural inheritance more explicit, Victorian advisers made a case for their evolution up from the "backward portion of the community." As intelligent man came away from the monkeys, according to Darwin, so did the "civilized" Victorian come away from the primitive "barbarian" according to social theorists popular in America, such as Herbert Spencer. By 1903, more than 368,000 volumes of Spencer's works had been sold in the United States. The barbarian was noted by superstition and folklore while civilized man knew science. Civilization's lineage could be traced back by collecting mere "survivals" of the folklore among "ruder publics." The peak period of etiquette books in the late nineteenth century coincided with the height of popular collections of these folklore "survivals." Showing their connection, many titles used the phrase "primitive

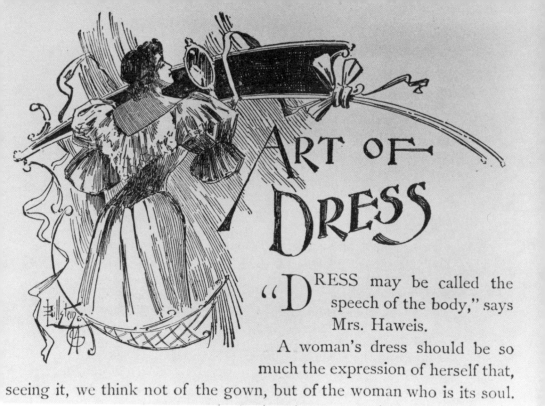

ART OF DRESS

"DRESS may be called the speech of the body," says Mrs. Haweis. A woman's dress should be so much the expression of herself that, seeing it, we think not of the gown, but of the woman who is its soul.

"Art of Dress," from *Social Culture*

manners and customs."[20] Often, etiquette guides and collections of folklore overlapped. The guides embraced novelty even as they sought roots for their traditions.

Besides *customs*, the manner books brandished the term *art*. The 1890s witnessed the publication of *The Art of Good Behavior, The Art of Good Manners, The Art of Pleasing, The Art of Being Agreeable, The Art of Dining, The Art of Speech and Deportment, The Art of Amusing, The Art of Entertaining, The Art of Dress,* and *The Art of Decoration*. The term art suggests high standards of skill, allowing the readers to elevate their dining, entertaining, and behavior to a lofty status. Art, too, is part of an upper-class rhetoric, underscoring judgments made by tastemakers. Art in the manner books thus became a symbol of social advancement, the creation of a taste culture. "It is not a thing to be set apart for occasional enjoyment," the authors of one social Baedeker declared, "but should be sought in everything we do." Another writer claimed: "If a dinner is to be served it is art which dresses the meat, determines the order of serving, prepares and arranges the table, establishes and directs the conventions of costume and conversation, and seasons the whole with that ceremony which, long before Lady Macbeth explained it to us, was the best of all possible sauces."[21]

Art expanded to the house, to furniture, to behaving. Art could enclose everything. Art was less something "done," however, than an overlay over something in existence. Art was framed and arranged. The advisers prescribed this sense of creativity in their art as a cure for a troubling social dis-ease. By assuring users that they were bound to be healthy in a protective art, the books allowed users to imagine a control over their larger environment. Here appeared a material mediation of the anxiety stemming from flux. Art imposed order on a problem; art appeared separate. By framing things as art, advisers gave control and something else. They gave "taste."[22]

The prescribed choices for these urban actors distinguished them as members of the new middle class. If not in inheritance, then in behavior and taste and in the ample time spent on developing a formal system of manners, members separated themselves from classes threatening from below and those stagnating above. Yet by emphasizing the choices as preferable for all, taste affirmed the choices as the proper standard for the future. *The Art of Beautifying Suburban Home Grounds*, for example, was "not designed for the very wealthy, nor for the poor, but principally for that great class of towns-people whose daily business away from their homes is a necessity, and who appreciate more than the very rich, or the poor, all the heart's cheer, the refined pleasures, and the beauty that *should* attach to a suburban home."[23]

Although art circles for the elite flourished in major cities, the civic surroundings appeared void of art. In response, the social advisers considered a sense of art in everyday forms essential. In the agent-client relationship, the environment would be designed. *Art in Every Day Life* was typical of the advisers. It defined design as "the selecting and arranging of materials, with two aims—order and beauty." The book's authors emphasized that "city planning is an art problem in which one man plans the layout on the groundwork of the design, and then turns it over to the public who put in the details of the composition."[24] Designers gave individuals their impression of order, balance, and harmony in appearance; advisers gave individuals a code of conduct.

The two came together in the home. Since the house is where people usually first learn how to behave and where immediate material importance lies, guidebooks were meant "for the home." One could obtain *Manners; or, Happy Homes and Good Society, The Home Manual, The American Woman's Home, Lessons on Manners for School and Home Use*, and *Rules of Etiquette and Home Culture; or,*

What to Do and How to Do It. In the middle-class home, men were assumed to be off at business. The woman's business was reshaping the home, as the man reshaped American business at the time. She managed the home. She designed its character.

The design of the house included the structuring of eating, furnishing, dressing, and recreation. "If our character could be resolved into its elements," one authority declared, "and these traced to their beginnings, the lines would all run back to home influence." Another adviser proclaimed: "Character, it has well been said, is seen through small openings, and certainly is as clearly displayed in the arrangements and adornments of a house as in any other way."[25] Therefore the moral influence of the house could be enhanced by employing an aesthetic system founded on prescribed principles of order, proportion, balance, and harmony. Recreation, for example, should be strenuous but somehow restrained. Hence, interiors compensated for the abundance of things in them by "attractive arrangements" suggesting order. Mary Elizabeth Sherwood would claim that "Indiana divorce laws may be perhaps directly traced to some frightful inharmoniousness in wall-paper. The soothing influence of an Eastlake bookcase on an irritated husband has never been sufficiently calculated."

Next to the Golden Rule was the "Golden Oblong"—a rectangle with two units on the short side and three on the long. Advisers connected the Golden Oblong to classical Greek tradition; thus it befit a new modern civilization while staying true to America's Christian core. The Golden Oblong fit the shape of a book. The principle of the Golden Oblong's ordered divisions reified the separation of public and private space and the emphasis on linear form fostered by literacy.

A telling episode of such design in action was described by sociologist Graham Taylor in 1915. In Gary, Indiana, just before World War I, United States Steel Corporation commissioned a decorator to paint the interiors of company-owned tract houses. Taylor described the reaction: "If you'll give us the colors we want Sophie will do the painting herself,' one of the workers replied. . . . And in the 'box' occupied by her family, Sophie had her way." Taylor added, "Outside it remained like all the rest in the row, but indoors . . . she painted the walls with borders at the top and panels running down to the floor." Taylor characterized this episode as the human story of Gary and other industrial cities: the conflict between some corporate body's "wholesale provision for community life, and that life itself surging in to cut its own channel for expression." The company tract "box" was meant to be a blessing for urban society, a leveler of class differences, making possible made-to-order cities. It stated simplicity, order, and harmony. It was a symbol of democracy, many claimed. Such hopeful theories notwithstanding, residents persisted in designing private symbols which apparently conflicted with the professionally conceived public ones, but which were forced inside.[26]

If the manner books contributed some of these public symbols, the metropolitan press picked up this role after the popularity of manner books dipped. Newspapers were more immediate and handy than the manner books. They fitted the faster pace of urban middle-class life and took on more importance as a conduit of information after the turn of the century. Like the manner book, the newspaper was divided into sections arranged by spheres of activity. Both covered the "latest trends." Beginning in the late 1880s, newspapers carried sections devoted to "women's topics" and "living." In 1896, "Dorothy Dix" (Elizabeth Gilmer) began an advice column in the *New Orleans Picayune*, followed two years later by "Beatrice Fairfax" (Marie Manning) in the *New York Journal*. The columns caught on, and increasing circulation of the newspapers cut into the need for an easily dated manner book. In 1915, the song "Beatrice Fairfax Tell Me What to Do" enjoyed success. The sheet music showed a question mark with five circles showing public situations such as dining, riding in a car, and dancing.

In the 1890s, publication of manner books remained at the rate established in the 1870s. The *Reader's Guide to Periodical Literature*, however, listed only eleven articles on etiquette. Covering the same number of periodicals, the figure jumped to fifty-two between 1900 and 1904. Between the years 1905 and 1914, more periodicals came on the scene, and eighty-two articles on etiquette appeared, while the number of new etiquette book titles dropped.

Coupled with the news of pressing events, the living sections of the newspapers appeared modern and essential. The *Philadelphia Inquirer* in 1890, for example, carried columns on "The Art of Dressing," "Brilliant Society Events," and "Beautiful Homes of the City." Magazines such as the *Ladies' Home Journal* and *Woman's Home Companion* underscored the need for conventional models of behavior for the middle class. "Ruth Ashmore" (Isabel A. Mallon) provided a column on social propriety for the *Journal* and received 158,000 letters in 16 years. Defending the *Ladies' Home Journal*'s policy of avoiding controversial topics with articles on the artistic design of the house, the managing editor of the *Independent* declared in 1908 that a periodical "must adhere strictly to the conventions if it would keep up its reputation as a safe guide for the multitude." The press made manners go public, but it was a public geared to a wider middle-class urban life.

The press nonetheless felt the ambivalence toward change, for, as historian Gunther Barth points out in *City People* (1980), the press "required walking a tightrope between social progress and traditional attitudes, between old journalistic practices and necessary innovations." The press did not have to give advice columns to fill the role of the manner books. Newspapers provided models of behavior through advertising and the reporting of news geared to an urban middle-class convention. Real-estate pages and illustrated features on housing carried through in specialized ways the themes established by the manner books. Especially after the 1890s, housing magazines such as *American Home, Sanitary News, Careful Builders*, and *Good Housekeeping* standardized taste and guided domestic behavior.

Especially for housing, the manner book and press suggested an environment urban in temperament and symbolically country in character. The house was supposed to be run like a business yet have the warmth of the hearth. The house was close to the heart of the city but still looked over the lawn. In the twentieth century, the shape of modern housing looked suburban. With the rapid expansion of public transportation after the 1890s, housing spread outward from the city. Building and loan associations attracted rising working-class families to secure a suburban home. "The Working Man's Reward," reads an advertisement for Chicago's largest builder in the late nineteenth century. A worker looks to a sun with a house inside its sphere, and above is the message, "Where all was darkness, now is light." The company offers a "cottage" placed in a suburban "subdivision."

Loan associations arose to attract working-class families on the rise, and they promoted the suburban expansion. In 1893, the founder of the United States League of Building and Loan Associations commissioned a painting of the "model American home." A healthy family greets a businessman in front of an ornamented suburban dwelling, with a backdrop of a New England schoolhouse, a Protestant church, and an American flag. The novelty of the dwelling is offset by its rural and colonial associations. Popular literature reflected the trend. In H.C. Bunner's *The Suburban Sage* (1896), the central character seeks a house that is as useful as a "country house" but will announce his social aspiration. William Dean Howells, editor of the *Atlantic Monthly*, had his protagonist in *A Hazard of New Fortunes* (1890) rail against apartments and uphold the "Anglo-Saxon home," where "all the family life could go on and society could be transacted unpretentiously."

The suburban house today owes to the manners of late Victorianism and is a reaction against them. The look of the suburban house has changed. It is now more streamlined, less adorned, more

Suburban homes combining modernist and colonial revival styles, Middletown, Pennsylvania

geared to the automobile age. Its basic plan has three rooms off a corridor and a low elevation with a sparsely adorned facade. Some of this technological feel stems from the rebellious academic movements toward the Bauhaus or "International" styles of the 1920s. As a result, builders emphasized simplicity, efficiency, and uniformity in materials and designs. Being more technological, writers observed, the house took on a modern appearance.[27]

The technological appearance was offset in many suburban dwellings by Colonial Revival styles. Since 1876, the year of America's centennial celebration, prominent East Coast architects had emphasized America's colonial past and future colonial power in exteriors inspired by Mt. Vernon and Independence Hall, among others. At first, the styles were commissioned by the wealthy for spacious homes in Boston, Newport, and New York, but later, builders appreciated the popular appeal of colonialism to a middle-class reasserting its nativism in the midst of heavy urban immigration. The ordered rectangular plan and symmetrical white clapboard facade still evoked a moral tone of restraint insisted on by Victorians, but it added a note of heritage. *Carpentry and Building* in June 1900 reported on "The Tendency in Home Architecture" by proclaiming the New England colonial model the epitome of the country's common heritage of practicality and egalitarianism. "The people really want a combination of wholesome, strong, simple effects, and especially good, livable things, with fair and moderate cost," the editors continued. "And that is what the present generation is getting at last."

The eclectic suburban house has escaped most academic efforts at typology, but today is nonetheless a familiar sight in and out of the city. Its very name suggests ambiguity. By being *sub*urban, it is part of—even as it is set apart from—the city. After World War II, it fanned out even farther from downtown, but in so doing has often served to define the very borders of the metropolitan area. Although generally nondescript, the suburban house readily enters conversation when describing types of modern houses.

The suburban house is rectangular. Its front is meant to be seen; its residents are in back. The house normally faces the road but is set back from it, usually with a plain, uniform lawn between the sidewalk (when there is one) and the house. The facade is commonly unadorned and porchless, capped by a plain pitched or pyramidal roof. A single front door is usually set in the middle of the front facade and is balanced symmetrically by two or more windows. Often a garage in proportion to the house rests alongside the facade. The usual exterior materials are brick (common bond or veneer) and aluminum. The house rarely exceeds two stories and typically shelters a single family. All of these features define not so much the house as its setting and how people perceive it.

Step inside. The division of public and private space does more than persist in the suburban house; it has increased from standards set by earlier manners. A hallway usually opens to a living room, a dining room, and a kitchen. Probably toward the rear of the house are the bedrooms and the family room or den. You expect the rooms to be in proportion to one another, with plain simple walls that demarcate private and common areas. The partitioned rooms reflect one another as rectangular studies in dry wall. Usually in addition to the front door there is a back door or an entrance through the garage or side. The door you enter signals whether your deportment is intended as casual or as formal.[28]

Despite references to the democratic spirit of the suburban house, other values are implied. Besides its racial overtones, the flight to the suburbs is, after all, largely a movement toward the identity of exclusive ownership, toward achieving status by occupying a single-family unit. Despite its uniformity, the suburban tract unit is about as close as most people can come today to building their own home, since ownership permits the individual to alter or personalize the occupied structure.

But such personalization can only go so far in a tract house. The suburban house shows a middle-class movement toward a private structural order and aesthetic within a preset public convention. The suburban house can be said to "behave" in a middle-class way, taking on a proper social role while maintaining an outlet for expression out of view. The house has a manner in part designated by its structure and in part by implicit expectations of conduct within. It has a character defined in relation to its surroundings and the company it keeps.

What does the house say? What can be told from its attire? The house outside has the look of a uniform. You recognize the status but you are not quite sure about the wearer. Once you enter the house the corridor tells you little. One suburban dweller described to me the value of the mute hallway as a place to say a few words alone to a guest without the physical distractions of the house proper. The hallway forces a division of space which inculcates the social value of private property and individual interest. The hallway gives a limited view of private space. The visitor must ask or be invited to "see" the house. Once invited to "sit" inside, the visitor is welcome.

Visitors come into a living room. The living room is typically a display piece. The family does not gather there. The living room contains furnishings signifying an expectation of socially acceptable fashion. Dining rooms these days also serve the guest, although a hutch often displays family or domestic possessions—perhaps china or silver. Farther back in the house, residents exhibit more personal symbols: photographs of family members, sentimental objects, favorite items of recreation, eccentric furniture, and so on. Each room of the suburban house serves a different function and is associated with different conduct. Eating in the kitchen assumes greater informality than eating in the dining room. Entertaining in the family room is more informal than in the living room. Each family member has a room. Although common areas such as the kitchen and family room do exist, the suburban house has developed into increasingly individuated and functionally complex areas.

Rather than being oriented toward the entrance of a person, the suburban house welcomes the car. Often suburbs lack sidewalks. The garage entrance, the common "front drive," and reduced, "car-eye" scale of suburban houses underscore the social and physical impact of the automobile. Despite the pivotal position of the car in suburbia, streets often curve in the manner of the countryside and take on bucolic names of trees and rural locations. In Harrisburg, Pennsylvania, for instance, suburban developments carry antimodern names such as Paxton Hollow, Tree View, Village of Pheasant Ridge, Village of Pineford, Village Knoll, Lakewood Hills, Colonial Crest, and Brookridge. One ad runs them together as Rose Garden Briar Cliff Italian Lake Hill Crest. Yet advertisements also underscore modernist words such as *completely equipped, contemporary,* and *modern.* At Locust Ridge the copy reads "Park Like Atmosphere Total Electric Living."

Suburban parents normally do not expect their grown children to live in the same suburb. They often do not themselves expect to live in the same suburb for long. Children are nonetheless expected to create their own private space on the model established by the form of the house and the conduct of the parents. The symbolically private house, in which children have their own rooms, implies an emphasis on private property. Yet the social convention of the suburban house and its typical setting also allow for adjustment to necessary and frequent moves. Suburbs are largely interchangeable, so that if a family moves in or near another urban center, suburbia and its structure will be familiar. The order of the suburban plan is more than a response to movement and a desire for distinct private spaces. It also bespeaks conditions of change underlying suburban life for both parent and child.

The partitions of the house signal different uses. And we are adding more uses daily. I hear residents talk of the washroom, the playroom, the guestroom, and the workroom. Often, rooms are given different levels of importance. The living room, as a public room, must be kept especially clean and orderly. It has taboos placed on its use, whereas the family room or the bedroom is allowed to be less tidy and regulated. Architect William Hubbard has speculated that the shape of differentiation in the house has something to do with authority: "In a more authoritarian society, the children might have to pass through the parent's room to reach theirs—or at least symbolically to pass by their door. Neither happens in the typical suburban house-plan."[29]

The aesthetic order imposed structurally, like the codes of the manner books, is a symptom of and a compensation for flux in the urban setting. Yet the uniformity brought by the order is itself often disturbing. "No one wants their house to be the same as everyone else's," a New York woman told me. She regularly alters the plan to suit her changing "tastes," as she refers to them.[30] She, like Sophie in Gary, Indiana, "designs," building a personal channel for expression which will still allow her to feel comfortable socially. She exercises control over an environment she did not create. This is how tradition functions in today's prevalent agent-client relationship.

Other enclosures similarly endure modification. I recall asking a friend about her new car. She replied that it would feel more like hers when she had familiar objects strewn inside it. She chose the style to her liking, but personalizing was still a social convention which she sought to manipulate further. "I've always had a blue car—it's a regular tradition," she said. Her feeling for personally satisfying form differed from that of others, yet it was important for her to maintain a bond with those who also had her "style," her reminder that she was not alone, that she was connected to a taste culture. The alteration and decoration of cars, related to the house because it encloses occupants, has long been a potent modern symbol of freedom through control, an alliance of personal aesthetics and social identity.[31]

People remark, too, about regularly changing furnishings or coloring in the house to provide a pleasing texture or arrangement. "That's neat," my sister stepped back and said after altering her dining room. In her choice of the word she conveyed the importance in her world of *arranged*, rather than *wrought*, order. Violation of arranged order implies a radical statement, as in "bohemian" houses, such as domes and other circular spaces, underground houses, and bottle houses.

When people dress they choose colors, fabrics, and styles to suit or compensate for season, occasion, audience, loyalty or mood. They have a look, they seek a personal fit and feel to their clothes, yet they do so within social constraints and influences or with a certain social strategy in mind.[32] The traditional tripartite division of the man's two-piece suit and tie, for example, is adorned with pins or designs that express his occupation, outlook, status, or aspiration. Rooms in the house are expanding, especially the bathroom, to accommodate the preparation of attire and appearance, which like the house divides sharply into formal and casual.

Perhaps the most notable extension of the aesthetic system embodied in the suburban house is in dining. Historically Americans have moved from a communal attitude toward eating—taking food from a communal dish and having utensils that serve multiple functions—to a highly individualistic orientation. Each person today expects a private place setting and a straight-backed seat. The implements for eating have specialized uses. We have a fork, a knife, and a spoon. We may even receive a soup spoon, a salad fork, a teaspoon, or a steak knife. The silverware balances the plate, and food is usually placed on the plate in tripartite symmetry: the central meat is flanked by vegetables and potatoes or rice. The serving of the food has become increasingly differentiated and moves forward linearly. We expect several sequential courses, rather than having the salad, entrée, and dessert all at once, and a different beverage corresponds with each stage of the meal. It is not uncommon today for members of a household to have different main courses at the same meal. Despite this individuation, unconsciously enacted patterns of ordered form are followed. The most common dining table is still rectangular, with a centerpiece, perhaps balanced symmetrically by candles or shakers, prevailing as a design motif. Social status also finds expression at the table since the "heads" of the table are commonly reserved for the household heads, who balance the central seating of children or other household members.

Many suburban households separate dining into public and private symbols. The dining table often has its own room and is public while the kitchen has a smaller and less elaborate table reserved for private interaction and aesthetics. The look and the texture of the food involve artistic elements in the meal's preparation, presentation, and consumption. Even before eating, the diner draws a connection between the food's surface presentation and the food's taste by commenting "That looks great!" and then affirming afterward "That was great!" "Just like Mom used to make" includes how Mom expressed the specialness of the dish through her personal touch, an expressive touch we often celebrate symbolically in emotionally significant ways on holidays and other customary occasions. Do you have to go to the bathroom after the meal? Chances are you will find a "family" bathroom and a "guest" bathroom. In sum, the development in dining and other house forms has been toward separation of public and private modes, establishment of order and predictability, differentiation of function and structure, and emphasis on individualistic interest within social conventions.

While it is difficult to realize tangibly our community or region, which are abstract concepts, it is easy to talk concretely about our house and street. References to aesthetics in material culture establish boundaries, keeping others out but within reach. One has a need to materalize social connections.[33] By creating a distinctive setting, residents establish concrete references for their sense of place and belonging. That is common to Western industrialized nations, but perhaps applies especially to the American suburban scene because of its reaction to the urban image of pressing disorder, the feeling of rapid motion and extension, which may simultaneously bring excitement and discomfort and a sense of freedom and restriction.[34] The manner books fitted into this idea of division maintenance as well, for they also reacted to the urban situation and externalized class differences, underscoring especially those differences with the class below.

Design helps to clarify, dramatize, or at least externalize ambiguities. Some of the ambiguity of the suburban dwelling has been mediated in different ways. Some "add-on" or "re-do" their homes, thus affirming control of their environment. Others are attracted to the control offered by Thoreau's ideals: they "build and do it themselves" and follow principles of "country living." This is still a bourgeois movement, as advisers such as *New Shelter* and *The Whole Earth Catalogue* bear out.

There has also been a trend toward more independence for suburbs from central cities, thus encouraging more "community" consciousness and a redefinition of suburbs. The very centeredness of cities has come into question. Others seeking mediation have gone the other way, back to the city. Like the "back to the earth" movement, the "back to the city" movement is underpinned by antimodernist sentiments. There is a celebration in housing, especially, of historical roots, and a yearning for an intense reality and historical authenticity lived by urban working-class groups. Ex-suburbanites reclaim rowhouses and set about "improving" neighborhoods. Yet such gentrification has mixed blessings for the social balance of the city.

The trends are reactions to the emergent dominance of suburbs in metropolitan settlement patterns. In 1910, 76.7 percent of the metropolitan population lived in a central city and 23.3 percent lived in a suburban ring. In 1980, 40.4 percent lived in a central city and 59.6 percent in a suburban ring.[35] Middle-class culture embraces fashion but resists mass appeal. A worry arose among many residents that escalating costs of suburban housing would hinder upward mobility, often visibly defined by moving into a neighborhood with a higher social status. Inflation slowed new purchases of single-family units. Many children of homeowners looked to urban alternatives. In so doing, many young, new members of the bourgeoisie (euphemistically now called "professionals") have invoked culture. This middle-class set has often sought its definition of culture elsewhere, looking to lower-class or elite groups for models. As the Victorians called upon classical and medieval metaphors, this movement, yet again dubbed modern, called upon the rhetoric of the Victorian and Renaissance eras. The perception of art once again provided a central role. To provide symbolic action to analyze, consider what happened on a small street in Harrisburg, Pennsylvania.

"Urban Renaissance," the headline read. Harrisburg's *Sunday Patriot-News*, the city's most widely read newspaper, took notice on 15 May 1983 of the changes occurring in midtown and used art metaphors to describe them. "Penn Street Rowhomes Exemplify the Fine Art of Recycling Houses," large letters announced. A photo showed one side of the 1500 block of Penn Street, and was captioned, "Whole streets in historic residential sections of Harrisburg are looking 'up' these days and much of the credit can be laid at the doors of city housing renovators. One professional couple who live in a renovated Penn Street house say the area is reminiscent of Back Bay Boston." Capping the photo was a quote from a bank official, "Saving historic buildings and recycling existing homes for people and neighborhoods that need them are the foundation of a rejuvenated Harrisburg and its economy."[36]

Fred Raleigh, occupant of a home that was pictured, thought enough of the article to put it in his front window.[37] That was the house I moved into less than two weeks later. Fred worked in state government as did most on that side of the street. "You know, there's folk art here," he proclaimed to me, "and I'm not the only one to think so. Across the street, take a look at Cal's house." If Fred's renovated house was the "fine" art, the contrast, the "folk" art for him, was a decorated house on a side not pictured, but a side worthy of attention for what it says about how personalized housing responds to socioeconomic change, and how "art" answers to politics. Here in close quarters, what sociologist Ira Katznelson calls the "city trenches" aesthetics are the armature for one's social reality in the city.[38]

From June 1983 to June 1984, Cal's house and the street on which it stands went through changes in appearance, changes that held symbolic importance for the social life of the block. I had a good

Renovated houses, Penn Street, Harrisburg, Pennsylvania

Cal's house front, Harrisburg, 1983

vantage to study the scene because I lived there and could keep abreast of activity, yet as a boarder could avoid being linked too closely with either side.

Harrisburg is the capital of Pennsylvania. Its main employer is government (32 percent). Manufacturing and service industries dominate the rest. The Greater Harrisburg Area takes in three counties and almost a half-million persons. In the last five years it has experienced economic and population growth when most Pennsylvania cities have been in decline. The striking cityscape of Harrisburg stretches along the Susquehanna River, once the economic lifeline of the city. The residential strip by the river is bounded by a parallel strip to the east of railroad lines and industry. The city rests on the East Shore. White suburban settlements in the past ten years have risen dramatically on the West Shore (called in the vernacular the "White Shore"). Harrisburg traditionally has subdivided sharply into neighborhoods. Residents easily circumscribe black sections (called the "Hill" and the "Strip"), the Jewish section (called "Little Israel"), the gay section, and the gentrified WASP section (called "Shipoke"). Center City Harrisburg is dominated by the Capitol Complex, but north of the complex, back from the river, is a series of narrow streets with neighborhoods in transition, neighborhoods seeking identity. They hold the highest concentration of residents in the city and have what is commonly referred to as a cloistered atmosphere. Houses on the side streets are being claimed and resettled after the upheaval in the 1970s caused by a ravaging flood, the threat of a nuclear accident, change in political administration, and white flight from the city.

One of these old, narrow streets is Penn Street. Two blocks over is much wider Front Street and the river. There, old mansions and stately buildings left over from Harrisburg's Gilded Age now house insurance, real estate, and legal firms, and lobbying groups. Second Street, just above Front, is the main thoroughfare northward out of the Capitol Complex. Residences share the wide street with professional associations and legal firms. The narrowness of the streets above Second, a leftover from the preautomobile age, has fostered more of a sense of neighborhood than on Second. The 1500 block of Penn Street, however, has been slower to develop than others on Penn. The 1600 block, in the minds of residents, is gay. Third Street, just above Penn, is black. Further down on Penn Street live the mayor, many "bohemians" (musicians and artists), and laborers. The 1500 block of Penn has a mixture of young urban professionals, mostly state government workers, laborers, and persons on relief. Reiley Street, running perpendicular to Penn Street, has several stores that cater to specific constituencies. A gourmet shop, and a restaurant

Center City Harrisburg's skyline

that preceded it, serve the gay community. A corner grocery is frequented mostly by laborers, a vegetarian café attached to an art gallery serves mostly Bohemians and young urban professionals, and a convenience store on Fourth Street is considered black. Historians refer to these few blocks as the "Hardscrabble" section of the city, but the term, more common at the turn of the century, has no significance today for residents.

A disastrous flood in 1936 partly saw to that. It changed the complexion of the riverfront residences. Before the flood, city leaders had already laid the groundwork for change. From 1902 to 1915, city administrators, under the influence of Mira Lloyd Dock, a wealthy burgher, undertook a City Beautiful campaign—an outgrowth of the nativist House Beautiful movement of the 1880s and 1890s. The House Beautiful and the City Beautiful campaigns were intended to reform urban environments and their working-class residents by imposing symbols of a bourgeois order—"good taste and order" defined by decor reminiscent of descent in old-stock American families.[39] The burghers of Harrisburg, mostly Protestant Republicans, called for "physical improvement" which would "elevate the urban population." Speaking to the Board of Trade on 20 December 1900, Mira Dock told of the "hideous conditions" of Harrisburg, and she called for establishing "good taste," common, she said, to Boston, Milwaukee, and European cities. Cleanliness and the genteel beauty she wanted to build up had "cash value," she argued. An "attractive" Front Street, by the river in full view of traffic, would bring business.

Opposition to the vested interests in the "Front Street Scheme" grew, but the proponents' faking of a typhoid epidemic, the drumming up of a threat by the legislature to move the capital to Philadelphia, and the spread of leaflets accusing opponents of being "tight-fisted clams" secured the bond issue. Supportive middle-class wards out-voted working-class wards that were against the issue. The construction of roads, parks, and golf courses encouraging middle-class residence went ahead. By 1915, J. Horace McFarland, a burgher backing the campaign, could announce that Harrisburg was "a made-over town."[40]

The combination of the 1936 flood, the sharp growth of automobile traffic, and a rise in the black population led to the second stage of planning in 1939-40, the "City Practical." For a nation that did not work well during the thirties, the imagery of the machine suggested efficiency and rationality. In the face of impoverishment, art connoted wastefulness. The cities geared up. Harrisburg's City Practical was designed to accommodate "automobility" and business, synonyms for middle-class values, especially on the riverfront. As before, planners singled out the aesthetics of worker housing for attack. Planners found no valid reason for narrow streets and lots. They rejected older histories which commended the caring tight-knit neighborhoods fostered by the layout. The streets, the planners complained, led to "endless rows of monotonous houses" without "architectural merit." The rowhouses would be undesirable "in the eyes of the coming generation, which is witnessing construction of an increasing number of attractive single-family dwellings, set on adequate sized lots." The planners called for slum clearance and new "Neighborhood Units," including neighborhoods zoned for whites. Ensuing administrations encouraged the occupation of the northern riverfront by white middle-class residents.

Despite recessions in 1950, 1954, and 1955, employment stayed high and the economy grew steadily during the 1950s. Suburbia grew. Historians divide over whether this was a symptom of good times or of rising racial conflict. The black population increased by 32 percent from 1940 to 1950, moving into neighborhoods formerly occupied by poor European immigrants and rural migrants. The number of families under the poverty line increased, but city leaders voiced the rhetoric of prosperity. Construction was at an all-time high, unemployment was low, Front Street looked good.

The Regional Planning Commission Report of 1958 was self-congratulatory: "Prudent use of natural resources along with growth as a transportation and government center, followed by the development of commerce and industry, has created a thriving metropolitan community of a quarter million persons." Much of this had to do with the automobile. "With the development and improvement of the automobile, the area became a major terminus for people travelling within the Commonwealth as well as the cross-roads of some of the busiest highways in the eastern United States." The planners felt a whir of change. The river no longer provided the lifeline of the city. Not serving any transportation or economic value, the river was replaced by the central business district as a hub. The river could, however, the commission claimed, be of use as a sporting area. Plans for building the governor's mansion were made further uptown. They called for a colonial Virginia plantation design in brick, strangely out of place in Pennsylvania but in keeping with the nativist symbolism Williamsburg held for the nation.

Seeing the future of the city in taking advantage of its role as an auto-traffic crossroads and its nativist middle-class heritage, the commission complimented "the old Colonial architecture" and "well-planned residential areas." The commission criticized the "narrow streets" of "older communities." Striking out at traditional ethnic and working-class communities, the commission asserted that "the toll of blight is observed where neighborhoods are small and isolated by heavy traffic ways." Neighborhoods should be defined not by social group but by economic needs and proximity to thoroughfares. To effect these changes and entrench the commercial interests of the middle class in the city, the commission called for increased city control of housing and building and the expansion of highways and streets. But the commission failed to foresee that accommodating the automobile in the city would also encourage the automobile-owning middle class to leave more easily.

Penn Street retained its narrowness, and it sheltered a rooted white working-class neighborhood. Population shifts were quietly occurring, however. More blacks and lower-class whites were coming to the city. More middle-class whites were leaving. Still, a relative calm prevailed. Whites could give evidence of the town's conservatism by reminding one another that in the liberal landslide of 1964, Harrisburg had the only black ward in the nation to vote Republican. But in June 1969, race riots broke out on the Hill near Center City. Harrisburg, which thought of itself as quiet ("dull," the *Philadelphia Inquirer* liked to quip), and conservative, found conflicts rising to the surface.

With the national publicity given to the Harrisburg Seven trial in 1972, one civic leader, M. Harve Taylor, wrote in his diary, "You know, there's more radicals in this town than you'd think." There were other signs of discontent. Over 26 percent of all families in the city in 1969, the U.S. Census reported, had incomes under the poverty level. Yet the total average income was touted as reasonable because the 13.2 percent who made better than $15,000 had pushed the figure upward.

In late June 1972, Harrisburg suffered its worst flood as Hurricane Agnes stormed through the Northeast. Taylor wrote, "The mess is horrible, and I'll tell them the smell afterwards is going to be even worse." Many middle-class residents saw the damage and left for the suburbs. Harrisburg's population dropped by ten thousand between 1970 and 1978. Harrisburg, having concentrated its middle class along the riverfront, lost its City Practical. Penn Street's houses were left empty shells.

In 1973, a community survey done by the Greater Harrisburg Chamber of Commerce lacked the singlemindedness of past reports. The survey reported that the stability of the region lay in employment by state government. Its growth lay in industry, but its roots were in the older neighborhood tradition "where people take the time to meet other people as fellow human beings." The survey encouraged "industrial management"—the upwardly mobile bourgeoisie—to come back to the city. It boasted of "an art association, a performing arts company, and a cultural society." "Come to Harrisburg," the survey concluded, "if you want a city in which you can really live and work." "Really," because the city hoped to expose the unreality of the suburbs. But reality in the city was discouragingly sullen; it meant a working-class harshness. Another flood in 1975 fed disillusion.

Whole sections of the city lay tattered and bare. A reporter from a national network commenting on Harrisburg after the Three Mile Island accident in 1979 told viewers that residents must be in shock because no one could be seen out downtown after five. "But no one ever is," a resident chortled. They left for the suburbs. Shopping and entertainment lay in a ring of shopping malls along encircling highways. Working-class city dwellers depended on high-priced neighborhood stores. Meanwhile, local reporter Paul Beers came up with eight long-standing commandments for the city: "obsession with eating, prudent conservatism, congenital obliviousness, small-talk enterprise, clear gender distinctions, contented prosperity, hatred of the cold, and a dark underside."[41] The first few were now openly challenged and the last was looming larger.

Harrisburg was a worrisome place. It was a city to work in but not to live or play in for the middle class. Harrisburg was left, temporarily, to the lower class, many working in menial, unskilled jobs or existing on relief. Penn Street's empty shells were favorite haunts for crime, drug use, and squatting. Of the original twenty-eight families in row houses on the 1500 block, only four remained around 1975. When the middle-class organizations of the American Association of University Women, Harrisburg Branch, and the Historic Harrisburg Association Incorporated sponsored a promotional historic tour of Harrisburg, they skipped over the old Hardscrabble section. It was not presentable.

The revival of the inner city was tied to the success of "Harristown," a commercial venture to consolidate decaying small businesses into large modern enclosed shopping centers which would attract professional clientele downtown. Its name gave it an antimodern tinge, but its subtitle of "Redevelopment Authority" gave its real intent. This was the third stage of planning, the City Renaissance. It received unsuspecting reinforcement from a local history project sponsored by the public library entitled, "Harrisburg: City of Change." Aimed at lower-class middle-school students, the program highlighted the progress of business and architectural development in Center City where the library was located. Art and economics were linked again.

It seemed odd to the students that the riverfront, with its constant threat of destruction by flood, would house the "gentry" of residents and businesses. Didn't they know better? Didn't they have more to lose? Yes, but they wanted to be seen. The appearance, the front on Front Street, was a conspicuous presentation of status. In addition, there was the suggestion of an unconsciously accepted cycle of destruction and construction which worked to generate investment of capital and the process of modernizing. Further back in the trenches, destruction did not lead to the large-scale capital investment of rebuilding and new developments. Houses there, dating back to the nineteenth century, depended on overlays of repairs, never quite complete. This was slow human-scale, community-wide, hands-on change of rooted workers, rather than the short-run, corporate-scale, client-oriented, contracted, ready-to-be-lived-in change of the mobile gentry. Businesses rebuilt; housing developments and renovations with $70,000 price tags on new "single units" sprang up in Center City, although not fast enough or popular enough to suit city leaders.

While commercial interests were working on Center City, some working-class families were moving to Penn Street. They took advantage of low rents and easy availability. Repairs were often needed, but residents regularly took parts of empty shells to improve their structures. Cal was one of those residents. Before the Urban Renaissance, these working-class residents were renovating using *bricolage*— making personal ornamentation and repair from overlays of locally obtained objects.[42] Residents were resurrecting an older open community based on communal aid and frequent face-to-face relations. Their notion of work was similar. They sought manual labor and applied it at home.

The row houses had a mixed jelly-bean look. Although the structures were similar, diverse colors, porch additions, facade ornaments, and sidewalk alterations gave this sidestreet cityscape a variegated appearance. Yet the *bricolage* approach marked the connection of the residents, and the control they were establishing by manually and informally altering their environment. New architectural faces speaking uniquely for their occupants, faces made out of the rearrangement and alteration of old parts, reshaped the old middle-class structures. In the process, the social texture of the community changed. The way the buildings were done and the way they looked bespoke entrenchment of an alternative social organization and occupational value system. For many working-class residents, the back streets marked urban villages of racial, ethnic, and aging networks. During the summer, they came out on their walks to sit and talk. They borrowed freely from one another, especially tools and materials. Many backyards became storerooms of house parts.

On Penn Street, Cal elaborated on his house, well aware of other embellishments he had seen in town. He brought in a fence to put out front. He changed partitions inside and painted them in bold colors. He dug up the sidewalk for a garden by his front window and constructed rough window boxes. Further up the street, with their painted blue car parked nearby, Carol and William Paine were painting their bricks a navy blue with white outlines. "It just comes natural," he told me, "something to do between sleeping and working." Their sidewalk garden had recycled tires and cans, painted blue, to create a distinctive environment. John Voss boxed in his front porch to make another room, marking his expansive goals. His neighbor took discarded concrete blocks to build up columns on his porch. Michael Williams's garbage cans got a jerrybuilt shelter with a familiar Greek Revival pediment from one of the flood's architectural casualties. Victor Ross's house stood out: it was painted orange and had awnings not original to the house. To George Henry, whose painted brown house had a hewn cross on its front, "Every house here is different." "Do you like it like that?" I asked him. "That way you know it's yours, and with who you belong."

In the late 1970s and early 1980s, new state and city administrations came into power promising to "clean things up." The old dark underside of Harrisburg, they chided, included political corruption, economic decline, and urban squalor. The new agenda stressed encouraging businesses and their managers and high arts to the city. A slick campaign entitled "Harrisburg: The Celebration of a Renaissance" was launched by the city's Office of Business and Industrial Development. People Place, an arts promotional agency, changed its name to MetroArts and moved into city hall. The mayor made moves to require city workers to live in the city. But the trend had already begun. Incoming administrations brought waves of professionals new to the city. Many looked to the city for appealing housing. Turning away from the sterility and "unreality" of the suburbs, they found nineteenth-century rowhouses that could be owned easily and altered to suit their middle-class tastes. They found "services" to do specialized tasks on the house much as they performed services for government.

The trend took on a name, "the back-to-the-city movement." In 1980, U.S. Secretary of Housing and Urban Affairs Moon Landrieu announced, "Americans are coming back to the city . . . . Renovation, in and of itself, will not meet our urban housing needs and put a halt to urban economic disinvestment."[43] What would? He didn't say, but his use of "disinvestment" linked urban decline to economic decline. The answer in most city administrations was providing greater economic and cultural provisions for middle-class professional interests.[44] It was planning by professionals for other professionals—a shared taste culture. The emergent group took on an appropriate name—Young Urban Professionals (YUP). A popular satire of them was published as *The Yuppie Handbook*. Poking fun at the group members' preoccupation with modernity, art, and renovation, the subtitle read *The State-of-the-Art Manual for Young Urban Professionals*. The young urban professional is a city person who is between twenty five and forty five, and "lives on aspirations of glory, prestige, recognition, fame, social status, power, money, or any and all combinations of the above."[45] "Lives on them," the author asserted, for the truth is that they are still climbing, never feeling quite settled or hegemonous. Essential to the label of the young urban professional are housing and art—the renovated Victorian rowhouse. The rhetoric of the "House Beautiful" could be heard again in descriptions of "Homestyle." Art is "an obvious gauge of taste. Yuppies choose carefully and use sparingly." This heightened attention is commonly matched by concern for economic revitalization. Their investment in the "physical improvement" of "living spaces" would "elevate" the city. Suggesting Victorian ornament yet sporting plain brickfronts, the house combined historical and modern design. Influenced by minimalist art of the 1960s, spaces were often opened up, dry walls removed to reveal rough brick, and wood floors bared.

Harve Taylor, who was involved in Harrisburg's City Beautiful movement early in the century, now questioned the new movement in 1981. "Today if your neighborhood's old, you're in luck. Used to mean you were just poor. But the bricks aren't the main thing—a town is people. And I wonder if all the newcomers will be givers or takers."[46]

Fred Raleigh was the first young professional to come to the 1500 block of Penn Street. He was lured by its short distance to work in the Capitol Complex and the building's potential for investment. Renovation meant giving the building a clean, Victorian look, usually engineered by hired professionals. They sandblasted the brickfront and removed inside dry walls. A new door in a turn-of-the-century style with a brass knocker went up. He removed floor coverings and highlighted the bare wood. These flights back to the original were offset by modern touches such as the removal of a room on the second floor to create an open space to the third floor above the kitchen. A modern globe lamp hung from the third floor ceiling down into the kitchen. The focus of the house was directed away from the street. The house was made for privacy and a public image of genteel taste. It was ready to live in, and he hoped "maintenance free."

Fred influenced three other government workers to buy houses on the block in 1981. Two lived next door. They explained their choice: "We're from the Boston area where we were very familiar with what could be done with old homes. So when we came to Harrisburg, we were looking for something energy efficient, something in town close to our jobs and something for a reasonable price. We wanted space that we could 'grow' into and a house in an 'improving neighborhood' where we might even be able to get a return on our investment. The biggest plus, however, is that other professionals and many of our friends are nearby." Their brickfront had a "clean Victorian" look similar to Fred's. Macrame and plants hung in the front window. Their focus, in contrast to the houses of Cal and his neighbors, was away from the street.

Fred encouraged other professionals to come and renovate their houses similarly, because "it improves the neighborhood." He explained, "Being in the city, there is a security in a community social network." The network was based on a perception of shared professionalism, economics, and education showing in tastes. Egged on by the city administration's optimism about the future, a special bank subsidiary to promote middle-class ownership of downtown row-houses, and the promotion of the river as a leisure area, two more professionals moved in by the end of the year. The north end on one side looked uniform. They were subdued, and to the inhabitants, renewed and "real."

The houses of the professionals tried to reclaim a past heritage and therefore create a present reality, but difficulties arose. "I was in the grocery store," an airplane pilot who lived down the street told me, "and I realized that no matter what we do, we're the outsiders, the moved-in set, even though we consider ourselves residents of Harrisburg." Their tastes ran to antimodern, favoring handicrafts and premodern music, yet the professionals were treated as symbols of suspicious modern change.[47] They were assumed to be guilty of "snobbism." Fred came from New York, Patricia from Atlanta, Mike from Philadelphia. Harrisburg was below them.

Cal's house appeared especially indecorous, "folk" to them. It was not all that different from other working-class homes in its appearance, but it was more outspoken about its *bricolage*. It more openly defied middle-class sensibilities. Its carpeted steps and garden accommodated the loitering of visitors. Its garish decorations were jerrybuilt from local, often discarded, materials. Its taste was not prescribed by popular fashion or professional advisers or put in place by the "therapy" of "do-it-yourself." Rather, it was put in place by using skills related to the residents' jobs. Cal's house showed his mastery of paints and boards. It faced outward, rather than inward. The street was Cal's parlor. Visitors, coming at odd hours of the day and night, appeared to be shiftless workers or wards of the state.

Cal rents his house with two brothers, but Cal attends to its upkeep. Born in 1947, Cal was raised in Harrisburg with four sisters and four brothers. His father was a roofer and his sons learned to work on houses from him. Cal "made things" in childhood. Sand statues and sculptures of bricks and boards filled the yard.

> Then somebody said why don't you learn how to paint, so I started painting dog houses and parts of barns. As time went past, I started painting cars, old cars like a junk yard and sometimes I used to take paint and in my pastime just paint the cars up and all that. So then people see how good a job I did on the cars and everything, so they asked me do I want to start painting houses as I was getting older and all that. So, I said, I might as well, because I had nothing else to do. So, I started painting this grocery store down on Capital Street and everything. I painted a good job there so the neighbors kept on giving me jobs after jobs. I kept on doing that and then pretty soon my old man got me a job working for him and everything, fixing roofs, putting windows in, and all that you know. So I got more creative as I was going along, so I decided I might as well take stuff off the houses and put different parts of the houses together on paper and see how creative I can get as to how to build the house. So I started to putting things together here and there, find out what I can get a hold of.

Cars, like houses, were things he could not own.

"What do you mean by creative?" I asked him. "You know like when people tear down balustrades and throw the wood away, I like to keep all the wood and make some kind of design out of the wood that they throw away. I don't like to throw nothing away if I can use it on a house. I like to keep adding to the house, make more designs on the house."

The designs were not just for him. He carved guns and numbers for a woman across the street to put on her brickfront because she liked John Wayne's guns. For a religious neighbor he made a cross and it went up on the exterior brick, near the door. Pearl, who hangs an American flag from her front window, received a patriotic eagle made by Cal. Cal adorned his house, inside and out, with carved horses. "I just like horses so I made a horse tacked on my house." The backyards, too, had objects made by his hand—wheels, whose design he learned from a Chambersburg carriagemaker, and small animals. Looking out at the small yards from the narrow walkway behind Penn Street, Cal quietly murmured, "They all belong to me; I made them all." His objects connected him to people and extended his influence.

Unable to own a house, Cal altered his residence as his way to own it. His objects on the houses around him gave the area a feeling of community. Asked if he thought he could own a house, he replied "No, but I dream about it. I had this dream house I built of sticks, but I looked at it and got mad, and smashed it." His creativity dealt with conflicts, often tried to resolve them, but as it did, it could also raise conflict.

Cal's father had given him technical skills, but encouraged him, as Cal said, "to create my own mind." "He thought I should learn it by him but do it by myself." Grown, he did odd jobs. He could fix bicycles, roof a house, replace a window, or paint a wall. A *bricoleur*, he never had a nine-to-five job. "Do you want one?" I asked him. "Not really. I like to have more freedom doing the things I'm doing now. A nine-to-five job is just like prison to me, closed in and everything. I like to be out in the open."

The first addition Cal made to the house was to paint the outside bricks blue and outline them in white. "Then I was building a couple of beds, and I said the hell with it, I made one shorter than the other. So I said I might as well tack them on the front of the house and just see how they looked. And then this guy down here was cutting down a balustrade, so I just cut the railing part in half, turned it up a little bit, and just tacked them on there, just cut out the ends on the pieces of wood I was making a bed out of, just tacked them on for designs." He painted the windows on the third floor with alternately colored rectangles and he painted his interior walls with a red and white brickwork pattern. He added wooden geometric designs to his front door frame, and he painted his transom with a sunburst design around the house numbers.

A metal "No Parking" sign placed in front of his house by the city offended him. He built a decorative wooden box around it, then around the others on the street. City officials took them down. He kept the one in front of his house. He filled it with dirt and planted greenery. Then he painted a fancy "One Way" sign on the paving. He put painted bricks around the city's trees and outlined and numbered parking spaces. He imposed some order on the street, a street fighting to accommodate both landscaping and cars. He expressed local control by enclosing spaces and applying a covering of paint. His neighbors picked up on parts of the aesthetic system. Strips of carpeting, in different colors, went up on front steps. The owner of the house next door to Cal asked Cal to paint his brickfront. A loud red and offwhite mix went up. On summer days, residents would sit out on their carpeted steps and face one another.

When the professionals moved in, Cal and his neighbors were suspicious. "I don't fit into their category and then I feel I'm a reject or something like that." He felt that they didn't respect the work he did. To be sure, Fred thought they didn't "really work," and I heard references to the people down the street as the "funny" or "stupid people." Social contact between the two groups was either to make a curt greeting or some joking remark, like "hot enough for you?" Cal commented, "When I'm joking around them, acting the same as they do and everything then I feel right at home. But if you don't get into conversation, you realize you're left out and everything else."

Cal went about marking his right to home. He outlined his property by painting the curb in front white and extending the block of the garden to the end of his brickfront. The growing uniformity of the north end of the street made him feel uncomfortable. "I don't like to see something plain," he said out on the street, and neighbors nodded in agreement.

Cal's house was never his work alone. Brothers, children, and neighbors told him to add or take away objects and colors. Cal asked for and took advice. He covered the blue and white on his bricks with red and white. Often, he "sleeps on an idea." "If it feels good to me while I'm dreaming then I'll go ahead and do it." "When I work on other houses," Cal says, "I have them [residents] go by the work I do around the neighborhood. Usually there aren't complaints."

But some complaints could be heard from the professionals. A city administrator who moved in across the street from Cal scornfully commented to me, "I suppose that's an original work of art." Another referred to the side of the street as a "veritable petri dish," and the term caught on. When one of the professionals wanted to sell his house, he worried what the houses down the street would do to his house's marketability.

After the "Urban Renaissance" article appeared, two more professionals moved in. Of the fourteen row houses on the north side of the block, three remained shells and seven were occupied by upper middle-class professionals. After moving in, the professionals quickly made their brickfronts conform to the clean Victorian look and thus reflect their status. Cal's house was in the middle of the south end of the street on the opposite side from the concentration of professionals. Seven rowhouses on his side were occupied by laborers with incomes on the low end of the scale. The other side of the south end had two professionals sandwiched by three laborers and two families on relief. Cal's paint, handiwork, and carvings had by now touched all the laborers and relief recipients on the south end. He had never touched any of the professionals' houses.

Because newcomers, mostly professional, sought neighborhoods already occupied by laborers, a conflict revolved around class-bound tastes. In Harrisburg, the establishment of the renovated homes as a "fine" art and the consequent local designation of the others as "folk" or "non-art" by their absence from coverage put in place a hierarchy with the professionals, as in times past, setting standards tied to economic stability. Cal and his neighbors countered by using a display of improvised creativity, but the trivializing of their effort reduced their effectiveness. Professionals on the north end trivialized their decorative work by questioning its value and by using the lack of formal education of the south end residents to back up an image of communal shiftlessness. The south-enders provided a contrast to a mobile bourgeois, more national-thinking, aesthetic. They were a benchmark of localism.

The "Urban Renaissance" article caused Cal to comment. He was sweeping the street and he stopped when he saw me. "What do you think of that?" he asked. "I noticed your house wasn't in it," I replied. He turned to look back at his house. "Well, in a way it looks like art to me, you know. Just like a guy going to take a stone from somewhere and carving a statue out of it. My kind of work is art to me, you know—the way I'm doing it and everything." "What makes it art?" I pressed. "Different parts that hook together make the designs and all that."

Cal worked on his box around the parking sign. He tacked extra boards on it and expanded the base. Its loud red and white colors had a bolder texture. He put soil in the base and planted greenery. He planted a large bush in the sidewalk garden. Complaints followed, so he repainted the box a neutral gray. He continued to paint the front door, curb, step, and garden partition gray. But the color's blandness dissatisfied him. In August he painted the rectangular blocks on the box a bright red and gave a similar red and gray design to his shutters and window boxes. He built up his garden partition and painted red rectangles. He replaced his old orange carpet with a bright green one. His living was more forcefully outward.

The professionals became more vocal in their protest when Cal brought in a white garden statue of a scantily clad woman and put it in a barrel filled with earth and concrete (to prevent its theft, he said). His answer to the complaints was to greet the coming autumn with a subdued brown covering over the wood on his facade and sidewalk. He replaced the green carpet with a brown one. The statue, now adorned with black yarn for hair by a neighbor, remained in place. Just before Halloween, Cal took a door from an abandoned house and replaced his old one with it. It had a long vertical window and Cal put a large paper skeleton hauntingly on the pane. His neighbors got in the spirit and filled their windows and doors with showy decorations. The professionals hung quiet reminders of autumn, such as fall corn husks, or nothing at all.

Complaints continued. The owner of the house, usually absent and unconcerned, left a note telling Cal to subdue his outside decor. Cal painted his shutters white—the absence of color to him. "I got tired of them always saying, change, change it, change, so it went white." But his silent protest, he told me, was to leave some of the shutters unfinished. The house looked confused, and the neighborhood at the south end was less visible too, as winter sent residents inside. Cal placed large green concrete blocks around his steps to make barriers around the space where he usually sat. He turned inward too and materialized his feeling of enclosure, after failing at his attempt to add depth to his house.

At Christmas the south end came alive. Bright decorations, considered tacky by the professionals, went up in front windows. Up the street simple wreaths were hung on doors. One professional hired a professional decorator to arrange greenery inside her house. A Christmas party at Patricia's brought together all the professionals on the north end. Conversation turned to the "veritable petri dish" down the block. Cal was a "character," one said. Another responded that "he's no different from the others down there. He just puts more of it up front." "When does he work; what does he do?" another asked. The group speculated on the new resident of an empty rowhouse formerly owned by a university professor. "I hear it's a professional woman."

Cal painting his house, 1984

After a powerful snowstorm in January 1984, Penn Street was neglected by the city. Neighborhood residents pitched in to help remove snow and ice, Cal being most active. Cal felt inspirited by the experience. On a blistery cold day he put on his coat, took a color suggested by his sister, and covered the shoddy white with a dark brown. "She said it should be one color. It feels good to be out doing something, making stuff. It's not bad now," he said. The house was calm. No complaints followed immediately, but tensions remained.

In February, heavy rains threatened to push the river over its banks. Eyes nervously turned away from Cal's house to the river. The crisis passed and a stronger feeling of community emerged as a result. The grays and browns of winter gave way to spring, and Cal greeted it with new paint. Bright brown and white covered the brickfront. Just before Easter, the south end's windows and doors were covered with bunnies and eggs. Cal draped a six-foot stuffed bunny, a discard from his sister, above his doorway. People took notice. The city administrator asked Cal if he took the bunny out of the rain, and Cal said, "No, he has a raincoat." Fred took a look and said, "I think I prefer it

Cal's house front, 1984

Cal in his portico

to Jackson Pollock." Dawn, a fellow state government worker, said, "I guess he has nothing better to do with his time; he must be bored."

The next outward step for Cal was to paint his bricks in three tones: white, dark brown, and light brown (plate 2). The white bricks gave an impression of scattered order. "It's different," he smiled. "It" was not just the design; "it" was the social organization it represented. Here were his community relations tangibly captured: scattered, yet connected; marked by overlays and borrowings. At a conference on vernacular architecture, Alice Gray Read reported on a working-class neighborhood in Philadelphia where residents similarly relate and personalize their brickfronts, and one had a design almost identical to Cal's.[48] Cal's design was further than the other laborers would go with their friends, but they liked what he did. They quietly recognized its connection to them.

But such outward moves meant some compensations too. The feeling of enclosure he began to materialize with his green concrete blocks grew. Cal added more blocks and repainted them brown and white. Wood walls went up over the blocks. A roof came over the whole structure and a curtain came over the front (plate 3). Cal would sit in his structure, enclosed on three sides but open to the south end, feeling safe, feeling in control. I asked him why he added the curtains. "I decided I wanted privacy." But the privacy existed out on his carpeted steps, still oriented toward the street. The final touch was a picket fence made out of scrap materials from neighboring lots and put on top of the whole structure. Cal reversed Thoreau's dictum; Cal's seat became his house.

With his protection in place, Cal was ready for more. His box became protected, too. He solidified and expanded the base by putting bricks around it. He felt driven. "Build crazy," Jim, a retired laborer living on the south end, called it. His friends would join Cal on his stoop. But Cal would be out in the stifling June heat touching up his bricks. I could hear his brother Mike say, "Take it easy, I'm afraid of going to sleep and waking up painted." Cal replied, "You get loaded, I paint." His brother escaped; Cal expressed.

In mid-June an unprecedented heat wave swept across Pennsylvania. It didn't slow Cal. He marked out his sidewalk with lines. He then painted them with reddish-brown paint. It ended up looking uncannily like real bricks on his sidewalk. Fred and Karen walked over it, and bent down to touch it, just to make sure it really was paint. His house facade blended reality and unreality. The street was real. His model was the altered sidewalk of Patricia's up the street. Done by a professional, her brick walk was an extension of the plain, clean Victorian look. Cal aped the *haute* fashion of the professionals and

Cal's house: painted sidewalk and flower boxes

showed the power of his paint. His paint, like his box around the parking sign, could overlay and convert the material already put in place by some authority. The artificiality of his paint made the appearance of brick all the more affecting. Cal commented, "Looks like real bricks, don't it? I think it's better than that there down the street." Cal expanded the paintings of bricks on the concrete-block foundation and steps of his stoop structure.

Soon after completing the brick sidewalk, Cal made another wheel out on the sidewalk. "What are you going to do with it?" I asked. "Give it to my sister or put it in the country." "How did you learn it?" I continued. "You know the trick, and the rest is easy. The tricky part is putting the spokes in. There was an old buggymaker in Chambersburg where I grew up. I watched him. I can do that, you know: watch somebody and know how to do it." He associated it with the country and with the workings of nature. As he worked on the wheel, he brought in a tree to replace the smaller bush in the front garden.

A passerby stared at Cal's house. "Looks like the Alps." "What do you mean?" I asked. "Garish, like a chateau," he replied. He yelled over to Cal, "You building that for the Alps?" Cal didn't reply. He didn't know what the man was talking about. Cal's concern was with the neighborhood. His models were taken from it and the surrounding countryside. His domain was local.

Cal didn't hear many more complaints (although the police were called out to quiet his stereo which was blaring into the street). The airline pilot hired Cal to do work on his house. The pilot reported, "He does things others don't want to do, but he does it well and he seems to enjoy it." Cal put in an air conditioner for Patricia. The professionals, on the move again, were not raising new conflicts. Patricia, Fred, and Richard were contemplating moving on to higher positions elsewhere. Cal covered the eye-riveting white with a more subdued brown. He added two boxed brick frames around a square of flowers. The brick frames were placed in a line with this stoop enclosure. They visually extended the passage from his entrance to the street, and provided frontal balance for his "seat," with him in the middle. They emphasized stability.

In the drama that occurred on Penn Street, the architectural backdrop became especially symbolic because it was constantly used and it was so visible. It immediately told of the occupant's level of self-control and his connection to others. To cultural critic Lewis Mumford, architecture's symbolism takes on importance, too, because it essentially reflects a wide variety of social facts and "the empirical tradition and experimental knowledge that go into their application, the processes of social organization and association, and the beliefs and world-outlooks of a whole society."[49] The appearance of Cal's house, for example, proclaimed his informal learning and communal activity, and his ambivalence toward middle-class "work," both challenging notions. Indeed, the decoration he did was questionable "work" in a middle-class world view, since most materially rewarding and therefore meaningful work is done away from home. Labor at home is leisurely or removed from one's occupation. Using *decoration* to describe what he did implies something secondary and frivolous, but in the postmodern city, decoration connotes one's personal control of space and social connection to community, since the structure of the house is already predefined and selection, especially for those of the lower class, is limited. Across from the capitol, for example, building owner Ed Early was angered by his forced compliance with city architectural requirements in the historic district. He responded by threatening to paint his building orange and purple. Exterior decoration becomes important socially because it visibly identifies an occupant's propriety and therefore his rationality and social organization. Exterior decoration is, like the hallway, giving directions to the eye before full entrance to the house is given.

In the middle-class renaissance in the city, decoration easily moves into a corporate (rather than human-scale) agent-client market system and an overarching concern with consumption patterns. Taking pictures of the south end of the block, I was nervously asked, "Are you buying houses?" A sensitive balance existed. *Bricolage,* a common alternative system of lower-class homes, is presented as unusual because it works outside of officially dictated tastes or a dominant planned economic system. Based on a creative process of recycling, improvisation, informal learning, and communal activity, *bricolage* is patronized for its provision of "real" and "intense" premodern experience, while often alienated for its possible challenge to the prevailing economic and social system. Class distinctions are not confronted directly but referred to in the stratification of housing and art. "Moreover," Yi-Fu Tuan points out, "what is at stake are deeply held values concerning not so much the quality of the physical environment as the quality of life both social and personal."[50] Buildings can take an ethical tone.

In the bourgeois world view, moving forward and being modern are preoccupations. On Penn Street, Cal and his neighbors thought they too were improving and modernizing their dwellings, but the definition of those behaviors differed. A *bricolage* social organization persists, for it stresses social continuity and face-to-face communication. On Penn Street, it emerged in front. Although part of most social living patterns, the degree to which it is exercised differs. Given definition by the physical block Penn Street sought social identity.

"Even where the buildings are old and run-down," Yi-Fu Tuan states, "the social network may still function, not despite the character of the physical fabric but even because of it."[51] In Elizabeth Collins Cromley's study of housing decoration and alteration in Brooklyn, New York, she found that "home-grown facades" clash and are full of anomalies when judged by formal aesthetics.[52] Painting brick? Aluminum siding as decoration? Cal made his house clash and pose more anomalies in answer to normative pressures. Improvised creativity expressed problems in latent symbols. The clash simultaneously reified conflict and a quest for resolution. His creativity signaled his control of environment and his connection to neighbors. The professionals also used alteration and decoration to impose a sense of wholeness to their lives, but differences of world view became interpreted tangibly into differences of taste.

Cal's story lacks an ending but has an epilogue. His activity, his creativity, continues to act and react, clash and resolve. He is out again. He adjusts the arrangement in his garden, fixes the window in Pearl's house, sweeps the street. His brush touches more houses in the neighborhood as his reputation grows. Cars flow up Second Street and down Front, their drivers oblivious to the cultural currents on the side streets. Yet the currents deeply affect the structure of city life. On Penn, traffic bows to people and houses. People and houses hold center stage here. The river is quiet but it may yet again reach for the street, threatening to alter the reality people have wrought.

Whether building a cabin alone in the woods, communally erecting a brick edifice in town, rearranging a modern dwelling in suburbia, or elaborating a rowhouse in the city, residents have sought control, identity, and connection. The shape and appearance of their enclosing artifacts worked to enlarge upon their ideas and values. "Man was not made so large limbed and robust," Thoreau reflected, "that he must seek to narrow his world, and wall in a space such as fitted him."

3

Making Things

WHY BOTHER making things? Today, you can order almost anything, it seems, in a choice of colors and styles from a department store, catalogue company, or central warehouse. The thing is ready-made without delay, and with cash the transaction is "over-and-done-with." You never face the capricious craftsman. You know what you're getting and you can easily replace the thing. Every year we have new models and old ones become passé or scrap or, after time, vintage.

What would Edward Bellamy, author of the most famous utopian novel, *Looking Backwards* (1888), have thought? After all, he foresaw a contented industrial army which supplied goods to central warehouses for distribution to the public of the year 2000. This was a vision of progress and abundance, and stores not more than ten minutes away. Befitting his nineteenth-century concern over the upheaval of striking tradesmen, Bellamy downplayed the individual worker and told of an overarching, formal organization which replaced the old localism with a corporate nationalism. The architectural adornment of the nationalism, Bellamy wrote, was a "female ideal of Plenty, with her cornucopia," the very same emblem gracing the cover of Sears, Roebuck and Company's catalogues in the late nineteenth century. And there was an economic order about to match the social order: "Legends on the walls all about the hall indicated to what classes of commodities the counters below were devoted."

Although modern America has been described as an industrial giant and a mechanized society, other sides exist. Americans are too competitive, too libertarian, too possessive, to give all to industry and the state. They are too afraid of being reduced to one dimension. The conciliation was to publicly present the facade of progress and mechanization and to draw depth from traditional roots in the shadowy substrata of culture. Quietly, and out of the printed news, Americans looked for outlets of informal social exchange and creativity. Nonetheless, public forces of technology and mass communication can transform or displace those substrata. They can make the vitality of the substrata more hidden or marginal. They can change their surroundings and meaning or make them come out only occasionally in ritualistic symbolic ways. Symbolic? The occasional, intensive ethnic festival replaces the everyday immersion of ethnic life. At festivals such as that of San Gennaro in New York City you can eat Italian, play and pray Italian, and look Italian, and then return to the neutrality of Americanness. The festival draws attention to the Little Italy life that was. It is as much a symbolic homecoming as a religious event. At times like this, the handmade object—especially food and craft—is special, made and given for cultural display and for symbolic effect. Signs of technology dominate the view of most Americans, but ethnic, regional, occupational, religious, and community subcultures seem nonetheless to gain strength in symbolic ways even as at the top our membership in the global village is processed and put on computer.

A historical response has been to pay closer attention to the communities that compose the political entities known as cities, states, and nations.[1] "Local history" has had a strong material culture component because the shape of the community has often been influenced by the things made in it. The most immediate community is the family, and as families become more mobile, more dispersed, the organizational role family plays for the person and the community gains emphasis. Paradoxes arise. As family has lost its tight weave in the twentieth century, it has gained meaning in symbolic ways—the "family" holiday of Thanksgiving, the "family" campaigns of presidential candidates. Family history often becomes commercial history because the documents are there. And in America, the work one did became a sign of how one lived and the values one held.[2]

A smaller view of national history and material culture raises large questions. David Russo in *Families and Communities* (1974) asks by way of conclusion, "How did the preindustrial village society become transformed into the mass industrial society that threatens the very balance of nature itself? How did Americans lose the small, viable, homogeneous, sometimes intensely spiritual community that stifled liberty and gain a large heterogeneous, libertarian, mostly secular community that threatens to fall apart? How have Americans lost a patriarchal, hierarchical, stratified, but personal society and gained a more democratic but also more impersonal, bureaucratic, institutionalized, but still stratified society?" Many of these questions are brought out in the drama of the American "climax of modernization" which occurred during the late nineteenth century. The nineteenth-century "incorporation of America," as Alan Trachtenberg calls it, brought massive changes to the nature of work and living. Production became industrialized. Consumption became nationalized.[3] Or did it? Rather, these public domains pushed the meaning of self-production and social exchange out of historical view, but they remained part of the cultural picture.

There are things that don't have prices and stock numbers because they need to stay informal to have meaning. Children, our youth, provide object lessons. A chain made of gum-wrappers for one's boyfriend makes sense because it was made by hand from tradition. Not from a store, it comes from the world of faith and belief, from the heart. The dark underside of childhood—its spitball shooters, bolas, spears, and slingshots—has its own social codes. A treehouse stands proudly for the "made it myself" feeling it gives children. Like much of children's folk material culture, it can't be seen from the main road. Children's folk material culture stands out of adult and ethnographic view. It is often hidden, ephemeral, and temporary. Children may be made to feel embarrassed about making playthings themselves when toys supplied by Mom and Dad sit idly by, or may be discouraged from strange, crude (by adult standards, anyway) flights of fancy. Indeed, adults often take the attitude that the child's world must spring from adult hands and tastes. But children do think for themselves, and thought sparks creativity—a world of their own making. Growing old, we hope we've "made it," we hope we've had some success. The middle years provide ambiguity, taking cues from what comes before and after but, being the standard of adulthood, the middle years look out at culture without realizing their own.

The achievement of handwork can offer its own reward. Mothers like to tell me, for instance, of the amazing things children do with their food—mashed potato mountains and string bean roads. This is not to say that children's creations are not purposeful. With concept in mind, the child rigs together an object for his personal world that Toys "R" Us cannot appreciate. It can be a cootie catcher, a "top shooter," or a clover chain. Jonah is a boy I know in Harrisburg, for example, who shaped a boat out of clay. It didn't fit into anything his mother could recognize, but Jonah worked and reworked the boat according to a blueprint he had in his head. His sisters shared the excitement he felt over the creation, and gave advice. Playing along the Susquehanna River days later, the children piled variously shaped rocks to make elaborate sculptures jutting out of the shallow water. "Sculptures" is the clinical adult view. To the children they were castles, lighthouses, islands. Each child worked on an individual design, yet they carefully consulted one another on the form and function of the creations, and ultimately the things resembled one another. The children used the creations to express their ideas in material form.

Although folk processes will continue to hold sway in children's

Rock sculptors Sadie and Neva deWall, Susquehanna River

lives because of basic needs of human development, recent commercial influences add a powerful variable in the marketable world. Through various media, companies specializing in children's toys persuade the parent and child of what they should have at a given age rather than answering what they might need. The mass culture stresses consumption and novelty. Folk culture values construction and reuse. Mass culture's products tend toward uniformity and fadism, folk culture toward variation and tradition. In the mass culture you can be told what the fashion is. Companies therefore attempt to control the material culture of children and discourage the supposedly jerrybuilt folk culture. Often, folk products like the stickball bat, go-cart, and wooden puzzle are usurped and repackaged. The stickball bat I made as a kid out of an old broom now sells for $12.95 and comes in "official" and "professional" models. With sincerity, children's toy manufacturers claim educational, creative roles for products. Yet the same roles have been played in informal social exchange and self-production among children. Children are impressionable but they're not dupes of manufacturers. Children commonly alter factory-made products to suit their tastes. A deck of cards became to my childhood friends a marvelous thing with which to show off the patience and prowess needed to build a house or create a tower. These friends took Erector sets and communally figured out ways to use the steel rods and bolts on their homemade carts and boats. Such experiences emphasized their control, their personalizing of things around them. Allowing them to conceive, control, and create things informally helped them to identify more with the object, and ultimately to externalize their identity better.

William Golding in *Lord of the Flies* (1954) used the experience of children's production to make a point about social division. Shipwrecked and alone on an island, children created their own model of society with "littluns" and "biguns." The littluns "had built castles in the sand at the bar of the little river. These castles were about one foot high and were decorated with shells, withered flowers, and interesting stones. Round the castles was a complex of marks, tracks, walls, railway lines, that were of significance only if inspected with the eye at beach level. The littluns played here, if not happily, at least with absorbed attention; and often as many as three of them would play the same game together." The biguns mindlessly destroyed the castles, "kicking them over, burying the flowers, scattering the chosen stones." Yet they could not discern or destroy "the particular marks" in which the littluns were absorbed.

Times have changed, but littluns and biguns remain. Standards of handwork have been superseded by "quality of service."[4] The standard-bearers are not the yeomen of American mythology but "professionals," "entertainers," and "big businessmen." These categories appeared at the top of surveys done by Lawrence Chenoweth of success heroes in the popular press from 1917 to 1969.[5] The dramatic shifts have been the rise of professionals, at the bottom in 1917 and topping the list in 1957 to 1969, and the drop of small businessmen, third of ten categories in 1917 and at the bottom in 1969. The models of the 1890s are captured in Theodore Dreiser's bittersweet parable *Sister Carrie* (1900). It is a saga of changes and oppositions. "When a girl leaves her home at eighteen, she does one of two things," he writes. "Either she falls into saving hands and becomes better, or she rapidly assumes the cosmopolitan standard of virtue and becomes worse." The opposition was between hands and the cosmopolitan, but the cosmopolitan was the standard and a powerful one at that. It was the "evening" of the century as Carrie, like so many others, embraced the dawn. "To the child, the genius with imagination, or the wholly untravelled, the approach to a great city for the first time is a wonderful thing. Particularly if it be evening—that mystic period between the glare and gloom of the world when life is changing from one sphere or condition to the other." The ambition for her and of the time was "to gain in material things." The cosmopolitan man she meets is suffused with material symbolism: "The purse, the shiny tan shoes, the smart new suit, and the *air* with which he did things, built up for her a dim world of fortune, of which he was the centre." Away from her rustic, tactile world, the standards were visual, scaled-up, commercial. "Now am I lifted into that which is best," she believes until disillusionment sets in.

In real life, her Chicago had set a national standard with the 1893 World's Columbian Exposition. The dedication took place in the Manufactures Building—the largest building of the fair—and heralded the rise of the progressive White City decked out in a Roman Imperial covering. Around the building were the Government Plaza, the Electricity Building, and a basin holding emblems for the fair—the statue of the Republic and the Columbian Fountain. Off the basin, the Midway Plaisance was a long rectilinear walk that celebrated the ascent of civilization from the "dark savages" to the present industrial age. The lasting lesson, Alan Trachtenberg reports, is "that the new society required the corporate version of 'capitalistic methods,' including the array of culture before the senses." The lesson overshadowed an economic depression and the "Great Upheaval" of tradesmen's strikes in 1886 and railroad strikes in 1894. What emerged was the command of mechanization. Folklore, folk material culture, and art were represented at the fair to give depth, but one of background. As architect Henry Van Brunt wrote before the fair of the presentation of "modern civilization":

It is necessary that the Columbian Exposition should not only bring together evidences of the amazing material productiveness which, within the century, has effected a complete transformation in the external aspects of life, but should force into equal prominence, if possible, corresponding evidences that the finer instincts of humanity have not suffered complete eclipse in this grosser prosperity, and that, in this headlong race, art has not been left entirely behind. The management of the Exposition is justified in placing machinery, agricultural appliances and products, manufactures and the liberal arts, and the wonderful industrial results of scientific investigation, and other evidences of practical progress, in the midst of a parallel display shaped entirely by sentiment and appealing to a fundamentally different set of emotions. It is the high function of architecture not only to adorn this triumph of materialism, but to condone, explain and supplement it, so that some elements of "sweetness and

light" may be brought forward to counterbalance the boastful
Philistinism of our times.[6]

Despite the wish for balance, Brunt's opposition of the "practical"
productiveness of "wonderful" machinery to the "sweetness and
light" of art and other handwork and, for that matter traditional (as
opposed to modern) groups, laid out the hierarchy of the fair's values
as those of the nation. The International Folklore Congress held at
the fair confirmed the view. Summarizing the progress made from
1853 to 1893, the welcoming address set the stage: "For forty years
the peaceful procession has moved on from the remotest corners of the
earth to a few common centres. Quaint faces, strange costumes,
unintelligible tongues, have blended with the dominant civilizations
of Western Europe and the New World beyond, while venerable races
have made obeisance to the material prosperity of younger and novel
institutions."[7] The 1901 Pan-American Exposition at Buffalo culmi-
nated the ideal: in its center were the Court of Plenty and Fountain of
Abundance.

Those who make things today may be perceived as fulfilling childhood passions or escaping reality and labor, living in the past or
indulging in a leisure pursuit. These are modernist and materialist
notions which patronize, or occasionally celebrate, handmade objects
without usually illuminating the sources of their production. For
that, we need to be at beach level in communities where things are
made and symbols—"the particular marks"—are built. Further, we
need to look up at ways the biguns interpret and convert such marks.

I begin again in the 1850s, in a small town in southern Indiana, this
time in Jasper, of Dubois County. About seventy miles south of
Ellettsville, Jasper marks a center of nineteenth-century German
Catholic immigration. The immigrants left their homeland to escape
religious persecution and improve their economic status. They built
villages in America based on an independent rural economy and
revolving around dominant Catholic churches. They left too for political reasons, since Europe of the late 1840s was in turmoil.[8] The
authority of monarchies was being challenged and reaction and coun-
terreaction created social havoc. Some shrewd promotion of the American Midwest by German priests enticed many Catholic devotees to
settle in a new vision of a harmonious religious-economic order.
Although Jasper had sixty Anglo-American settlers by 1833, Father
Joseph Kundek's establishment of St. Joseph's Church in 1838 and
his soliciting of settlers from Germany brought an influx of immigrants who eventually dominated the area. Kundek oversaw the
construction of a courthouse on the central square in 1845. In 1866

Jasper incorporated as a town, in 1915 as a city. Today, the central courthouse square, St. Joseph's Church, and furniture factories jump out at the observer as identifying markers of the city. Its welcoming sign announces, "Jasper, Nation's Wood Capital." Around the city, the countryside rolls out handsome corn fields and attendant old barns.

Smokestacks and somber brick factories remind one of the tradition of German industriousness and of the heritage of American industrialization. Kimball Piano is here, as is the Hoosier Desk Company. Town chroniclers attribute the success of the town's furniture production to inherent German craftsmanship in wood and stone, its commerce to American craftiness.[9] Before World War I, German challenged English as the chief language, but in the wake of war, use of German rapidly declined. Nonetheless, in the last few years a popular revival of German customs has occurred in the Dubois County area. Locals can attend a *strassenfest* (street festival) where they eat homemade *sauerkraut* and *turnipkraut,* hear German band music, and watch old-timers who still remember how to make a chair by hand.

Some of the old-timers make music—a combination of German polkas and American square dances. I heard one group, Gus's Gang, at a senior citizens' dance in Huntingburg, a few miles southwest of Jasper. Also steeped in German heritage, Huntingburg boasts a line of craftsmanship from the old wagon works to today's furniture factories. Gus Kerkhoff, the fiddler, is dead, but the band, in honor of him, kept his name. Frank Lehmkuhler calls some dances. Enos Lamers stops to talk to me, for he knows my companion Carol Blemker, the daughter of Lil Blemker, whose family, like so many others in Dubois County, has been there since the 1850s. Enos is eighty-six and still works on his farm. "But it's not the same," he tells me. "What do you mean?" I ask. "Farming meant something. It meant making things grow, working with your family, making the town grow. It meant being a carpenter, a wheelwright, a blacksmith. It meant dancing in the barn, not in a slick gym. Now we're from out of town, we're out of touch." He looked around at the worn faces in the room. "They remember; that's why we come."

Lil Blemker talks of her concern for the past and future. Her house, built by her husband's great-great grandfather Ernest Jackob Blemker in 1853, has the look and substance of the Harris House. Until a few years ago, the brick kilns which supplied the bricks for her house still stood. She runs an antique store in Dale, south of Jasper, and her husband is a retired furniture factory worker from Jasper. Her family life telescopes the nineteenth and twentieth centuries, for her German-born grandmother lived until the age of ninety-three with Lil and her children. Grandma filled the parlor with German songs and the kitchen with traditional German foods. Lil's kitchen now abounds with carvings by local men, and pottery from local works. Their makers are dead or gone now. Her children have gone to college and left town for careers. At Thanksgiving the family reassembles. Lil cooks the turkey in the old woodstove that stands retiringly in the back of the house. Appliances in the kitchen speed the rest of the meal along. "Well, you know those gadgets do make life easier," she offers. The boys meanwhile watch football games on the color television. "The place has tradition," she says to me, "but it has grown up different." She pauses and thinks a moment. She tells me of a memory of German tradition—the Durlauf family of stonecarvers. "They're related to me. They made stones to remember, you know—stones for the people." She hesitates, "Now, of course, you don't have that anymore." She is a modern woman, but her thoughts turn to her roots, and talk of death brings reverence for ritual and tradition and a life of community.

The story of the Durlaufs begins with Michael Durlauf, Sr., who came to Jasper from Bavaria in 1858. He felt lucky to have made it. Along the way, a severe storm whipped his ship. With another stone-mason he prayed. Should he survive, he promised, he would build a magnificent stone crucifix in their new church. Arriving safely, he put up the stone, although in 1928 it blew down in a storm. That got people to talking and the talk led to legend. Was it a sign of the changes in the traditional life of the community?

In Jasper, there was not the demand for architectural stonemasonry that there was in Germany, but among Michael's stonecutting skills was gravestone carving. Michael set up shop. In September 1859, he bought a lot in Jasper and sent for his son Michael Floren, born in Germany in 1856. In 1860, Michael, Sr., was one of three stonecutters in the county. He became a volunteer in the Union Army during the Civil War, serving as a company drummer. After the war, he resumed work on his stones and played for the St. Joseph's Church band. The Jasper newspaper carried only one article on him, a report of his arrest for "nuisance and disturbance of the peace" in 1876. Shortly thereafter he left for Germany and never returned.

Michael's stones were small but ornate. He took local limestone and built up its texture with a pick. On top of the rectangular limestone foundation, he placed an upright stone on which he chiseled in fancy German lettering. He usually set off the surname by creating a rectangular inset in the stone and chiseling away stone until the letters of the name appeared raised and smooth.

At the time, the stonecarver shared duties in the cemetery with the blacksmith. Iron crosses with decorative curves and flourishes could be requested. Lacking the solidity of the stones and connected more with Old World tastes, the iron crosses gave way in popularity to stone by the end of the nineteenth century. Some stones were made at home, especially by the poor. They tended to be crosses with shells, tacks, and pebbles attached. But as the stonecarver's work spread in the county, his artisanship became the standard, and the building of monuments became his specialty.

Learning the trade from his father, Michael, Jr., opened a shop in Jasper for selling monuments and gravestones in April 1888. The furniture-making shop which the Alles brothers had opened in 1869 had become the Jasper Furniture Company, and several chair and desk factories opened later. The town elaborated on its strengths: its forests, its strong sense of community and religion, and its residents' industriousness. Michael, Sr., never quite adapted, but Michael, Jr., sharing the German lineage and having an American consciousness, did. His answer to the growing industrialization was to make "special request" stones with the compassion of his handtools.

Michael advertised "double-arch tombstones," "tombstones with inscriptions in German," and "tree-stump tombstones." The customer could work with Michael to design the stone and Michael's hands could work in the details. Michael drew many of his customers from the orbit of families around St. Joseph's Church, and answered to other "town" Catholic churches in Huntingburg, St. Henry, and Ferdinand. The 1891 tombstone of Augusta Cox located in Huntingburg is an example. Built in limestone, the stone simulates a crib-work of half-notched logs supporting an obelisk formed of branches, trunks, and ivy, and capped with an acorn. Augusta's prosperous husband William, born and raised in Dubois County, had requested the stone. At the time of her death he had entered law practice. Later he would become a congressman. Michael's initials appear in a protruding section on one of the logs in the base. Michael gave particular attention to carving rings on the logs and contours of the branches and ivy leaves. For Cox's family, the stone meant Augusta's relation to nature. The Dubois County she and her husband knew was a place of forests from which log houses were built. The ivy and the acorn led thoughts to the future. But having attained the prosperity to raise an obelisk monument, her family did not want to forget the ground on which it was based. With that feeling came a different attitude toward death as the nineteenth century progressed. Death was a culmination of life's work, not a beginning of meaning. The deceased during this period, historian Kenneth Ames notes, "rested from their labors."[10] Death was masked in symbols of nature and was a chance to reaffirm social

Cox gravemarker, Huntingburg, Indiana

Detail of the Cox gravemarker

hierarchy, upward aspiration, and individuality. The inscription on Augusta's stone summarized the attitude: " 'Tis not death to live in the memory of those left behind."

Michael's "special request" stones celebrated life's work and the creative, touch-oriented world in which they operated. He would take note of the deceased's occupation and carve in the tools of his or her trade. Reaping hooks, mallets, axes, and firearms went on the stones along with religious symbols, such as a cross, or an anchor or naturalistic symbols—the durability of ivy, the fidelity of fern. And, residents will tell you, ivy means something in need of protection. For all this work, Michael insisted on his handtools, many inherited from his father, even as stonecutting technology moved toward mass production. Michael still crafted his own tools—the mallet carved from the hard wood of apple trees, and chisels from iron shaped at a forge.

Michael's creations attracted attention, for Michael did not work for the uniformity of the factories. The news of death in this traditional community in transition, a community where those that died were the originals, carried the need for a personal objectification. It

"SHE ENTERED ON UNTROUBLED REST."

A Victorian depiction of death, from *Social Culture*

was still a place where people knew one another, but a place where their roles were put in question as each new factory went up. Each carved stone was news. Shortly after Michael, Jr.'s, shop opened, the town newspaper took notice. It announced, "Mr. M. Durlauf completed this week a fine double column arch monument, of marble and granite, for the late John L. Hoffman of Harbison Township. It is one of the nicest monuments in the county, and shows there is no need of going away from home to get fine work of this kind. The base of Bedford limestone, is six feet long, and weighs 5,000 lbs. It certainly ought to stand solid after being put in place." For his work, Michael charged between $10.00 and $25.00. (Sears charged between $9.98 and $29.00 in 1900 for their common memorials, in 1902 between $5.10 and $15.15, plus freight.)

Michael's repertoire was not confined to gravestones. He carved gateposts for churches in Ferdinand and Jasper, a door and an archway for a church in St. Henry, and the Soldiers and Sailors Monument on the courthouse square in Jasper. The paper heralded the unveiling of the Soldiers and Sailors Monument with the headline "A Link to

Plan for the door of St. Henry Catholic Church,
St. Henry, Indiana

The door of St. Henry Catholic Church

The Soldiers and Sailors Monument, Jasper, Indiana

Window, Durlauf's shop

the Past." Michael's flare for design extended into furnishing and architecture. He designed new pews and a "majestic" steeple for St. Joseph's church that announced heightened ornateness and eclecticism in design. They took from Gothic, Roman, and Old World styles. In each work, Michael put in his distinctive marks. They showed the play of varied textures gained from picking tools and a careful eye for realism and naturalistic symbolism—ivy, ferns, and acorns.

In 1894 Michael bought the Daniel House, a brick hotel built in 1849 and referred to as the "most imposing structure of this style in the state of Indiana."[11] Michael lowered the first floor about six feet and built a partition between the shop and residence areas for his family. Living and working were still connected, much as with the older artisans he had known. They drew their business from word of mouth, served local demand, and could be called on at home. Meanwhile the publicity of distant supply houses reached into the heartland. They were willing to pay freight and charge, as Sears did, "the actual cost of cutting the work of the quarry with but our one small

Andrew Schum and his wife

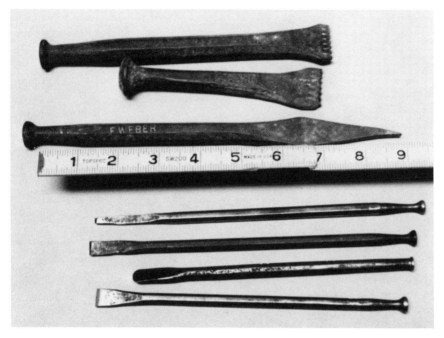

Andrew Schum's stonecarving tools

percentage of profit added." Michael felt compelled to advertise. He decided to make himself a living advertisement. He inserted a large semicircular window with a carved ornate arch. Framed by the attention-grabbing dome, he would carve and let passersby on the courthouse square watch the work of a master. The Jasper newspaper took notice on 20 July 1894: "Mr. Durlauf's large arched window on the Main Street front of the building is quite an improvement, and adds immensely to its appearance."

Michael had a central role in the organization of the community. His commercial success and social connection as a stonecarver and musician made him prominent in Jasper. His shop standing proudly in brick was one block from the central courthouse square, the hub of the town. He served on the town council for many years. He organized the city band. His work spread across the county and beyond, as did his influence on other carvers. Andrew Schum opened a shop in Mariah Hill in 1888, moving to Dale in 1914. Less experienced than Michael, Andrew would travel to Jasper to watch Michael work. Both were musicians, as were many of the artisans in Dubois County. They

The Durlauf family: Leo, Michael Jr., and Harry (c. 1890)

A tree-stump gravemarker, Gosport, Indiana (Warren Roberts)

played in bands together and during intermissions of performances they could be heard talking shop.

Michael brought his sons into the stonecarving trade. Harry, Leo, and Otto stood by him in the window of the old Daniel House and learned his techniques. They stood by him, too, in the town and church band. Following his lead they took up brass instruments. Leo was the oldest and most accomplished stonecarver of the three. Born in 1880, Leo from an early age helped his father in the Main Street shop. Harry showed artistic talent and had his eyes set on the new motion-picture industry. He left for California and worked on set

Stripped bark design and tools on a log gravemarker, Huntingburg, Indiana

designs. But he left his mark. As a playful lad he took his father's tools and carved his initials on the arch of the shop window as well as cornerstones around town. Leo and Otto meanwhile stayed in Jasper to carry on the trade and legacy.

As the nineteenth century came to a close, Michael began to specialize in a certain type of stone—the log and tree-stump tombstone. These stones capture the detail and contour of wood, and include adornments of tools, vegetation, and inscriptions. The log may lie on its side with an inscription found directly on it. The tree-stump is often propped up by a foundation and a stone announcing the name of the deceased. Typically, the log is upright and sometimes placed alongside a matching log to signify a married couple. Each log stands on its own but has branches that intertwine. When upright, the log stones are usually the tallest stones in the cemetery. A small stump next to the larger one often carries the inscription of a dead child while the larger one is the parent. Michael Durlauf's log and stump tombstones appear with the most frequency for the period between 1891 and 1915.

Books on the Marcus Smith log gravemarker, Gosport, Indiana
(Warren Roberts)

The log memorials are not Michael's innovation. They are found in
other locales, especially those with forests and limestone. Chances
are that Michael got the idea from Bedford, Indiana, where he went to
pick up his limestone. The area around Bedford has many log
tombstones similar to Michael's, several of which date earlier.

Stones around Bedford commonly carry open books, representing
the Bible or books generally, on top of the log or at the bottom. More
than being talked about, having a name etched in a book became a
new sign of being noticed, and one step above the usual alternative,
which was to put the name on an area where bark had been stripped
away. In the one a mark had been made in the woods. In the other a
mark had been made in civilization. Books suggested "individual-

A Victorian mourning picture (Eleanor and Mabel Van Alstyne Folk Art Collection, Smithsonian Institution)

ism." As Rhys Isaac explains, "When private readers withdraw into a secluded realm where discourse reached them in solitude, modes of silent thought developed—thus was engendered 'individualism.' "[12] Yet often the "top book" in a pile was considered the Bible, a "speaking book," thus maintaining social and spiritual ties to oral culture.

Manner books were among the strong influences on sentimentalizing death in the nineteenth century. They often called for naturalistic symbolism of willows and park settings and classical affectations of obelisks and urns. The height and upward spire of the obelisk were appropriate to an age that considered itself the height of civilization. Taken together, stones before and after this period never reached such heights. The heights to which stones reached were also a public presentation of social and economic status. The Victorian graveyard had several levels. Further above the obelisks were mausoleums and below were the crude markers of the poor. Enjoying the wordplay of

The cemetery as a Victorian park, from *Our Manners at Home and Abroad*

manners and money, one etiquette adviser stated, "Affection will dictate that all the marks of respect which you can provide should be paid to the memory of your beloved dead."[13]

Death's ritual effect moved from the deceased to the mourner. Mourning pictures, mourning stationery, and mourning apparel became popular.[14] As public, sentimental presentations of mourning and a private search for meaning in an ambiguous age grew, use of symbols proliferated. Material symbols were euphemisms for difficult and heavily publicized dilemmas between old and new, orality and literacy, localism and nationalism, handwork and machinery, small business and big corporations. Symbols were also attempts at mediation by externalizing the oppositions that had formed. The romance of tools like axes and spinning wheels translated into signs of an occupational culture based on face-to-face social exchange even as they pronounced the distinctiveness of the craftsman. The log stone, like the period in which it grew, reflected ambivalent feelings toward rapid changes taking place.

The cemetery took on stones and more monuments and "memorials." Although reflecting the hierarchy of Victorian cities, the cemeteries after the 1840s became parks, patches of rural sentimentality. Strong textures and rounded forms stressed natural forms and varieties of material designs, again not matched before or after the period. The stones called forth an intensity of experience provided by the "touching" environment. The suggestion of rural life and indeed the cemetery park movement were sentimental because the advisers were addressing an eastern urban, middle-class audience for whom nature and landscape were distant and nostalgic. The midwestern rural translation of the move away from fearsome Puritan views of death and to a sentimental notion of living and dying was to go one step further to the forests and their pioneering symbolism. The log with its cut branches was compelling because of its sentimental suggestion of cut-off life and because of its rusticity. The East had its share of log cabins and forestry landscapes, but the Midwest (extended into the upland South) is where the log cabin myth and the legendary man of the woods came to rest. It is the land of Lincoln and Crockett and where the log cabin campaign of 1840 took root. The iconography of logs was firmly notched to the midwestern frame of mind.[15]

Most frequently the log's symbolism leans toward the taming of the wilderness and the attendant craft traditions. The symbolism drew attention because of its resistance—details of wood made of stone. Here is natural and artificial, man and environment, counterpoised. An example is the upright log tombstone of Eberle Martin in Mitchell, Indiana. It carries carvings of a muzzle-loading rifle, squirrels, and dogs. The log is signed by the carver, C. Underwood, and announces the date Martin came to Mitchell as well as his date of birth. In Bedford, a monument in the Fraternal Order of Police Park done by the same hand is in the form of an upright log on which is carved a muzzle-loading rifle, powder horn, and shot bag. A squirrel is perched on top, eating a nut. Two dogs run along a path at the base in pursuit of a fox who enters a cave.

Claude and Silvester Hoadley of Gosport, Indiana, are stonecarvers of log tombstones researched by Warren Roberts. They were especially fond of carving spinning wheels, especially for women, on their stump stones. A stone for Malinda (1815-1895) and Marcus Smith (1815-1897) carries the carving of a hand passing a biscuit to another hand, a symbol of generosity according to Hoadley's nephew. As with the Durlaufs, the Hoadleys represented "a strong family tradition."[16]

Warren Roberts reports log tombstones from Bloomington south to Jasper with firearms, mallets, wedges, books, plows, and axes. The dates of the log stones run from 1889 to 1912. I found many such stones, too, in southern Michigan. One special arrangement is in Springport, Michigan, where two upright logs stand side by side with

Martin gravemarker, Mitchell, Indiana

Peiger-Godfrey log gravemarkers, Springport, Michigan

branches crossing each other about two-thirds of the way up. Ivy runs around both logs. At the base of one is the surname Peiger and on the other Godfrey. Above Peiger is inscribed Jacob and Frances, and above Godfrey is inscribed George and Eunice, with various dates of death from 1899 to 1915. In a rectangular formation around the logs are five small logs on their sides giving names of "Mother," "Father," and children. Up from this arrangement is a log tombstone carrying the name Soule on a large book, and flanked by two small logs on their sides. I could not find such a frequency of log tombstones in fieldwork in Pennsylvania, New York, Delaware, and Mississippi, and these stones have not been reported in substantial numbers outside of the Midwest.

Benno Schum, son of Andrew, described the customers of the tree-stump tombstones as mostly union men and members of the fraternal organization Modern Woodmen of the World. The labor and individuality of the deceased drew more and more attention from the carvers. The deceased were less eighteenth-century children of God than nineteenth-century knights of labor. A sign of post-eighteenth-century secularization, the attitude toward work was noticed by Viennese immigrant Francis Grund who observed of Americans in 1837, "Active occupation is not only the principal source of their happiness, and the foundation of their national greatness, but they are absolutely wretched without it." And as Ralph Waldo Emerson added, "Labor: a man coins himself into his labor; turns his day, his strength, his thoughts, his affection into some product which remains a visible sign of his power."[17]

The rural-urban split no longer held so well. Jasper was rural and industrial, ethnic and national, religious and secular. The rise of an overarching working class called for differentiation. That was found by pointing to the individual's trade. One's productive activities became a mark of worth. Putting tools on one's stones was more than showing one's occupation. Tools proclaimed continuity and skills, especially handskills, at a time when such skills and their distinctiveness were being questioned by mass production.

The tool, the extension of one's hand and the means by which change and control are exercised takes on extra meaning in this period. Workers' parades often emblazoned their tools on banners and staffs. For many trades, tools were the most conspicuous piece of property they owned. Industrialist Henry Mercer, in compiling his attention-getting "Tools of the Nation Maker" exhibit of 1907, acknowledged the changes taking place: "In so far as the equipment of man with tools and utensils is concerned a greater change has taken place in the last two or three generations than took place in any fifteen or twenty generations preceding."[18] The old craft tools he found connected the last generation to traditions thousands of years old and, for industrial America, connected the pioneer spirit of the nation to industrialism.

For immigrants—a large portion of the working class—tools provided security, a reminder that work was at hand. Owning tools provided the opportunity to do piece work, which offered some independence from manufacturers. But manufacturers sought to control ownership of tools. In 1903 an especially bitter battle between iron molders and metal manufacturers in Philadelphia turned in favor of

Hand and machine labor in sewing are contrasted, from *Eighty Years' Progress* (1868)

the metal manufacturers, who formed a protective association to insure control.[19] In addition, Sears boasted, "We do not have our work done by the piece, but only employ day labor." The control, the standardization, of the product was in the hands of the organization, not the individual. Widely circulating "progress" books that boosted industrialism while passing as history texts affirmed the theme. Rarely having single authors, they were corporate ventures that emphasized progress in the title. One of the most popular, *Eighty Years' Progress* (1868), proudly declared that "a mule spinner, operated by one hand, carrying 3,000 spindles," did the work of "3,000 girls," who had done the "spinning by hand with a single spindle." By inference, progress was equated with machine control which produced greater quantities. It was a corporate vision. *Eighty Years' Progress* added poetry to make the point:

> No longer is wrought the *gusset and band*
> With ceaseless stitch and wearied hand;
> For sewing is *pleasure* by magic art,
> Since curious machines well play their part.

Setting the pace for advertising through the early twentieth century, the poetry's message made handwork appear dullingly utilitarian.

Machines added "magic art." Now giving "pleasure," machines appeared therapeutic.

Department stores and mail-order catalogues used the therapeutic theme by playing on their authority shown in mythical size and the pleasure of buying from a central place. Sears advertised "Capital and Surplus over ONE MILLION Dollars" and "From 5 BUILDINGS We Supply Careful Buyers of Every State and Territory." Invoking the structuring of etiquette guides, Sears and others called their catalogues "consumers guides." Changing the exclusiveness of craft labor, they devalued tradesmen's tools. Previously a custom-made or specialty item, tools were offered "at a price so low that there is no excuse for anyone not being supplied." Sears offered a carpenter chest with thirty-five tools for $14.58, a wood butcher's set with thirteen tools for $5.55, and an "every day tool set" with fourteen tools for $2.55. The advertising told the customer to forget the specialist artisan: "Do your own carpenter work and save five times the cost of this outfit by keeping your property in perfect order, saving time and carpenters' and wagonmakers' bills."

Henry Mercer claimed a special importance and a "momentous character for the old tools in the United States because of the country's 'influx of immigration.' " The tools thus provide, he said, a "broader object lesson" than they would in Europe. The lesson was one of assimilation and modernization. Popular author Elizabeth Bartol Dewing agreed. In her novel *Other People's Houses* (1909), she too compared American and European changes. "In America," she observed, "civilization had travelled; and to such purpose that it had forged ahead of humanity itself, which in the mass had builded better than it knew—accomplished feats which in their greatness belittle the individual workman." In Europe, she claimed, the individual workman still held sway. The Americanizing influence did not escape the press. In 1883, *Lippincott's Magazine* noted the large contingent of German craftsmen in America and their devotion to keeping up older traditions. By 1910, *Everybody's Magazine* announced that the Germans and Irish "coming in huge waves decades ago, have toiled slowly up into the skilled work of our industries and have united by thousands with the American born." The immigrant had used old handtools, Mercer added, until "a wave of inventive mechanical genius having seized him, he cast them all aside, and equipped himself with the products of a new machinery."[20] Convinced of the inevitability of industrialization, Mercer labeled the tools a thing of the past, hoarded them in museum collections in the name of preservation, and thus underscored their obsolescence, although such tools and the crafts they were used for were still active in the country.[21]

Ollie Schuch's workbench and tools

The other "influx" was of women into the workforce. Observing the shift, moralist writers expressed worries about the emasculating effects of factory work.[22] Men's traditional control of trades came into question, and hand tools and making things came to symbolize masculinity. In a job where the worker "*makes* nothing" without the control of tools, clergyman R. Heber Newton complained, the man "sees no complete product of his skill growing into finished shape in his hands. What zest can there be in the toil of this bit of manhood?"[23] By the 1920s, craft tool metaphors used for masculine boasts of sexuality became pervasive in "party" records. "The Every Day Man" and "The All Around Man" both claimed that they were no miller, auger, or butcher's son, but that they could use their tools and do their tasks of grinding, drilling, and cutting equally well.

The things made by hand by the worker for himself became more symbolic, more homebound. The factories heightened the separation between work and residence. Workers took materials home from the factories and used the skills of their trade on creative objects, although now that such production was nonutilitarian and out of the mainstream, the objects became "art." Upholsterer Linus Herbig of

Jasper made miniature chairs and put them in bottles. He carved a wooden horse with a chain in front. Furniture factory worker Ollie Schuch carved miniatures of German-style benches and chairs and made pocketknives out of wood. Stonecutter Jesse Corbin made chains out of stone. Furniture factory worker George Blume also made chains, but of wood, and he carved scaled-down replicas of handtools. Miniaturization, material displacement, bottling, and chaining connoted reduction of freedom or importance. Yet by drawing attention to the symbolic resistance of the object and the exceptional possibilities of handwork, the workers enlarged on their experience.

The log tombstones provided some enlargement on experience too. In southern Indiana one can walk through the Loogootee graveyard and find a replica from 1898 of two barrels and a cooper's adze or go to Bedford and find a stone dated 1917 containing a stonecarver's bench with mallet, hammer, and chisels. That World War I is an approximate terminus for most of the logs-with-tools tombstones is a sign of the withdrawal of the crafts tradition as a business. The flame of the revivalistic Arts and Crafts movement for furniture and house design flickered around the turn of the century but was extinguished by 1915. The eulogy for nineteenth-century craftsmanship came in 1914 from the pen of Thorstein Veblen in *The Instinct of Workmanship, and the State of the Industrial Arts*. "The machine technology," he declared, "took over the working concepts of handicraft, and it has gradually shifted from the ground of manual operation so afforded to the ground of impersonal mechanical process."[24] By this time, traditional crafts, although still persistent in isolated regions and among ethnic groups of the country, had been relegated in the popular mind to museums whose stated purposes included serving industry and promoting nationalism.[25] This period marked the decline in distribution of manner books, a sign that the social flux caused by an urbanizing, increasingly middle-class society, a swell of immigrant ranks, and a rapid industrial change was not felt as strongly. The strictures of etiquette had eased and a modern formula for living had become standardized.

In 1915 Jasper officially became a city after an election in which the margin of victory was two votes. Many precincts, especially those with older German-Catholics, did not favor the loss of community control which incorporation as a city would bring. George Wagner, a manufacturer and financier, became the city's first mayor. Leo and Otto moved the shop to a smaller space two blocks off the square out of the center of the town. The artisan shops had fostered the use of German to conduct business. American nationalism and the corporate demand for standard English in the factories accelerated the removal of German from public use. The decline of German as a public speaking language broke down many of the informal, community-bound ways of doing business, since the oral language supported face-to-face exchange and reliance on an ethnic connection. The only other artisan left on the square, a tinsmith, moved from the square in 1909.

Leo Durlauf preferred less ornate, sparser backgrounds than those on his father's gravestones. Still, Leo retained the Durlauf manner of lettering, technique of picked textures, and presence of naturalistic symbolism. His father Michael died in 1931. The Jasper newspaper carried the news on its front page with the headline: "M.F. Durlauf, Well-Known Musician Dies." But before his death, Michael had made plans for the community and his family to remember his trade, his tools, and his life. He had asked Leo to carve him a log footstone.

The footstone would be a memorial to Leo's father. It would be Leo's tour de force, a touchstone, and a monument to a past era. Leo worked five months on the carving to be placed in St. Joseph's cemetery. It contained Michael's stone-carving handtools: a tooth axe, a pair of dividers, a mallet, chisels, a pitching tool, a hammer, and a double-pointed sledge or scabbling hammer. Amidst the tools, ferns, acorns, ivy and oak leaves line the bottom of the six-foot log. For son Jerry, this was Leo's sign that the tradition needed protection and should last forever. A musical lyre rests atop an apron with strings. The apron and tiestrings in Michael's life were handmade by his wife Elizabeth. Leo carved in seventy-four rings in the ends of the log to give Michael's age at the time of his death. Eight cracks intersect the rings for his eight children. To daughter Irene, the ferns indicated an unfinished goal in life: "Dad always said he needed another seventy-two years to do everything he wanted to do." On the back of the stone is the inscription in raised lettering, "Carved By Request of Our Dear Father by Leo F. Durlauf."

The stone and the memory of Michael gained renown, although Leo's trade failed to prosper. Leo continued to carve special request stones, although carving of the logs ceased. One request that received attention was the tombstone of Eddie "Penny" Rottet. Eddie had carried the Jasper High School team to a state championship and died shortly thereafter. The loss of an athletic youth is tragic anytime, but especially in a state where basketball is taken so seriously. Using Eddie's basketball, Leo carved a replica in limestone bearing Eddie's team number "5" and "J.H.S. 1934."

Leo suffered a stroke a few years later, forcing him to stop carving. Demand for Durlauf stones persisted, so Leo agreed to design them and have the carving done by the Schums of Dale. Leo and Otto

Michael Durlauf, Jr., gravemarker, Jasper, Indiana

finally closed the shop during World War II. Leo died in 1954, Otto in 1962. Their children did not take up the business, and a cable television company occupied Leo's shop. A plain slab with Leo's name, a lyre, and a cross rests next to his parents' headstones. The Schums continued their business but accepted mass production techniques. In Benno's office sits a stone done by his father's hand. His father's handforged tools rest proudly at the base.

At the Good Samaritan Nursing Home, Henrietta Steinhart sits up in bed to talk to me. She is Leo's sister. Now ninety-three, she has primped for our meeting. Sparkle comes to her eye as she recounts the family music, the family trade, the town and church band, the traditions she has known. "I guess you can't blame the children for not carrying it on. It took too much time and cost too much money to do. Leo had to work hard. But at least the family still has those old stones to look at and remember. The stones now aren't much to remember. God, you don't know who made them."

The "stones now" to which she refers are sparse, carrying at most a name and dates. They line up with slick blank faces in rows in monument shops. The shopper moves across to choose a desired

Michael Durlauf, Jr., gravemarker: side view

Rottet gravemarker, Jasper, Indiana

Leo Durlauf gravemarker, Jasper, Indiana

A cemetery park, Harrisburg, Pennsylvania

shape. They are then relegated to cemetery parks, where death lounges quietly in the shade amidst neatly trimmed grass. No longer a testimony to life's work or community travail, death is a measure of time spent, rarely of tasks accomplished. Sentimentalism and personalization have given way to rationalism and egalitarianism in the shape of the stones, mourning at the cemetery to recreation there. The effect of the parks is visual, not tactual, circumstantial rather than cultural. Bellamy's vision is perhaps most pronounced here. The cemetery landscape is more uniform and routinized. The individual stone is scaled down; the size of the grounds is scaled-up. Death has become more removed from view in the late twentieth century. "The living," David Dempsey points out in *The Way We Die* (1975) "carry on as though nothing had changed."[26] So does death's material culture. It has been removed from the individual and given to the economical mass, without a mark, and has thus been made less affective, less tied to community and family. "But it makes life easier."

If the story of the Durlaufs shows the ebb of making and feeling things, then the twentieth-century story of Anna Bock is a reminder of its tide. For her story, I move to northern Indiana, leaving rolling hills for flat stretches of farmland. Here we find another ethnic settlement, but one that has chosen to resist the "modernizing" influences of industry. Anna lives in Elkhart County, the center of Mennonite settlement in northern Indiana. The county's 11,000

Mennonites live in several close-knit communities that share a common occupation—farming—a common religious belief—Anabaptist—and a common cultural heritage—German. Like most of their non-Mennonite neighbors, the Mennonites began migrating to the area in the 1830s from Ohio, Pennsylvania, and New York. The speech of the region still reflects the eastern influence, while German influences are still discernible in bank barns, place-names, and foods. Meanwhile there are constant reminders of modernization—commercial strips arising along expanding highways, suburban expansion, tourism. Twentieth-century Mennonite families in Elkhart County perpetuate their German agrarian heritage, although younger members often work in nearby trailer and recreational-vehicle factories.

The area's Mennonites are more than members of a religious organization who share a fundamental belief system linked to the Bible. They are a cultural group who possess common values of family, *communitas,* and tradition. Two goals related to the preservation of these values are "separation from the world" (explained by Anna as maintaining a group identity apart from modern society) and "plain living," that is, avoiding ostentation in dress, housing, and life. Such goals are part of *Ordnung,* or "order" and "regulation," in the lives of Old Order Mennonites. *Ordnung* does not appear in written form and is not dictated by a higher bureaucratic authority. *Ordnung* is perpetuated as a set of customary norms.

Maintaining traditional ways of life helps achieve religious goals by solidifying the group in its resistance to change. In this respect, language serves as one distinguishing feature of the area's Mennonites. Anna explained, "Our ancestors who came from Switzerland spoke the same language we speak and it has been handed down for nine or ten generations. A man from the old country heard one of our church men speak and said, 'He speaks Swiss Dutch.' It was the Swiss dialect of Pennsylvania Dutch, and he after all these many years recognized it which I thought was really something." A prescribed form of dress—simple clothing and bonnets—also sets the Mennonites apart as does their preferred means of transportation—horse and buggy. These features distinguish members of the group from nonmembers and symbolize group unity. Moreover, material culture marks divisions within the group—such as sectarian differences among the Old Order Mennonite churches in Elkhart County—although these markers are usually more discernible to members of the local Mennonite community than to nonmembers. Theirs is a touch-oriented world of face-to-face social exchange and spirituality. Theirs is an extended community, for it relies on regular visits between Old Order Mennonite settlements in Pennsylvania, Ohio, Illinois, and Iowa.

Anna, the daughter of farming parents, was born in Wakarusa, Indiana, in 1924.[27] Handicapped at an early age by diminutive height and other physical problems that hinder her movements, Anna's painting has allowed her, since 1946, a means of support without traveling outside her home, and an outlet for creative expression. Anna never received formal training in drawing or painting, but as a child her family recognized that she possessed an unexplained artistic talent beyond that necessary to produce utilitarian objects. The Mennonites value humility, and this value prevented her from formally developing her talent. "If I went away and made a big deal," she said, "if I tried to show off, I would get in trouble." Anna accepted the strictures. She cherishes its offering of identity and structure to her life.

Anna's environment fostered Mennonite and German values. She was raised in what she calls a "double home," one that housed her parents, grandparents, and at one time even her great-grandparents. Such a living situation, which manifests strong family ties, has been crucial to the retention of Mennonite traditions in the face of modernity, and the preservation of both "separation from the world" and "plain living." A dialect of German, or "Pennsylvania-Dutch" as Anna calls it, was and still is the primary language used in her home. Her mother and grandmother were both adept at rug hooking, quilting, and foodways, which had customarily been part of the woman's world among nineteenth-century American Mennonites. Anna's uncle and grandfathers carved traditional decorative objects such as fans and chains out of wood. Her father farmed, using skills passed down through many generations.

While in her early twenties, Anna began decorating jars and plates with flowers and geometric designs. Having difficulty keeping paint on glass, she contacted an older Mennonite whose work she had seen locally. The two women met in Lancaster County, Pennsylvania, and from the older woman Anna learned painting techniques. Anna's art changed when her sister-in-law brought her a canvas. She began painting genre scenes of everyday Mennonite life. Anna described these early attempts as "crude." She humorously recalled, for example, a team of horses that she painted with their knees inward. Despite these detractions, she painted more daily scenes because she was dissatisfied with depictions by "outsiders" (non-Mennonites) of her community's lifestyle: "They couldn't get anything right—the buggies were all wrong and everything. We live what I paint and I paint what I see." Her material culture held a symbolic power for her

"The Sugar Camp," 1971 (24″ x 30″)

"Apple Butter Season," 1973 (24″ x 30″)

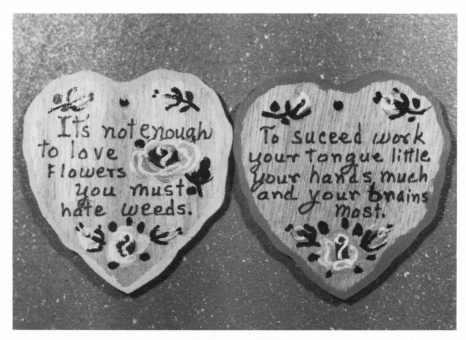

Wall plaques, 1979 (4″)

"County Line Church," 1979 (8″ x 10″)

and its distortion by outsiders—aliens not just to her regional milieu but also to her ethnic and religious background—motivated her work.

Today, which Mennonite scenes she paints are determined largely by what will sell. She personally prefers the "mountain cabin, nature, and water" scenes, but they sell poorly. Scenes such as maple sugaring, buggy drives, and farms are strong sellers to local non-Mennonites, while smaller scenes and decorated wooden objects including matchbox holders, memo rollers, wall plaques, and salt boxes sell well to Mennonites. The Mennonites buy such wooden objects as souvenirs or gifts for children when they visit distant Mennonite churches. The objects are appealing because they are inexpensive reminders of a visit and are utilitarian as well as decorative. Anna signs her name and gives titles to the works for non-Mennonites. For Mennonites it is usually not necessary; they know who she is, they know what she is depicting. She is part of the community.

Many Mennonite viewers consider Anna's larger paintings too ostentatious. When asked to identify what was too much art for Mennonites, Anna paused. She tried to explain: "When God formed the earth, he put decoration in it—plants and flowers and things like that—just nothing artificial. It's puzzling to outsiders but we know it." Her own walls are free from decoration with the exception of a pendulum clock and small paintings she did of her house and churches. A pillow decorated with a tulip design worked by her sister lies on a nearby couch. A woven rug rests in front of the couch, and a hooked rug with a flower design made by Anna's mother lies in the living room. The modest furnishings epitomize humility and plain living.

Anna makes some objects she does not sell. "Painting gets on your nerves," she says. "You get tired all over. I like it but I just don't know what to make next. After painting pictures for about two weeks I change off—take a break—and do easier painting, the wooden wares for a while. Once a year I get a streak to do something different." One year this impulse prompted her to make colorful, circular braided rag rugs, which she placed under two rocking chairs to protect the bare floor. What divisions did she make between the things she made? Pointing to the rag rugs, she said, "Oh, those are just for use. They serve a purpose." "Aren't they art, too?" I probed. "The art part is knowing what you're doing," she replied. "You got to have the right system, know what colors to put in, you have to know how to do it." Art to Anna is skill, but she makes distinctions between purely decorative objects such as paintings and useful items such as rugs. But precisely because the rugs are everyday, traditional items that require great skill to make, she can use them as outlets for creative expression within the limits of her religious values. Anna recognizes

"Rural Life by H.B.C.," 1853 (17½" x 24") (New York State Historical Association)

that creativity within tradition, any tradition, can be taxing—
"painting gets on your nerves," she notes—because creativity involves anxiety. Indeed, creativity involves the uncertainty of making
a novel expression that follows social standards, making something
with personal meaning and having it accepted socially, the risk of
attempting the unprecedented or of successfully repeating a design.

Anna paints scenes of farmsteads and houses that are a combination of imagination and memory. She also receives specific orders for
particular farms. She prefers to work from a photograph because she
can then work in her own home. She measures the size of the objects
and then multiplies them mathematically to keep the painting in
proportion. On those occasions when Old Order Mennonites commission farmscapes, she must travel to paint them because the *Ordnung*
forbids photographs. For Anna, this work is her visible testimony to
the connection of community. The work is her public show of labor.

The commissioning of farmscape paintings has appeared in rural
areas for at least two centuries in America and longer in Europe,
although urban encroachment and photography led to a decline of the
practice in the late nineteenth century. Farmscape painting, however,

continues to be popular among Old Order Mennonites. Asked why, Anna explained, "Mennonites like farm scenes; I painted one for my brother. I don't know why—I guess it's a my-farm type of thing, and to see how well you can make it like it really is."

Anna's depiction of farmsteads and houses is hardly mechanical. Her ability to portray the life around her is based on her intimate familiarity with her physical and cultural surroundings. This point became especially evident when two friends of mine asked Anna to paint an eight- by 10-inch picture of their one-story house in Bloomington, Indiana. The house did not conform to the typical house she was used to, and she admitted difficulty. She termed it a "funny" house because it looked different from those with which she was familiar. She claimed that one Mennonite even asked, "Is that the President's house?" She then showed me the painting. "Did I leave anything out?" "Should I change anything?" "Is there anything that's not right?" She was uneasy about depicting life beyond her community and outside her ethnic experience.

Anna's scenes encompass many of the familiar benchmarks of Mennonite life and life in northern Indiana. She paints any of a stock mental list of common scenes, with variations determined by the size of the canvas and the complexity of the scene desired. Her paintings emphasize selected activities and cultural landmarks, not individuals. Figures in her paintings lack distinguishable facial features: "I can't paint anyone to look like anyone. I'm just not good on people. I couldn't paint a portrait even if I wanted to." She puts people and activities in her farmscapes and other paintings where figures seem secondary. She explained, "Helps to sell them. You wouldn't want buildings without the buggies or people." Her remarks parallel those of another genre painter who told me, "I don't sell paintings, I sell scenes."

Such scenes hark back to a Victorian American appetite for picturesqueness. The picturesque provided a sentimental contrast to the efficiency and streamlining of American visions. To middle-class tastemaker Andrew Jackson Downing, writing in 1841, "We find the Beautiful in the most symmetrical edifices, built in the finest proportions and of the purest materials. It is on the other hand in some irregular castle, . . . some rude mill nearly as wild as the glen where it is placed, some thatched cottage, weather stained and moss covered, that we find the Picturesque."[28] The picturesque came to be associated with the lower strata of culture and their lore. T.F. Crane in *Popular Science Monthly* in 1881 presaged the currents of things to come when he wrote, "Mr. James enumerated the items of high civilization which are absent from the 'texture of American life.' To

"Harvest Scene," 1971 (10″ x 16″)

these might be added an item of low civilization, but what for the purpose of the imaginative writer, is of greater utility than the court of Epsom—folk-lore."[29] For twentieth-century moderns, the Old Order Mennonites provide some of that picturesqueness, some of that reassurance that depth of everyday living is not gone.

The emphasis on daily activities can be seen in a list of Anna's scene titles. They typically involve traditional productivity in a communal, touch-oriented world, as for example in foodways: "The Sugar Camp," "Making Taffy," "Bringing Pumpkins for Grandma" (plate 9), "Apple Butter Season," "Butchering Day" (plate 11), "Cider Making." Other paintings portray the closeness to nature provided by farming: "Fall Farm Scene," "Spring Farm Scene," "Hurrying before a Storm" (plate 10), "Haying Scene," "Harvest Scene." Another set of paintings emphasizes the picturesque material culture of Mennonites in the region and their suggestion of heightened social connection. Examples are "Covered Bridge," often shown with a courting couple, "Bonneyville Mill," associated with picnics, and "Bachelor Buggy," also with a courting couple. In still another set of paintings Anna underscores the value Mennonites place on hard work, especially as it relates to the intimate relationship between farm and home. "The Busy Season," "The Hard Workers," and "Grandpa's Clean Up" idealize times of the year when Anna's family and others traditionally begin spring cleaning or prepare foods for winter. "The Hard Workers," a fall scene, shows a five-horse team plowing a field while the women make apple butter near the house. Anna modeled the team after one that belongs to her family minister. The same team appears in "The Busy Season" (plate 7), a painting of a farmhouse beside which many quilts hang on a line, rugs and mattresses air out, a kite flies in the background, and horses help a man do his farming.

The presence of customs insuring social connection draws attention in "Sunday Company," which shows the Mennonite custom of visiting neighboring families for midday dinner after church services. These regular meetings reinforce shared traditions. The elder women of the host family supervise essential food preparations and in the process train their daughters in the preparation of traditional foods. The men visit in the living room while the children play socially engaging games such as New Orleans and Mother Witch. To Anna, "Sunday Company" objectifies "part of pleasure." To non-Mennonite customers, it is part of the picturesque.

Anna's paintings contain images having personal meaning. Exaggerated trees in "Fall Picnic" reflect her love of nature and the outdoors. Anna described a farmscape she painted from memory: "It had a creek and an apple orchard, but I put flowers on the trees in the

"Sunday Company," 1973 (16″ x 20″)

painting to make it nice." Another important personal image is the mailbox, especially prevalent in "Anxious for the Mail" (plate 12), which reveals her reliance on correspondence to reach beyond her home. She is unable to travel easily because of her physical handicap, and like most Old Order Mennonites she does not have a telephone in her home.

Anna is well aware of material symbols of Mennonite identity and she applies them to her paintings. She points out buggies, windmills, plain clothing, white houses, and green window blinds. Looking at a harvest scene with tractors, I asked her "What's Mennonite about this painting?" "They're steel tractors," she replied. "They have steel tires. If they have rubber tires they can go like a truck on the road. The steel keeps it home." The stress on home allows Anna to feel part of the productive community, despite her handicap. Paintings such as "Anxious for the Mail," "Fall Picnic," and "Sunday Company" reflect the joy that Anna derives from observing everyday life which flows, and her depictions compensate for her inability to participate fully or fluidly in those activities.

Like many artists, Anna manipulates forms to control error and to provide repeated, procedural standards. In various versions of "The Sugar Camp," for example, the essential form—the sugar house—is surrounded by other objects such as a horse pulling a sled packed with barrels, a Mennonite couple standing in front of the structure, prominent trees, buckets hanging from trees, dogs observing the scene, and a woodpile lying on the snow. Anna can alter those paintings she considers "flops" to sugar camp scenes by inserting a large sugaring house in the center of the canvas and adding other items, depending on the size of the canvas. Her use of repetition to control error and to reduce anxiety from creativity is also visible in three paintings she had in progress in February 1980. Each canvas depicted a Mennonite house flanked on one side by a prominent tree and on the other by a barn. One painting had a house with three windows over two, two rooms deep with a central door, while the others had a typical I-house shape—one room deep, two rooms wide, two windows over two, and a central door. One house had a porch while the others did not. As the three paintings lay on her easels, she pointed out how she could add Mennonite symbols—green window shades, buggies, or sometimes green roofs—and provide a repeatable formula, in short, a controlled, sequential process for making things.

Several other patterns underscore Anna's artistic control. Her roads usually run perpendicular to each other, and she uses the same pattern for fence and building formations. Houses consistently have two stories and a central chimney. For smaller canvases which often feature covered bridges or buggies, she places the basic unit in the center of the canvas and balances it with smaller units on either side. She used a similar pattern in her only still life, "The Parlor Lamp," where a lamp is in the center of the painting and a hat and gloves are on either side. The result provides an inner triangular frame for the painting's elements. The product is predictable in form, manipulable in symbolism.

Although "separated from the world," Anna functions in a market economy. She keeps careful records of all her transactions. She notes the dates of purchase, the names of customers, the types of objects bought, and the prices paid. Although she earns more money from her paintings, she sells mostly wooden objects such as plaques. Yet she claims to have more orders for paintings than she can handle. Nonetheless, her income is still minimal. And like Michael Durlauf, in the role of artisan she has accepted special requests. Special orders have included such jobs as painting a nearby harnessmaker's sign and decorating tinware. She does not hang out a sign for her work and she does not advertise. Knowledge of her work spreads by word of mouth in the community. The work proceeds from face-to-face encounters.

Asked how her Mennonite neighbors felt about her artwork, she replied, "They like it, and they try and help me out because they know it's all I can do." In her mind, she serves four distinct groups, each with particular tastes and demands: Amish, Old Order Mennonites, new Mennonites, and outsiders. The differences among the groups, according to Anna, are their conservatism and its manifestation in material culture: "The Amish are a little more conservative than us in things like plain dress and such, and we're more conservative than other Mennonites in keeping the Old Order with horses and buggies and dress, while outsiders drive the cars and such." Anna considers herself firmly in the Old Order Mennonite community: "I paint the scenes around me usually and the life I live or that type of picture, and if you come down into these parts you may find our life style is not as rare as you now may think. I realize it may be where you live." Anna's situation is similar to that of many ethnic artists. Although a member of a recognizable group tradition, she depends on people external to her tradition for a market, and her work increasingly reflects the demands of that market.

The market economy notwithstanding, Anna's paintings express her sense of possession of the scenes and objects portrayed. Similarly, her sentimental comments about the memory paintings of her original double home convey pride, belonging, and a certain wishfulness. It is as if she has painted a world of Mennonites and nature, one without "outsiders." She paints Mennonite-built structures, and when she paints regional structures such as covered bridges and mills, Mennonites are the only ones in a scene, thus implying possession. Buggies are the only vehicles on her roads, and moreover, buggies appear in the center of the roads, rather than hugging the sides as they do in real life. Occupying the center is what her paintings hope for.

Residences in her paintings represent the general—any Mennonite house and farm with their characteristic green blinds, windmills, and red barns without white corners. Her sympathetic but stylized renderings of horses, gardens, food processes, and mills are material symbols of the Mennonites' community cohesion and their work ethic. The courtship rites, picnics, Sunday visits, and family gatherings represent community-bound activities in a constant flow of life.

Anna refracts reality in her paintings to convey the interconnected meanings of a distinctive life given visibility by material culture. In reality, activity and objects are integrated. In her art they are segregated. Material symbols stand alone to draw attention to themselves.

Anna heightens the effect of a distinctive material life by manipulating *proximity* and *balance*. Her paintings literally create framed categories by clustering social activity and material symbols around a central artifact. In "Hurrying before the Storm," the eye is drawn to the intersection of perpendicular lines of imagery. A buggy moves left to right and children walk from right to left. The center of the line is provided by a vertical walk and a mailbox. Just above is a haywagon with a pair of similarly depicted Mennonite laborers. Lightning just above the wagon points attention downward. Similarly sized trees flank the whole composition. The backdrop is crowded with nature.

Anna serves as community documentarian and artist, functions which contribute to group identity, and the art gives her an outlet for personal needs of creativity, activity, and economy. Non-Mennonites view her paintings as symbols of the region, identified by a people close to their land. Like westerners' desire to have American-Indian artifacts, the paintings appeal to a sentimentalizing of America's heritage which accepts modernization as a standard. The rugs and quilts made by the Mennonites do not sell as well or as often, but the visual painting mediates between the hand and the machine, the old and the new.

If influences exist from outside, there are also ones from the inside. Her family plays a strong role. Members criticize her art and look for what they perceive to be mistakes. Her father, for example, pointed out that her kite in "The Busy Season" showed one wind direction while her windmill revealed an opposite one. Her mother similarly commented on such details as quilt patterns depicted. Westward migration by Mennonites from Indiana looking for cheaper land or more seclusion has sparked memories for them to take with them and fostered their commentary. Anna talked of painting the harness shop on the next farm over, for example. "That sold real quick. Any time you do something *really* from the community it goes. Especially to people going away like this boy going to Germany, and *our* people going to Wisconsin to look for cheaper land."

Typical of informal learning, Anna solicits suggestions for changing her depictions to alleviate some of the uncertainty inherent in communally inspired creativity. When painting "Meadow Valley School," a Mennonite schoolyard scene, she used as models sketches of the school made by Mennonite schoolchildren in addition to her memory of the school. She included a schoolyard baseball game in the scene. Unsure as to how baseball is played, she asked me whether the batter and players were in the right positions. They were. Anna nonetheless remained unhappy with the painting because "the building didn't set the right way." On another occasion, at a customer's request, she painted a "stream, fishing, and a mill scene" that excluded buggies. In another painting she added a dog. Anna adjusts her paintings to audience preferences by substituting or deleting and adding certain features. Her formulaic techniques allow for artistic productivity answerable to shifting demands.

Colors are important to Anna. She favors "red, white, brown, blues—and black for the buggies." She painted one fall scene that she claimed was too bright. "It should look natural," she said. Her comment underscores the value she places on closeness to and beauty of nature, which is also a religious value to her way of thinking. Just as Anna presents scenes and objects in a repeated, formulaic process, so too does she use colors in a repeatable and predictable manner. She has a standard way of coloring leaves for each season. When she tries out a new idea such as painting a sky to depict an oncoming storm, a degree of experimentation occurs before she settles on a repeatable procedure. This is the twentieth-century version of craft as business. It is acceptable to Anna because its order follows from the social regulation governing her life.

Anna's emphasis on typical scenes of community life parallels many works of nonacademic rural artists elsewhere. Indicative of the view of rural women's domestic attention to monitoring everyday operations, and less solid and harsh, less representative of ideas of male strenuosity in stone, wood, and metal, the genre painting of women such as Queena Stovall of Lynchburg, Virginia, Theora Hamblett of Oxford, Mississippi, and Anna Robertson Moses of Hoosick Falls, New York, possesses common themes. Whereas the specialness of male craft products ran through descriptions of the trades, these genre artists share a notion that it was "the familiar that rural America loved and rural America was loved for these very things." Quilts, canned fruits, and rag rugs provide aesthetic satisfaction in subtle ways. The genre painting, often being a twentieth-century women's craft, retains everyday subtlety and a consistent interplay of plush, fertile nature in harmony with a humanly built world. Painting, for Grandma Moses, Otto Kallir writes, "was always subordinated to the duties and obligations of everyday life."[30] Painting came into bloom when housework became too strenuous for her. Having lived the "everyday," the regulation of children and adults' activities revolving around farm and home, the artist objectified the life, trying to draw out its meaning. Hanging in Anna Bock's workshop, for example, are paintings she did of the structures she has frequented most: her own house, County Line Church (destroyed in 1950), and Yellow Creek Church. Like Anna, the other genre artists number among their popular paintings depictions of apple-butter making,

"A Painting for Home Decoration," from *Social Culture*

butchering, farming, school and church scenes. With each, the artist is at some remove from the scene, either in time or in action. The flat, restrained, and pictorial material culture of women has fared much better in the twentieth century than the craft products of male tradesmen. Women's material culture already resided in the private realm least affected by industrialization. Advisers such as *Social Culture* (1896) encouraged the domestic entrenchment of women's material culture. Less threatening to a social and economic order, literally less cutting and suggestive of labor, more visual and sentimentalized, women's genre painting appealed not just for its picturesqueness, a carryover of Victorian sentimentality, but for its "impression of depth," as Kallir states, "its atmosphere of compelling truth and closeness to nature."

With the publicity for a tradition of decorative effect and cottage handskills lacking for men, women's artifice generally adapted better than men's to the secondary decorative role which handwork now played in society. Catharine Beecher and Harriet Beecher Stowe's successful adviser *American Women's Home* (1869) stressed the "professionalization" of women's domestic skills, including "Sewing, Cutting, and Mending," "The Care of Yards and Gardens," and "Home Decoration." In 1883 the *Ladies Home Journal* followed by *Home Decoration* in 1886, served a women's audience indulging in handicrafts. Later, these crafts became arts, as they appeared to become a leisure-time pursuit. *Home Arts* appeared in 1909 followed by *McCall's* in 1913, which put out a supplement of decorative arts and needlework. A testimony of the effect of the separation of men and women in handskills came in 1886 with a report published in *Popular Science Monthly* on "The Hand-Work of Children." Surveying Yonkers, New York, schoolchildren, the author found that by second grade handwork done at home by girls "begins to show the effect of training at home, and is more commendable than that of boys. The specimens included white undergarments, neatly made and turned; aprons of various styles; knitted dolls' heads, base and crochet work; baby's clothes, crazy work hats, dressed dolls, beanbags, pen-wipers, and pin cushions." Boys "found themselves too unskilled to make good specimens, and were too proud to exhibit poor ones." Although providing "good moral influence" and the "exercise of self will-power" drawn from "completing one thing," it was evident that handwork was nonessential, a pastime done at leisure. The author writes, "There would be found in almost every individual aptitudes for hand-work of one kind or another, which would afford pleasurable pursuits in hours not occupied with the *serious* affairs of life."[31]

Women's buildings at world expositions stressed domestic hand-skills. In the comical *Around the Pan* (1901), written about the 1901 Pan-American Exposition in Buffalo, a cartoon shows a man and woman going in separate directions, and the woman speaking. The caption reads, "I think you're horrid to compel me to spend the whole day looking at machinery." Women who did wage work were considered most capable of doing delicate work requiring patience and hand dexterity, especially in the textile industry. Men's tasks were scaled up to reflect the constructional and synthetic duties of machinery. *Popular Mechanics,* starting in 1902, gives recognition to this notion for its male audience. Men's tasks were "occupational" and "essential," geared to the mechanized society.

Otis Mason's *Woman's Share in Primitive Culture* (1894) confirmed through the "science of anthropology" that the modern age of industrialism and militancy belonged to men. But he claimed that the origin of industrial pursuits lay in the handwork of women, militancy in the aggressiveness of men. "In contact with the animal world, and ever taking lessons from them, men watched the tiger, the bear, the fox, the falcon—learned their language and imitated them in ceremonial dances. But women were instructed by spiders, the nest builders, the storers of food and the workers in clay like the mud wasp and the termites."[32] Women persisted in their handwork even through industrialism and it is for them, Mason implied, that men toil so hard. If women became leisurely and domestic, it was because their major work was behind them. "It is in the apotheosis of industrialism," Mason wrote, "that woman has borne her part so persistingly well. At the very beginning of human time she laid down the lines of her duties, and she has kept to them unremittingly."

Men doing domestic handwork were most visible in Allen Eaton's America's Making Exposition in New York City done for the Russell Sage Foundation in 1919 and traveling widely afterward. Located in New York's Armory, the exhibit attracted over a million visitors. The men shown doing crafts were immigrants who had contributed greatly to the making of America, Eaton showed, but who were meant to "Americanize." The exhibit was followed by surveys of rural crafts through the 1930s, once again showing male basketmakers, carvers, and furniture makers. But 67 percent of those reporting to the survey were women. The existence of crafts among immigrants or rural people was a sign of a "great industrial country," Eaton contended, for they can be found working in a mode reminiscent of the early life of the nation. Yet he considered the beauty, depth, and meaning of their work essential to urban consumers: "The stream of hand-made objects flowing from rural communities to the towns and cities is of real importance to countless Americans who, coming into possession of these objects, have an opportunity to express their tastes and indulge their tastes and indulge their aesthetic preferences in ways never before within the reach of the average purchaser." Eaton could have found crafts within the industrial belt of the Middle Atlantic states but chose to study areas away from these centers. The areas of New England and the Southern Highlands fitted well into a primitive agrarian myth that supported an urban ideology of progress by separating domains of work.[33] Disillusionment with factories shutting down and equipment forcing debt helped draw attention to Eaton's economic argument for the commercial viability of handicrafts. Indeed, many workers did return to the traditional skills that they knew would produce marketable goods, and even mechanical magazines ran articles on whittling and old-time practical skills. The 1930s was also the time that women genre painters came to national attention. In painting, the primitive agrarian myth and women's special role in symbolizing it came to the fore. Often, though, such painting took place in old age, in leisure, after a woman's labors were spent.

Around the turn of the century, men were known to paint, much as Anna did for her community, but they usually did so more directly as a matter of labor or as a sign of membership. In the General Conference Mennonite community of Buhler, Kansas, Emil Kym painted genre scenes of his Swiss homeland on walls of neighboring Mennonite homes from 1896 until his death in 1915. Another artist, Olaf Krans, worked in the paint shop of a religious-communal society at Bishop Hill, Illinois, from 1850 to 1861. He painted houses, signs, and curtains after he left the society in 1861, but he was most noted for his genre paintings done from the 1890s to the 1910s based on his memory of Bishop Hill community life. He died in 1916. Like Anna, their work materialized a communal way of life. The very surge of creativity that produced this lasting testimony to communal unity was also a sign of dispersal.

Given the dualistic nature of the Mennonite community, as part of, yet separate from, modern American society, tensions naturally exist. Hence, Anna's productivity is an expression of and for Mennonites, yet its survival depends on pressures for her to produce material conforming to non-Mennonite preferences. It is a balancing act, to be sure, but one accomplished with some success because of the Mennonite communal concern for finding roles for members of the community. The aged in this community are not separated as they are in modern American society, but integrated, relied upon for passing on knowledge. Anna's art allows her to work. It serves her community in a traditional, symbolic manner, and it maintains continuity with Mennonite traditions. In its closeness to nature and its regulation, her art embodies religion by objectifying communal and spiritual values. Beyond the Mennonites, "plain living" is the catchphrase for much of folk material culture. It became the cornerstone of the popular *Foxfire* series and its many imitations, stretching from the 1960s to the 1980s.

Spiritual values in America became attached in the early twentieth century to a closeness to the land and to the technology of the past. The other center for traditional handwork besides the home and family was in religion. Such thinking was encouraged by a barrage in print bemoaning the secularization of America.[34] The essays asked for the materialization of sacredness in a technological society based on faith not in spirit but in science. Anna's expression of religion as living is too vague and consuming for most Americans. Religion had become compartmentalized, given its time in the appointment book. But the search for spirituality, separate from a discussion of religion, still concerns those who make things.

Like the image of home, religion's imagery draws closely on body and mind. Often, people who make things speak of being guided by the hand of God, of feeling a spirit, of seeing a vision. Making things involves conversion. The machine, usually feeling distant from manual control, is more existential. It appears, finished. How it works, how it came to the final step appear inconsequential. It lacks the incrementalism, the slow transformation, of the handmade object. The converted work, whether a child or wrought iron, often takes on persuasiveness or even sanctity, and implies a moral connection. Blacksmith Philip Simmons would preach, for example, "Raw iron ain't worth nothin', you got to shape it for it to be something. Same with a child, you got to make something of him."[35] The performed spoken words of the Testaments were given the "power of the word" when converted into the Bible, its confirmation of truth given by placing one's hand on it. Those who controlled processes of conversion—the blacksmith, carpenter, farmer, and stonecutter—had extranatural beliefs attached to them and provided metaphors for the messages of ministers. Puritan poet Edward Taylor rhetorically asked, "Upon what base was fixed the lathe wherein He turned this globe and rigolled it so trim? Who blew the bellows of His furnace vast?"[36] One could cite Ecclesiasticus 38, "All these put their trust in their hands, and each becometh wise in his own work. . . . they shall maintain the fabric of the world; and in the handiwork of their craft is their prayer." Indeed, Calvinist conversion stressed the lump of clay of man turned by the hands of God into a refined, shaped product.

But a change that occurred with industrialization was a shift from the religious rhetoric of work to leisure, a shift from the working class to the leisure class. The *Christian Union* founded in 1870, consistently criticized the overwork of tradesmen and industrial work and called for repose in "the duty of play." In 1882, Henry Ward Beecher wrote for the publication a widely-circulated essay on "The Moral Uses of Luxury and Beauty." Workers could find their models in the pursuits of the upper classes, he intimated. "If we are doomed to be tradesmen and nothing but tradesmen," Unitarian Henry Bellows wrote in 1845, "let us not mistake it for the kingdom of heaven."[37]

The craftsman ideal lost some of its moral meaning. It was left to so-called radicals such as John Ruskin and William Morris in England and Gustav Stickley and Elbert Hubbard in America to push for the moral influence of handwork in their Arts and Crafts movement. By the 1910s, however, the products of the movement came in line with industry, designed to improve it rather than change the way people lived and prayed. Art historian Edward Lucie-Smith comments on the result: "The heavy, rooted solidity of Stickley's artefacts, particularly his furniture, came to seem impossibly clumsy and out of tune with the needs of the society which mechanization had produced. . . . His furniture was factory furniture, designed to be manufactured on a large scale." Short-lived magazines in the movement such as *Handicraft* and *Craftsman* reported on traditional societies still creating crafts for social exchange and religious functions, rather than commerce, but ultimately considered them anachronistic.[38]

More in keeping with the incorporated work force, religious leaders called for congregations to enjoy recreation, art, and leisure and have time set aside for church attendance. No longer builders of churches, the *Nation* observed in 1886, ministers needed "managerial, executive abilities."[39] The kind of regular contribution of labor that stonecutters and blacksmiths gave to St. Joseph's Church ceased by the late nineteenth century, replaced by "wholesome" activities of band performances and church picnics.

It was at this point that scholars took notice of folk religion and its manifestation in material culture. A widely traveled exhibit organized by Stewart Culin of the University of Pennsylvania in 1892 took the theme "Objects Used in Religious Ceremonies." Although the objects were contemporary, the exhibit, according to the University of Pennsylvania president, was showing "the aspirations and affections which are guiding it painfully upwards and onwards through the stages of its evolution." Time was manipulated. These objects were of the period, but of an earlier time and stage of culture. Their use of

Cal's house on Penn Street,
Harrisburg, Pennsylvania:
Above (1), August 1983;
left (2), April 1984.

Cal's house: *Above* (3), June 1984; *below* (4), May 1985.

Cal's house in August 1985: *Above* (5); *left* (6).

Paintings by Anna Bock (a pseudonym): *Above* (7), "The Busy Season," 1980 (18″ x 24″); *below* (8), "Evening Ride," 1979 (18″ x 24″). Photos by Darrell Peterson.

Paintings by Anna Bock: *Above* (9), "Bringing Pumpkins for Grandma," 1971 (18″ x 24″), detail. *Below* (10), "Hurrying before a Storm," 1979 (18″ x 24″); photo by Darrell Peterson.

Paintings by Anna Bock. *Above* (11), "Butchering Day," 1979 (16″ x 20″); *below* (12), "Anxious for the Mail," 1980 (12″ x 16″). Photos by Darrell Peterson.

Ross Butler's furniture store mural, Harrisburg, Pennsylvania, 1983. *Above* (13), side; *below* (14), front.

Murals by Ross Butler, 1983. *Above* (15), appliance store mural; *below* (16), Agate Street mural.

handwork and their use in religion called attention to them as apart from modernity. Indeed, evolutionist Charlotte Burne's chapter on "Things Made by Man" in *The Handbook of Folk-Lore* (1914) was devoted to "not only the art of making, but the thing made, or the instrument used, that may excite religious veneration."

Invoking evolution was an influential rhetoric, for it established industrial standards as the height of progress, the mark of an all-encompassing civilization. Influential works such as *The Origin of Invention* (1895) by Otis Mason, *The Evolution of Art* (1895) by Alfred Haddon, and *Primitive Industry* (1894) by Thomas Wilson confirmed that handwork was primitive and anachronistic. Invention, industry, and art were touchstones of civilization. They were the Anglo-Saxon, urban standards by which other peoples were judged. The emergence of diffusion was a threat to this scholarship because it challenged the social order. It argued a spread of culture, rather than its rise. It was given notoriety by the works of Moses Gaster, Franz Boas, and Joseph Jacobs. Immigrants and Jews, they fought a two-front battle against the evolutionary school and the rising tide of anti-Semitism. The implication of diffusion, Stewart Culin remarked in the 1920s, was to downplay nationalism and the hegemony of Western technology.[40]

The relation of evolution to mechanization and materialism did not go unnoticed in the popular press. Joseph Le Conte, writing in *Popular Science Monthly* in 1888, announced that the period was witnessing "a deadly life-and-death struggle between religion and materialism."[41] Evolution was the most materialistic of all doctrines, he declared, because it assumed that it was the last doctrine, the triumph of the rational and mechanistic over the organic. Defending evolution in *The Childhood of Religion* (1876), Edward Clodd assured readers that with "the displacement of many beliefs without fear, . . . the great verities remain. . . . The process of destruction is removing only the scaffolding which, once useful, now obscures the temple from our view."[42] Religion, like other cultural institutions, split into modern and folk. Frank Riale answered the question "Why So Many Definitions of Religion?" with the answer that it was a matter of surroundings and internal differences, a matter of reflecting on personal destinies.[43] Urban, progressive religion was the standard by which others were judged.

Informal practices and splintered folk sects arose during the late nineteenth century. The holiness movement of the period drew on disenfranchised groups—blacks, poor white workers, immigrants, and isolated farmers and laborers. It led to the rise of Pentecostal churches, women's Virgin Mary and saint cults as a form of folk Catholicism, and faith healing and charismatic revivals, especially in the Midwest and South. Although informal in its forms of social exchange and worship, the folk sects commonly called for more regulation and order in one's life according to holy virtues, and in reaction to progressive technology, a stress on fundamentalism and on the community serving the "common laboring man and woman."[44] Most of the twentieth-century objects reported in *Religious Folk Art in America* (1983) came from this tradition.

People still insisted on making things to show their faith, but these objects were often relegated to the home or the bedroom. In Dubois County, one finds "dresser-top shrines" complete with a statue of the Virgin Mary, crucifix, beads, and candles. Home altars and crucifixes commonly call for the handskills of a woodcarver. People say they still hold things sacred in the informal, private world of devotion. The *Encyclopedia of World Art* even makes the claim that "sacred objects and representations originate out of such aspects of private worship as prayer or the veneration of images, and they are most widespread in the sphere of folk art."[45]

I probably would not have begun thinking about the relation of sacredness to the handmade object had it not been for Leo Klueh of Ferdinand in Dubois County, Indiana. Ferdinand is a sleepy town overlooked by the imposing presence of St. Mary's Catholic Convent and Church on a high hill. Leo had been a farmer and carpenter. Born in 1898, he was retired but still made things. He would build wheelbarrows, whirligigs, and puzzles. He especially liked to make pliers out of one piece of wood. Some forty years earlier he had come across a hobo who taught him the skill to make the pliers in exchange for razor blades. It stood out in his repertoire, for here was an improbable construction—a hinged tool that had no sign of artificial interference. It also provided symbolic resistance with its metal, artificial subject in the natural material of wood. Leo showed me several pliers of different woods and sizes, but one he held more gingerly. He reached for it slowly and spread the bottom handles tenderly. The top of the pliers moved back like curtains to reveal a tiny, delicate cross. "That's a becoming object," he whispered. "Becoming?" I asked. "It's pretty, you know, and I suppose it's not quite done." "What does it need?" I quizzed. "A blessing, a sign—spirit."

Religion, in its folk forms, fosters the handmade thing because of its connection to mind and body. It invokes localism and virtuous labor. Speaking on aesthetic experience in religion, philosopher Geddes MacGregor noted that attitudes toward works of art resemble feelings for holy people. They are both revered, enshrined, and beyond understanding.[46] But although art is extrinsically holy, the holy thing needs to be intrinsically sacred. To Leo Klueh, his object had

Leo Klueh's wooden pliers with cross

Madonna and child on a rock, Jordanville, New York

shape, an outside, that sufficed for its use as a creative object, but it lacked a divinity inside. This divinity could convert his "becoming" objects into the more sacred state of being. It gave his artifice an incremental goal to work toward. That feeling of intense experience makes it kin to other forms given consumable status as "folk" by middle-class blandness. But for Leo, the effectiveness of the object depends on its informality, its use as a social instrument, not an economic one. He would give the pliers to priests, family members, and friends as friendship tokens.

Magical or religious, being is measured by human experience. In Western culture the state of being is given to experience that is miraculous, unexplainable, and transcendent. The body is typically given as the spiritual benchmark—of the soul, the spirit, the sacrament. But Western culture contains prohibitions on overt bodily expression; one expects the body to keep still. Groups compensate by externalizing aesthetic action. They invoke objects and use settings which permit such behavior to occur.

The primary object is the individual. In rites of praying, faith healing, and devotion, individuals hold fixed positions in imitation of statuary objects. As an object with a patterned form, a person feels in commune with others sharing the design. Invoking tradition, privately calling on community with a shared form, the person is active, the person is becoming, waiting for the feeling of being. In official religion, the feeling is more existential; the person is devotional by being present. The effect is of service, not of product. One goes to services, not meetings.

Crafted objects play similar roles. The maker gives the object a fixed, customary position. Human qualities or symbols are commonly attached. In the evolution of art, the *Encyclopedia of World Art* reports, the crucifix and the Madonna are the most common motifs. In my fieldwork, I often run across Madonna figures placed in bathtubs immersed in the ground and surrounded by flower gardens. The result is a shrine. In a Russian Orthodox cemetery in Jordanville, New York, a handpainted rock showed a Madonna and child. The rock and its design emphasized circles and ovals. Next to the rock was an egg placed on the grave to symbolize life. The bathtub and gravemarker Madonnas attach to private devotion. The femininity of the Madonna image coupled with the closeness of handwork lends compassion to the religious symbolism. In their recycling of materials and their proximity with nature, the bathtub and gravemarker Madonnas announce the folk feeling of becoming.

I also find many carved crucifixes in my travels. Often the woodcarvers who cut out a chain or caged ball for me have a crucifix in their repertoire. The crucifixes are made mostly by men. Indeed, the crucifix is the symbolic expression of an outstretched human form usually thought of as masculine. Beyond associations with gender, however, the tactile quality of the hewn crucifix invites clutching. It brings devotion inward, in addition to invoking nature and compassion. Like the ovals of the Madonna, it relies on strong geometric designs.

Religious folk art commonly implies relations between human and geometric and natural forms. The invisible deity when made visible by the artist is given human form and conceived as a supreme, that is, a model being. In common pictorial representations of the Garden of Eden and the Peaceable Kingdom, humans are placed among other forms but standing above them. The typically upright religious object has the power to see or is seen by all; it is touched and touching. Artificial objects—bills, letters, and pictures—are often placed upon the object. Hands and eyes are often exaggerated in pictorial representations. In rituals, the object is moved and moving. Processions provide climaxes to many religious festivals because they announce

A nineteenth-century church steeple, Charleston, South Carolina

the transformation from matter to man. The object is then placed in a home or a stage to enact dramatic episodes. Made by the compassionate and often driven hand, the object externalizes and releases human prohibitions and limitations. It emphasizes the release by its very large or very small shape or its ritual setting. It can take on spirit by embodying and transcending human form.

The body gives shape to the religious object, but its idea is projected by a concept of mind. Religious folklore refers to the godhead, the temple of the mind, the apex of the mind's Carmel or Sinai. The mind is appealing as a metaphor because of its suggestion of boundlessness and expansion even though an appearance is given of a fixed form. Since human thought is believed to be the highest power in the animal world, its extension should be the ultimate power in the spiritual world. Geddes MacGregor notes that a ritual like spreading incense in a group shows "God in their active mind, by a spreading of incense, hitherto confined in this inner chamber, throughout the mind's temple." He later concludes, "There is something belonging to the mind which is God himself."[47]

Artists materialize the mind as a spiral, pyramid, or inner core or circle. The strong geometric form of the circle with its supernatural connotations is translated into the halo. The dome gives the halo depth. Its imagery of a cap on a head lends credence, for instance, to the beehive as a Mormon religious symbol. The pyramid and the spiral underscore the top point of the head in relation to the body. Their direction of the eye upward underscores expansion and supernaturalness. This combination also made spirals, obelisks, and pyramids especially popular in the late nineteenth century. Church architecture today uses the steeple as its prime symbol, but has scaled down its repetition or texturing. In such rituals as dancing the *giglio* in Italian-Catholic neighborhoods in New York City, a huge, decorated steeple-figure is hoisted by a body of men and moved down the street. The leader of this procession is the *capo*, the head. The effect is to underscore the supremacy of the spirit over brawn, to unify community around a common mind.

Textures used in religious symbolism convey tactual and emotional feelings. A particularly good example is the religious environment created by Father Philip Attavi and the men of the Providence Home next to St. Joseph's Church in Jasper. The official church no longer fostered the handskills common in the nineteenth century. The men of the home built their private devotional environment of deeply textured geodes. Attavi, an Italian immigrant, and the men built grottoes reminiscent of the Old World folk shrines he remembered. Fountains, stations of the cross, and walls went up with geodes

Grotto, made from geodes, Jasper, Indiana

collected from local river banks. Betty MacDowell reports such environments from Alabama to Wisconsin and gives common dates of construction beginning in the early twentieth century. Typically, they are "cave-like settings composed of various rock and mineral materials. Such settings serve as backgrounds for biblical figures and scenes, before which the visitor may pause in private prayer and meditation."[48] Informal, they commonly built up areas for communal worship. For the communistic Harmonists of the nineteenth century, the grotto—rough outside and beautiful inside—"is a symbol of man showing that physical appearances mean nothing, that it is the spiritual that matters."[49]

The ethnography of religious art shows that the mind is often given an independent existence. The major exhibit "Religious Folk Art in America" (1984) included the work of James Hampton, who was "convinced that God came regularly to his garage-workshop to guide him in his ambitious undertaking." Gertrude Morgan of Louisiana and Minne Evans of North Carolina both felt that God or "something" moved their hands.[50] Dreams and "flashes coming into the mind" also provide inspiration. The mind with its suggestion of spirit becomes a place to deny self and declare community and spirituality and in the process to justify creativity. The mind is made an entity to direct and dramatize the creative impulse. Internally, the mind's power, mystery, and ambiguity permit the transcendent leap to spirit and being. As an external force, the mind is used by many artists to connect them to a larger community that might not otherwise be available. Many so-called folk artists are marginal figures in their physical communities. They become central in their built world of a spiritual community. For other artists who do work without a pattern of tradition, a motive comes from fulfilling a private devotion or vision within the boundaries of a local group.

Such religious symbols, being connected to a communal, touch-oriented world, often become political. The civil rights movement used symbolic gestures of holding hands, "having a dream," and "being on the mountain." "Religious Folk Art in America" featured the work of S.P. Dinsmoor, born in 1843 and living through the crucible of change in the late nineteenth century. "Between 1907 and 1927 Dinsmoor constructed his two-part environment, the *Garden of Eden* and *Modern Civilization,* around his Rock Log Cabin home at Lucas, Kansas. Built of cement and limestone, the dual environment includes not only the familiar figures of Adam and Eve, Cain and Abel, and a hovering angel, but also the Devil, God's all-seeing eye, concrete trees and flags, and *The Crucifixion of Labor* by members of the professions: a doctor, a lawyer, a preacher, and a banker."[51] The common cityscape has also become a dual environment with the secular declaring itself dominant. Harrisburg is typical. Church spires still rise above downtown rowhouses, but the towering secular rectangles of downtown office buildings symbolically declare their authority. Government, meanwhile, has taken over the dome.

The interplay of religious and political symbols is shown in the work of Harrisburg's Ross Butler. A janitor in the downtown post office, he lives in the city's black ghetto. The strip on Sixth Street is filled with many storefront churches, mostly Pentecostal. Abandoned buildings and boarded fronts fill the streetscape. Butler had painted the walls of his own apartment to provide, as he says, "beauty to an ugly world." He painted swirling designs and plants. The living room wall received a huge dome with a cross. "Domes are religious, you know," he said. "The churches don't have them now, but they're really expressive, 'cause they enclose so much." He expanded by painting boarded windows on abandoned buildings across the street from his house. Around the corner, an appliance store sat empty, a victim of

A symbolic cityscape, Harrisburg, Pennsylvania

State Capitol, Harrisburg, Pennsylvania

vandalism. Butler painted the front, and vandalism stopped. The dominant imagery was of overlapping domes. A central dome toward the bottom had a cross on top and flanking it were smaller domes. Over it was a larger dome with sky around it. The crossed dome was the church, the larger dome God's presence. In the doorway he continued. A red circle was flanked by classical pillars and capped by a dome. His work was noticed by neighborhood children and adults. His house was a gathering center for the block. The storefront was his creation but it was a communal symbol. Children asked him to sign their names in the design. Adults meanwhile gave it religious meaning.

An abandoned furniture store became Butler's next public artwork (plate 14). On the Sixth Street side, a large dome reads "Harrisburg" and beside it sits a cityscape with the prominent capitol dome dominating the scene. He included other governmental and authority symbols: a harsh white, rectangular United Nations building with a stark brick edifice next to it standing above the variegated cityscape. On the other front panels, hierarchal strips of imagery again run across. At the bottom are pots with plants in them and a black face

Ross Butler working on a street mural

A housefront mural by Ross Butler

with hair in an Afro style. The strip above has smaller domes enclosing rectangles. The one above that has flowers. The top strip has a dome with a wrench where one would expect the cross to be. Yet on the side, away from the wide street view, is a large black dome with GOD written in it. It is flanked by many smaller domes. The cap of the dome is white and in the background stand white mountains.

What inspired this work? Ross raises his hands and says, "That's just what's in my mind." The work dramatized his relation to his world and the worlds around him. He comes back to the storefronts to touch them up. He enjoys the facade of beauty he has made. He inspects them, wondering what they mean beyond that. His is the imagery of blacks in a center of government. It is informal religion capped by officialdom.

In Ross Butler's life, religion provides a communal authority that government cannot give. Religion provides the protection, legislation, and structure that government, in his mind, will not. In exchange for that formula for living, Ross Butler works and materializes payment. The so-called expressions of folk religion in the United States are measured by the "official" standard of white middle-class Christianity, with its managerial, executive abilities. Old World Jews, rural fundamentalists, ethnic and racial sects have systems of spirituality that provide formulas for being, for authority. They stress the preservation of material symbols in the face of a leveling society. They commonly practice in a private communal world.

Government has its own religious symbolism. Capitols sport domes, and their legislative sessions are given benedictions. They have executive heads, judicial arms, legislative bodies. The core of the White House is the president's oval office. His bishops are his inner circle. His cross is a seal with the symbolic eagle. The separation of church and state has always been a tense one in the United States, and the power of technology has brought its influence to bear on both. Religious philosopher F. David Martin complained, for instance, that "technology tends to arrange reality so that we do not have to participate with it. Thus technology can so externalize our lives that we become alienated from ourselves and others, our artifacts, and nature."[52] Away from the center of power, artifacts become more creative, more touch-oriented. At the seat, expression and texture are not as necessary because one is secure. Having become a standard mediating between high and low, official religion rarely gets a qualifying adjective. That is reserved for alienated groups who are often set apart by the description "folk." Yet the impression of what is taken to be folk is necessary to combat the artificiality that modernization has wrought in the public mind.

"Folkness," picturesqueness, and tactility are abstractions for calling upon nature, the rustic past, and the ethnic present to offer reality and wonder. Their manifestations in material culture provide depth, rootedness, and intense experience. Artists are longed for who can craft spiritual meaning through the direct control of their hands in the security of community. The wonder with which artists make ordinary materials become something new and the processes through which the materials go to take on being are coupled with social fears that modern people will become objects rather than make them. Religious folk art stores a mosaic of different values and beliefs, but more than this, it questions and acts on the transcendent nature of reality—physical and social.

So I thought as I pondered why a major religious folk art conference in 1984 should be held in St. Peter's Church in New York City. Here was an edifice connected to a shopping mall, an edifice barely recognizable as a church when registrants looked for it. Its hours coincided with the end of the business day. Above its altar is an open vertical window with clean lines and slick surfaces. It looked up at the towering clean lines and slick surfaces of skyscrapers which dwarfed the edifice. It seemed ironic for me to talk there about John Joseph Stoudt. Shortly after the turn of the century, Stoudt's father had written on his native Pennsylvania-German folklore. So as the "cultivated rose has been, by the gardener's skill, developed from the common wild rose," he wrote, so had folklore been the foundation for products of his overcivilized age. From his view, typical of the time, the folk are wild and common, but through their knowledge one may realize their "thoughts, their ethics, and their religion."[53] His son paid closer attention to material culture, to folk art. Trained in theology, he found religious values lacking in "capitalist art." "Capitalist art," John Joseph Stoudt argued, is based on geometric form and "dull middle-class morality." He found Pennsylvania-German folk art spiritual and appealing because it used natural form to "depict the transcendent world which lies beyond the pale of things which can be verbally or graphically expressed."[54] The translation for my audience was to view folk art without grasping it.

In the movie *Simon* (1980), audiences laughed at the thought of a church congregation praying to a television set, yet the satire drew on the worship of technology that the larger society perpetuates. It drew on the passivity and lack of creativity in a visually oriented world, a bourgeois blandness attached to flat, rectangular technological form. In real life, symbolic confusion exists. New steeples resemble oil cans rather than spires. The steeples of the pancake house and twenty-four-hour convenience store draw more people than the church. The imposing domes are not on capitols but on sports stadiums. The man or woman who makes something from a sense of transcendence is commonly called unusual or naive, "an outsider" or "a visionary."

Such cultural rhetoric of secular rationality has been heightened since the visible transformations in settlement and manufacture of the late nineteenth century. But through the eighteenth century, patterns of modernization were occurring or, more importantly, were believed to be occurring, with, as Rhys Isaac reports, "authority based on individual contract; government empowered by a printed constitution; the ascendancy of statute law over ancient custom; and an increase of scale that effectively provincialized local government. . . . In these changes can be traced the intensified impact of a print-oriented cosmopolitanism upon an already weakened localistic oral culture."55 "Weakened" may not be as apt a term as a process of "privatization." It was a question of access to and sanction by the mainstream, where the essential and fashionable were. It was an issue of centeredness that came to a head in the nineteenth century. More than the "forms" of building, making, working, and living changed. The ways in which standards were formed and conveyed changed. The ways in which standard-bearers were chosen and promoted changed. The public, "progressive" world that was wrought was urban, technological, and corporate—that is, institutional and *form*al. For the communal, for the *in-form*al, one had to make private outlets in family and home, community and spirit.

4

Consuming Things

RALPH WALDO EMERSON'S CLAIM of 1860 that in America "every man is a consumer" was balanced by his self-reliant idea that every man "ought to be a producer." But although the man who made things seemed to be less evident, signs of consumption were ever increasing. What was being produced was wealth with which to buy wares and services. The widely circulating book *Eighty Years' Progress of the United States* (1868) noted the consuming mood by citing that the annual production of wares rose to over one billion in 1850, over 40 percent above what it had been 1820. "With the large immigration of skilled workmen from abroad," it said, "a greater breadth has been given to all branches, and progress is very rapid, the more so that the general prosperity enables consumers to extend the best possible encouragement to producers, by buying their wares."[1]

By 1899, Thorstein Veblen was talking about *conspicuous* consumption, the show of wealth and status through the wasteful, extravagant purchase and display of goods. His biting book *The Theory of the Leisure Class* helped the term enter popular jargon. For Veblen, the relation of the consuming of goods to the consuming of foods was not coincidental. In feasts, hosts gave expensive presents and served an abundance of food. Christmas, for example, especially during the late nineteenth century, was a time when families enjoyed ample, showy foods and presents. Conspicuous consumption could be found especially in the purchase of luxurious narcotics and beverages by a class able to afford leisure and to depend on consumption because they do not produce. The "gentleman of leisure, then, not only consumes of the staff of life beyond the minimum required for subsistence and physical efficiency, but his consumption also undergoes a specialisation as regards the quality of the goods consumed. He consumes freely and of the best, in food, drink, narcotics, shelter, services, ornaments, apparel, weapons and accoutrements, amusements, amulets, and idols or divinities."[2] In consumption of both food and goods, the consuming is personal and social. It satisfies one's personal comforts and tastes, yet relies on social influences and events. The thing consumed belongs to you. One is taken internally, the other is taken in externally. One is a natural process, the other artificial, but both are given to social dramas and functions other than subsistence. Both food and goods involve a recognition of what is necessary and what is beyond necessity. Both involve waste. Both involve choices and appearances.

Sister Carrie in Theodore Dreiser's novel of 1900 notices the metaphor of consuming food. She enters a restaurant where "once seated, there began that exhibition of showy, wasteful, and unwholesome gastronomy as practised by wealthy Americans, which is the wonder and astonishment of true culture and dignity the world over." Yet Carrie becomes taken with it. "The tables were not so remarkable in themselves, and yet the imprint of Sherry upon the napery, the name of Tiffany upon the silverware, the name of Haviland upon the china, and over all the glow of the small, red-shaded candelabra and the reflected tints of the walls on garments and faces, made them seem remarkable. Each waiter added an air of exclusiveness and elegance by the manner in which he bowed, scraped, touched, and trifled with things."[3]

For Veblen the scene was most likely to occur in the cities, where mobility was high, crowding was dense, cash was the primary value of exchange, and the claim to status and gentility was most important. The crowding and vagueness of position in the rapidly changing cities meant that acquiring and displaying distinctive, fashionable goods offered recognition of taste and status. The flexibility of class division in urban America created a desire to externalize, to materialize the status attained or aspired to. This was especially important for the members of the rising middle class, who did not have the advantage of "family legacy" among the gentry to dictate social position and behavior. How do you show the production of wealth? Spend it on displayable goods which suggest leisure and management. Consumption differs in places where one relies on small groups and in communities where personal acquaintance and word of mouth are more the run of life. Canons of taste differ.

An example is a story of turtle soup consumption. Sister Carrie noticed it in her chic restaurant, but it is not on most menus today. It is one commodity that has resisted mass consumption. Rather, turtle consumption is relegated to either informal use, often in isolated, poor, and rural areas of the country, or to epicurean, elite tastes. The symbolic confusion became an issue in the presidential campaign of 1852. Accused of pomposity Virginian Winfield Scott came under ridicule for his desire to "swim in the sea of society," the result of a poor boyhood in which he was fed "hasty" plates of turtle and oyster soup."[4]

European travelers to the New World reported the eating of turtle meat among American Indians in the seventeenth century. Drawing a comparison with the Plains Indians, one account boasted the turtle among the Gulf Coast Indians as the "buffalo of the Caribbean," consumed for medical treatment and nourishment.[5] Reporting on the Carolinas in 1682, Thomas Ashe found that English seamen had learned of the turtles from Indians and had begun harvesting turtles for export to the West Indies and England. "At the season when they most usually come ashore, which is in April, May, and June, the seamen or turtlers at some convenient distance watch their opportunity, getting between them and the sea, and turn them on their backs, from whence they are unable ever to rise, by which means the seamen or turtlers sometimes turn forty or fifty in a night, some of two, three, four hundred weight." Ashe recommended the taste, nourishment, and possible medicinal value of the turtles. Indeed, he said, it "makes as good and nourishing broth as the best capon in England, especially if some of the eggs are mixed with it."[6]

In the eighteenth century, turtle consumption was common along the American coast. The *Oxford English Dictionary* took notice of literature during this period concerning the turtle, especially turtle soup, and cited the 1755 quote, "Of all the improvements in the modern kitchen, there are none that can bear a comparison with the introduction of the Turtle." Turtle soup was a common feature of "civic banquets," the dictionary reported, and indeed, during the eighteenth century, "giving a turtle" meant giving a banquet. Its novelty and its reptile form gave it a manly, ceremonial value. In 1790, Virginia Colonel James Innes, for example, invited Williamsburg friends for a special dinner: "I arrived safely . . . and found all well at home, the Turtle not excepted. Tell Barraud it dies on Tuesday next and will be interr'd with the honors of War. Will you & he come up and grace his Funeral?"[7]

Turtle barbecues were popular ceremonial fare in New York, and turtle eating really took hold in the South, where various species of edible turtles were abundant. William Byrd in his *Natural History of Virginia* bragged that "the meat of all these turtles is as good as the best veal, even better, either boiled or roasted or baked, or in a ragout. I have often sampled it." The first printed southern cookbook, *The Virginia Housewife* (1824), devoted several pages to the butchering and preparation of turtles. Soup was the common form for consumption of turtles, but "should you not want soup," in the best southern tradition, "the remaining flesh may be fried, and served with a rich gravy."[8]

Turtles, especially the fatty green turtles, were being imported to England, and as an import item, were expensive delicacies. As a contrast to the predominant "hogmeat and cornpone" diet of southerners, turtles became an unusual, decorative item on wealthy tables. The table in the big house on the Alston plantation on the Carolina rice coast had "Turtle soup at each end," and "two paralled dishes, one containing a leg of boiled mutton and the other turtle steaks and fins. Next was a pie of Maccaroni in the center of the table and on each side of it was a small dish of oysters."[9] Further north, people turned away from turtles as the diet came to emphasize the hog-corn complex and, among more prosperous diners, beef. Another reason for turning away from turtles was its association by an Anglophile population with French cookery. Turtles became connected with the "queer" eating of another reptile part, frogs' legs, and the preparation of French ragout. Patrick Henry publicly attacked Virginian Thomas Jefferson for his taste for French cookery and its elitist connotations. Consuming turtles became a more expensive matter, too, as the defenseless animals were killed off.[10]

Manner books in the early nineteenth century stressed feminine, genteel dining as a mark of status, and the messy, fatty, "repulsive" reptiles became less desirable, or more reticently accepted on special occasions, where they could be treated as "luxuries." Eliza Leslie, author of *Miss Leslie's Behavior Book* (1859), wrote in her *Directions for Cookery* that only mock turtle soup would do. "We omit a receipt for *real* turtle soup," she asserts, "as when that very expensive, complicated, and difficult dish is prepared in a private family, it is advisable to hire a first-rate cook for the express purpose. An easy way is to get it ready made, in any quantity you please, from a turtle-soup house."[11] Most took the attitude of Madame Prunier, who genteelly said, "It is unlikely that most of us will ever have to deal with a turtle, or even to cook frogs or snails. . . . It is not very likely that private houses or indeed many establishments will ever want, or be in a position, to make turtle soup." The consumption of turtles was foreign to middle-class Anglo-American cooking and was not supported by a system of commercial dissemination such as restaurants or catalogues.

With the "professionalization" by women of cookery within the home, called for by the Beechers, came a removal of animals formerly cooked for their celebration of man's hunting and hand labor. The domestication of cookery during the nineteenth century excluded foods such as reptiles which suggested the dark wild and its creeping, slimy, and treacherous symbolism. Poultry, fish, pork, and beef came from controlled environments or lacked physical characteristics disturbing to feminizing middle-class sensibilities. Mrs. Sherwood of *Harper's Bazaar,* writing a new preface to the 1900 edition of *Manners and Social Usages,* bragged that women now "enjoy in a million humble homes the dainty breakfast, the comfortable luncheon, the stately dinner . . . and the young matron has a thousand domestic arts by which she embellishes her home." "In America," she claimed, woman as "the lady of the house" had taken over the role of conductor of "social politics," and her increased control of foods served, the settings created, and the implements used, made her the mediator of gentility in the home and the instrument in the removal of man from the wild and into business.[12] Printed humor from the Southwest in the nineteenth century served to heighten the old male stereotype. There was George Washington Harris's Sut Luvingood, for example, whose environs were set in rural, manly East Tennessee. Luvingood's placenames were Frog Mountain Range and Rattlesnake Springs. In stories such as "Parson John Bullen's Lizards" (1867), Luvingood is the reptile gatherer who is wanted "dead ur alive" by the Parson for "discumfurtin the wimen very powerful." Indeed, swallowing reptiles is an initiation rite in men's fraternities at many colleges. Until a few years ago consuming salamanders was part of a celebration called the Bowery Ball sponsored by a men's fraternity at the Pennsylvania State University.[13]

In the twentieth century, city dwellers diminished the fearsome qualities of rodents and reptiles by domesticating them. The tame little turtle under human dominion served to further distance turtles as sources of food for urban consumers. As far as *The Famous American Recipes Cookbook* (1957) was concerned, turtles were either emergency or epicurean fare, not acceptable on the restrained, standard-bearing, middle-class table.[14] To make turtle acceptable to American epicurean tastes, it was steeped in the exotic quality and perceived refinement of French cookery. *The American Woman's Cook Book* (1972), for example, listed turtle last in its fish section and suggested "Turtle Ragout" and "Turtle Á La King." Occasionally, government agencies tried to encourage commercial gathering of turtles, for example in 1893 and 1919, but their efforts failed because producers did not consider the specialized epicurean market sufficient.[15]

Producers were often unaware of, or unconcerned with, poor consumers in back sections of the country. But there residents maintained noncommercial consumption of the turtle. Although supplies of the green turtle had diminished, inland snappers were bountiful along streams and swamps, especially in the South. Like other "informal" foods commonly hunted and butchered, such as squirrel, opossum, frog, and rabbit, the turtle was a readily available, nourishing food whose consumption was sanctioned by local tradition.

Not everyone approved. In Florida, Marjorie Kinnan Rawlings wrote in 1942, "Here and there a Floridian turns up his nose at them, foolishly." Although she prized the eggs, most reporters described soup or fried meat as how the turtles were consumed. Near Rabun Gap, Georgia, *Foxfire* collectors found mud turtles fried and put into a stew. In rural southcentral Pennsylvania, men take lines to bring in the turtles and women make soup from the meat. In Alabama and Maryland, "terrapins" are boiled and the meat extracted to make "snapper soup."

Several accounts are found in Kentucky. *Food For Thought: An Ethnic Cookbook* out of Lexington in 1976 noted that preparing turtles for food consumption is a "dying craft"

There are two methods of catching turtles, and essentially two kinds of turtles: hard and soft shelled, or "snappers" and "leather-backs" respectively. The first method, "noodling," is for only the brave or foolhardy wader, who slides his hands under the banks of streams until he finds the tail of a turtle, then pulls it out. The problems appear if a turtle has backed, rather than burrowed, into the protective mud bank. The second method, "hooking," employs heavy cord line, a large hook from a hardware store, and tough beef shank for bait, cut in 1½ inch squares. The cord is hooked and baited, then tied around stumps or trees on the banks of a stream. When a turtle is hooked, the lines become taut, and with great effort, the turtle can be pulled from the bottom of the stream. Since turtles have notoriously bad vision, the stream should not be overly muddy, or the turtle will not see the bait. Cleaning is also difficult. After the turtle has been beheaded and hung beside a tree for several hours, it is scalded in a large pot of boiling water. The shell then softens and may be removed. The skin is scraped and removed several times, and during this process the turtle is scalded at least four times. As soon as bottom shell is removed, turtle may be cleaned in the manner of chickens or fish. When all skin is scraped, meat will be visible—except for the tenderloin which remains attached to the shell until removed. After turtle is cleaned, there are nine different shades of meat, each with its own distinctive flavor. If the turtle with its shell is larger than a dinner plate (about five pounds), the meat is too tough to fry. The best turtle meat is the tenderloin, a hard-to-remove circular section running from back to front inside the shell. Meat may be cut into pieces and fried like chicken.

In Harlan County, Kentucky, Leonard Roberts heard in 1955, "You know, turtles have all kinds of meat in 'em, chicken, duck, fish, cow, hog, and every kind of meat there are, and make awful good eating." A problem in reviewing such accounts is that the frequency of, settings for, and functions of turtle consumption are not given. What can be gleaned is that it is a male hunting activity commonly reported in the rural South and Middle Atlantic States.[16]

My experience in Dubois County in southern Indiana provides perspectives on the matters of frequency, setting, and function. The region takes many of its traditions from the line of migration from Virginia to Kentucky to Indiana. Abundant in streams populated by turtles and containing many of Veblen's "small communities" based on personal acquaintance, it might have been predicted to contain some turtle consumption. But the frequency with which turtles are consumed may appear surprising. Almost every weekend during the summer, great quantities of turtle soup are consumed at Catholic church picnics. During the week, restaurants serve fried turtles. Residents will tell you of men who gather and butcher turtles for home consumption of soup.

The picnics are major social events in the county. Residents check for their scheduling, often passed by word of mouth, and travel to the small towns for them. Family affairs, the picnics invariably have quilt raffles, various games of chance, fried chicken dinners, and, most conspicuously, turtle soup. The turtles are supplied beforehand by specialists such as Edwin Englert and John Lange, who hunt and butcher in the area. Formerly, butchering was a cooperative venture among members of the church congregation who would also contribute turtles, but in the last twenty years the picnics have increasingly relied on the specialists.

"Churches," folklorist Thomas Adler points out, "have long been among the most important community institutions, and they provide numerous social occasions through which foodways traditions can appear and be maintained." Doing fieldwork in Georgia, he was told, "And if it was church Sunday, you got up and you cooked dinner before you went to church. But most of the time, it was once a month, and everybody carried a basket and you ate dinner at church. There'd be a dinner-on-the-grounds at church. And the whole family went."[17] Although the numbers of southern "dinners on the grounds" declined, in Dubois County, Indiana, the coordination of festivities with

A church picnic poster

Consuming turtle soup at a church picnic

cooperative labor, reinforcement of acquaintances, the opportunity to consume without the burden of production, and the community bene-fits of raffling and gambling helped increase their popularity. They were also reminiscent of southern fish fries, where

> The men would go fishin', you know, and go out to some—like up to Whiddon Mill, or some lake somewhere, or some creek, and they would go and fish, maybe a day in advance. . . . Then the women and the children would go join them the next day, and they would of course take food, but, um, they would have fish fries. . . . Big celebration that day. The ladies usually would prepare a vegetable, but you didn't have a variety of foods at a fish fry, not too many desserts. It was mostly your corn bread and your fish, and grits or rice, something like that, and they would take some peas, or butterbeans, or whatever. And most of the time they did this during the spring or summer.[18]

In Dubois County, the church picnic is a celebration combining the ritual preparation and sale of turtle soup by men, assistance by women, and the value placed on family togetherness and community visiting associated with Sunday dinners on the grounds. The turtle, like the fish formerly, is an informal food, gathered by local tradition outside of commercial use. Women cut vegetables and other ingredients for the soup. Their quilts, too, are connected to the events of the picnic, since the quilts are made by cooperative labor for redistribution to the community. The opportunity to publicly gather, gamble, and play gives the picnic the mark of a social occasion where local events and traditions take primary importance. The gathering of turtles, an old, local, and special food, works to underscore that importance.

The men who do the hunting go to local swampy rivers and find hard-shell snapping turtles. They carry poles to force the turtles out of their holes, grab them by the tail, and throw them on the bank. Turtle nets are available and are occasionally used. The turtles are brought back alive. Edwin Englert keeps his turtles in the basement until he is ready to butcher them—usually for a period of two weeks. If he has an excess of turtles (if his basement is two and three deep with turtles), he will move some to wooden barrels and feed them table scraps for up to six months. "Just like fattening a hog," Edwin told me. "I only butcher turtles and hogs. I don't have the stomach for cattle." Another turtle butcher, Harvey Eckert, keeps his turtles in iron barrels. "I slop 'em like a hog," he offered. "The more rotten it is, the better they like it." Just before butchering he stops feeding them and changes the water several times to cleanse them.

Dubois County men usually butcher outdoors. To begin the butchering, Edwin holds the tail of the turtle while one of his sons, Gene or Melvin, pokes at the head with a pair of pliers. When the turtle's head emerges, Gene grabs it with the pliers and hatchets it off. The Englerts convey the commonly held belief that even after turtles are killed they continue to live until sundown. They tell several stories about particular turtles that were especially stubborn or lively. "There was one who grabbed my pliers, and even after its head was off, he wouldn't let it go. But you know, it's unlucky to kill a turtle unless you plan to eat it. Yeah, that turtle will kick. I like to hear my wife squeal when she's frying those feet and they start to scratch and squirm in the pan."

Edwin and Gene scald the turtle with hot water after removing its head. They cut the shell from the body with a kitchen or pocket knife and remove the meat from inside the shell. The shell can then be used for flavoring, much as bones would be used in other meat soups. The next step is removing the intestines followed by cutting the turtle into quarters and slicing off the neck—the prime choice of the turtle

Vats of turtle soup

Preparing jugs of turtle soup

Butchering turtles

Ed and Gene Englert gathering vegetables for soup

according to the Englerts—and the legs. The butchering lasts about one hour for each ten-to-twenty pound turtle.

After butchering, family members or neighbors begin preparing the soup. Each person contributes garden vegetables, homemade wine, beef, chicken, and pork. "Everything in the garden is thrown in," Edwin said. "The meats are there to kill the turtle taste. You can't taste the turtle when you fry it though; it tastes just like chicken. The turtle has seven different meat tastes." Few can name all seven, but they're sure seven or nine tastes are there.

Two turtles go in twenty-five to thirty gallons of soup. Only half the turtle is actually used for the soup. "It takes a lot of work," Gene complained, "and it's not really worth it." When I asked soup preparers at a Mariah Hill picnic why they no longer butcher their own turtles, they replied, "Too much work." It is also work that demands a careful hand with a sharp knife and, some will tell you, a steady stomach.

Problems arise in explaining the consumption of turtles here. One problem, emerging early in the course of interviews, is that while residents of a small area within southwestern Indiana continue to butcher and regularly consume turtles at church picnics, few of the people I talked to reported actually liking the taste of turtle meat or even recognizing it (the soup often is confused with vegetable soup), and even fewer enjoyed the work required to hunt, butcher, and prepare the turtles. A second and related matter is why an individual often expresses apparently contradictory opinions about the compelling and repulsive qualities of a food or its preparation, such as turtle soup.

If many people do not enjoy the gore of butchering turtles or the effort to prepare the soup or the flavor of turtle meat, I asked, then why is turtle soup featured so often and so prominently at social events? Neither this nor the second, related question is limited to turtle soup, both are relevant to other instances of food consumption. For example, vegetarianism has become popular enough to force additions to restaurant menus and to spur specialty houses. It has also given some cause for self-justification of eating categories, and indeed, many now take the compromising route of "I don't eat red meat." Other people refer to dishes composed of animal's organs euphemistically or with terms that disguise or direct attention away from the object. Lamb testicles, to give an example, are "lamb fries" or "Rocky Mountain oysters." Certain ethnic dishes, especially strong-smelling or unusual-tasting ones, served and eaten on special occasions, similarly produce conflicting feelings in people. Chitterlings, for instance, are both a symbol of racial pride and source of embarrassment for many blacks, who continue to prepare and eat the food despite the laborious preparation required. Many restaurants serve headless fish to alleviate the discomfort of customers who prefer not to face the creatures eye to eye. When they receive the fish, some customers drown it in lemon or sauce to remove the "fishy" taste. The paradoxical attitude was displayed by my companions on one trip to the area. They admitted being repelled by, but still curious about and therefore attracted to my examination of turtle butchering. Then they returned to eating their ground beef.

Acceptance of turtles in the diet of Dubois County residents has historical precedent. The county has always been predominantly Catholic; the restriction by the Catholic church against eating meat on Fridays did not prohibit the eating of turtle flesh. In an area where home butchering and wild game hunting are common, the gathering of turtles did not seem as unusual as it did in other "domestic-ated"environments. And I would hear, "Hell, I've always eaten it." The churches, keepers of community and family in the county, are able to suggest through folk production and consumption at the picnics a connection between the informality of community and a larger social order.

Turtle consumption gives the region a distinctiveness appealing to some residents. It is a food that sets them apart, like muskrat in Monroe County, Michigan, or crawfish in southern Louisiana, and lends a sense of locality to identities increasingly felt to be national in modern times. Beyond this local boosterism is competition between churches, which promotes consumption. George Blume, an ex-turtle hunter, told me that the people of the neighboring communities of Mariah Hill and St. Henry both "thought they made the best soup even though the turtles came from the same people, and often, the same folks prepared it." People who buy five- and ten-gallon jugs of the soup support through their purchases the claim of some local church members to the best soup available.

It could be argued that the socializing that occurs around turtle soup consumption helps override discomfort felt by some individuals at consuming turtles. At church picnics, preparing turtle soup requires the cooperative effort of many individuals. Men gather in groups while the cooking goes on, and women visit while making preparations for the soup—preparation which usually starts many days before the picnic. Adolescents participate by being responsible for stirring and dishing up the soup.

In preparing the soup, sexual division of labor is particularly pronounced. The men are the hunters and butchers; women are the preparers and preservers. In addition, men assume Sunday cooking and supervisory duties, a pattern common in America.[19] When they do, as in the backyard barbecue or the church picnic, cooking takes place outdoors, a man's domain, and involves some showmanship. Some of the men I spoke to at the Mariah Hill picnic did not think of their cooking as taking over the woman's task, but rather as taking a ceremonial role. "Guys always cooked the turtle for special occasions," I was told. "Keeps you coming back to the church." Having the choice of buying or not buying the soup allows members to participate in the social aspects without consuming the turtle. The soup sells quickly. One is told to come early before it is gone. The turtle soup is conspicuous consumption for members of the church, but rather than the show of status of affording luxury, this is a show of excess labor.

Could turtle soup consumption have an ecological justification, especially in an area with a farming background and where gardening is common? To the Englerts, turtle soup is appealing because it absorbs a variety of foods in the area. "Everything in the garden goes in." People in many areas have recipes that prevent food waste by calling for a "gumbo" style inclusion of various substances. Calling for improvisation, such dishes lend themselves to folk production and consumption. The common Brunswick and Irish stews come to mind, and in cowboy folklife, the "son of a bitch" stew: "Son of a bitch stew came under the head of no waste, for it was composed largely of those supposedly lowly internal organs which even today many Americans disdain."[20] Turtles also account for wastes because they consume "leftovers" when alive. To many butchers, they offer a convenient disposal system, much as raising hogs used to.

The pride felt for the success of specialists might be said to contribute to the continuance of turtle butchering and soup-making traditions. Some of the people I interviewed expressed great respect for successful hunters and butchers, because of the risky role these adventurous men play in the church picnics, and because they independently follow an older, rural model of behavior. Yet these figures are commonly peripheral to the community. The Englerts, for example, live on the extreme northern edge of their town on a road officially known as Cour de Lane, but colloquially, and revealingly, called Pig Turd Alley.

Hog butchering at home has almost died out in the county, as commercial slaughterhouses and legal restrictions, not to mention the difficulty of organizing cooperative labor, have caused many to give it up. Gathering the turtles, and associating them with the raising of hogs, maintains the sense of tradition and social function offered by butchering. The church picnics provide a community structure that sanctions the tradition. Substitution of the turtles scales down the butchering, makes it more private and specialized, but allows the productive activity to continue.

For many, butchering is a matter of control of one's food production and consumption, one's announcement of a close relation to nature, and an ethic of self-reliance. At one butchering I attended, I heard, "If another depression comes, we'll always have food on the table. We don't have to buy food, we'll get it." When it came time for the meal, Kentucky Fried Chicken was placed before the men. The informal, private gathering coexists with the commercial consumables, but maintaining some of the informality—whether in butchering, in participating in the preparation, or in purchasing the product—gives a sense of personal control and social identity. The future of turtle butchering is in question now, since the supply is not plentiful and hunters sometimes have to go as far as southern Illinois to find good turtles. It has been suggested that the soup has little or no turtle in it but continues to be prepared as mock soup simply because "people insist on it." Calling it "turtle" and making the activity sociable are the essential ingredients.

Are turtles exotic? In Dubois County they are not, but they are special. Since the point of the picnics is to raise money, publicly showcasing an item which cannot be consumed normally enhances the appeal of coming. The activities of the picnic are celebrations of folk production and consumption because of the stress on cooperative activities and maintenance of traditions not found on the grocer's shelves. Such behavior has risks and variations, a mood reinforced by the gambling, sports, and bingo playing which typically occur.

How about the ones who "turn their noses up at," or have mixed feelings about, the turtles? Some people express their dislike for the "turtle taste" of turtle soup jokingly, in the form of "nervous laughter," to make their dislike less threatening or less offensive. Others compensate for conflict by reacting in a way contrary to existing standards. That is, an individual may take pride in what others claim to loathe, thus making this person different and presumably above those who reject the attitude or activity. Though he himself may not always relish the butchering of a turtle, Edwin finds justifications—the activity brings him together with his sons, makes his wife squeal. Others who butcher turtles or eat the soup seem to be aware that not everyone does so and that perhaps the activity is abhorrent to some. Maybe this very fact is a source of justification. For some, butchering and preparing soup is a necessary completion of a process. If one hunts, in other words, one has to go through with the steps from the wild to human consumption to give that sense of wholeness defined by the self-reliant tradition.

A mechanism for dealing with a conflict that might exist in the butchering and consumption of turtle is to erect mental blocks to, and to establish psychic distance from, the disturbing activity or object. In this way one need not confront the image of the creature whose flesh is being eaten or admit to participating in its destruction (particularly if someone else is required to do the preparation and if the product "masks" the taste or image of the creature). Few individuals are actually involved in the hunting and butchering. That once-essential part of the process has given way in emphasis and visibility to the social activities of production and consumption.

The community does not create turtle soup. Individuals do in the name of community. Resisting marketing, embracing festivity and specialty, individuals together with the institution of the church have invoked tradition to aid production and consumption for social and symbolic purposes. The sanction by a local institution and the ritualization of consumption lend legitimacy to a food category which did not survive the domestication of cookery in the nineteenth century. Different participants in Dubois County's turtle-soup process—hunters, butchers, preparers, sellers, and consumers—play different roles in this cultural drama. They have formed a chain of producers and consumers linked to localism. It is not a "folk" food to them but a local one.

Such localism can become chic, as it has for crawfish in Louisiana. C. Paige Gutierrez reports, "Tail meat may be combined with cream, wine, mushrooms, or other relatively expensive ingredients to produce any number of refined dishes appropriate for posh occasions. Even a crawfish boil may be 'dressed up'; a south Louisiana department store sells special napkins, napkin rings, place mats, trays, utensils, and glasses for formal crawfish boils."[21] This has not occurred with Dubois County's turtles. But it has not been uncommon for the distingué to formalize local folk dishes and change their meaning. Pocket bread and black bread, once low-status ethnic foods, now find their way into elegant menus. Mrs. Sherwood's *Manners and Social Usages* (1900) told elegant housewives that "in many rural districts the butchers give away, or throw to the dogs, sweetbreads and other morsels which are the very essence of luxury."[22]

This is more than "one man's meat is another man's poison." When foods or things with local, informal connotations are taken from their original settings and surrounded by the trappings of a formal culture perceiving themselves as dominant, they often take on the label of folk, ethnic, and rural, setting them apart as real experiences, exotic and rare, or at least below the "surface of things," thus lending them the left-handed compliment "essence of luxury." Exotic or merely local, the consumption of turtles takes its meaning from use, from its role in reflecting and influencing cultural perceptions of appropriate activity. To be sure, it is one of many stories in a consuming society, but it is exemplary of a small, informal world within the larger social order. The story of turtle consumption in America illustrates how a once-popular food came to exist in two worlds—folk and elite. It is to this common process in consumption, the transformation of items from one social purpose to a different one, that I turn my attention.

"Morsels" can be things such as antiques, someone else's junk. Addressing the city-dwelling antique hunter, Walter Dyer in *The Lure of the Antique* (1910) shared dinner with a rural New England woman of tradition, and it made him reflect:

> Ridiculous little old woman! Living here alone, part and parcel of an age before steam heat was invented or electric lights even dreamt of. Faded little old lady, whose ancient lace belongs somehow with the old mahogany and Sheffield plate. I see you [the reader] smile, but I can see it is not a smile of contempt or of pity. Your city home was made beautiful by the most up-to-date decorator you could afford. You spent hundreds of dollars on "color schemes" and "vistas." Your Mission den cost more than this woman ever had to spend. Then why do you covet the old candlesticks on the wooden mantel? Why does your palm itch for the possession of her one magnificent Wedgwood vase? It is because they are real. They mean something.[23]

Collected properly, presented properly, and consumed properly, such things take on a social meaning for a different setting, for a different kind of community. Just as turtle consumption represents a link to tradition, so antique hunters in the emergence of the antiques market following World War I imagined the creation of real experience—"the pouring of candles into their molds," "the crackling of the back-log on the old fire-dogs," in Dyer's words. As in turtle consumption, the roles are varied, the actors connected. It is a canon of taste, based on collecting, display, and consumption. While turtle consumption operated under a system different from the dominant commercial consumer system, the antiques market arose as a subcultural, commercial alternative to mass production. Yet it was tied to the assumptions of mass-production control of handwork and its products. As Harold Donaldson Eberlein and Abbot McClure wrote in *The Practical Book of American Antiques* (1916), for example, "There is a sincerity of purpose about them that commands our respect. . . . An examination of their shortcomings, at any rate, is calculated to increase our appreciation of conditions existing in our own day." The

Newark Museum in 1928 invoked "The Superstition of the Antique," based on the belief that "there comes a moment in the history of every civilization when it turns back to look at the ground it has covered, before crossing the pass and plunging down to new discoveries on the other side. On the threshold of a new age it experiences an overwhelming desire to build an artificial paradise out of the ruins of the past. The forms in which this desire is satisfied are explicit and tangible; no sophisticated *recherche du temps perdu*, but an almost avaricious clutching at the material relics of yesterday."[24]

In exposition and book, antiques were an example of wealthy America discovering morsels of its own surface history and surrounding the history with evidence of the prevailing wealth and leisure, manners and social usages. It wasn't long before the search turned to indigenous art traditions. The stress on antiques of the American colonial period carried over from the centennial and the Columbian Exposition, and the entrance of America into colonial rule and world prominence. These forces influenced many in the vanguard of eastern urban society to put spotlights on early American crafts and arts. Critic Virgil Barker commented on an exhibit of colonial paintings at the Whitney Studio Club in 1924: "The discovery of our artistic past which is now progressing with increasing rapidity satisfies more than the collecting instinct, for such paintings and miscellaneous objects as were brought together in this exhibition have the tang of reality."[25] Not being schooled but being old and domestic, the art objects—mostly portraits and occupational carvings—were considered antiques in the early twentieth century. They were the products of the colonial forebears, representative of a national history.

Although dubbed a "craze" around 1916, consuming antiques had direct roots in the taste for the picturesque described by Andrew Jackson Downing. Middle-class Americans found it in numerous prints and pictures which became widely available. The Beechers in 1869 suggested setting aside thirty dollars for rustic frames and pictures by "the best American artists." They suggested "The Little Scrap-Book Maker" and Eastman Johnson's "Barefoot Boy." "By sending to any leading picture-dealer, lists of pictures and prices will be forwarded to you." Currier and Ives made their mark in the picture-dealing business by selling idyllic prints of rustic, pioneer America. In a crowded society which increasingly judged status by visual appearance and material accumulation, consuming pictures underscored a stress on visual surroundings. Encapsulated into small rectangular units, the pictures could be arranged and amassed, replaced and traded. In the home, pictures stressed naturalism—landscapes, rural dwellings, still lifes. The pictures suggested for, and gested for, and chosen by, the woman for her domain connected naturalism to femininity and domesticity.[26] The pictures simulated windows to an idealized, private, natural setting admidst public presentation of an artificial, modernizing environment.

To the Beechers and other middle-class advisers, pictures were valuable decorations for the feminine home. The home, being a model of domesticity and traditional rural values (while public places were given to business and manufacturing), emphasized placement of plants, pictures, and reminders of historic rusticity. The history to be stressed was the Anglo-Saxon colonial past. Dyer wrote of antique collectors, "Malign as you will, we are a home-loving people, and the things of the homes, and our reverence for the past around the hearthstones of our forebears. Also we are for the most part descended from Europeans, and there is born within us a respect for antiquity. We have no Rhenish castles here; no Roman roads undulate over our hilltops. The oldest we have is just coming of age, but we are glad of that, and do our homage." The interest in antiques included celebration of American productivity, as Eberlein and McClure boasted: "The quest for American antiques is more than a temporary craze. It is the awakening of a permanent interest in the beautiful and the curious hosehold arts of our own forebears; things which, therefore, have for us an intimate charm that no foreign products, however lovely, can ever quite replace."[27]

A major event which drew attention to the domestic, nativist spirit was the opening of the American Wing at the Metropolitan Museum of Art in 1924. From the exhibit came *The Homes of Our Ancestors* which states, "Much of the America of to-day has lost sight of its traditions. Their stage settings have largely passed away, along with the actors. Many of our people are not cognizant of our traditions and the principles for which our fathers struggled and died. The tremendous changes in the character of our nation, and the influx of foreign ideas utterly at variance with those held by the men who gave us the Republic, threaten and, unless checked, may shake its foundations. Any study of the American Wing cannot fail to revive those memories, for here for the first time is a comprehensive, realistic setting for the traditions so dear to us and so invaluable in the Americanization of many of our people, to whom much of our history is little known."[28]

The Metropolitan was defensive, though, because by their standards the material could not be called "great art." "In its general simplicity and fine workmanship," the museum nonetheless offered, "it has an interest to many to whom great art creations cannot appeal." But the "great arts" system was being challenged. At the end of the nineteenth century folklorists and anthropologists brought art,

Sorting ethnological art at the United States National Museum, 1890s (National Anthropological Archives, Smithsonian Institution)

exotic and primitive yet striking and beautiful, before the American and European public. Otis Mason, curator of ethnological collections at the new United States National Museum, first referred to a "folk fine art" in his presidential address to the American Folklore Society in 1891, published the same year in the society's journal. Eskimos, Indians, and Polynesians had their traditional designs heralded as art in extravagant expositions in London in 1891, Chicago in 1893, and Atlanta in 1895. On the one hand, displaying art of primitive societies allowed the Victorians to contrast crude and exotic images with their view of their own products as refined and advanced. Assuming that they had climbed to the top of the cultural ladder, Victorians often used primitive art to gauge how far they had come. On the other hand, the Victorians began to accept art as a cultural product, something learned and shared by members of a communal society.[29]

The convergence of cultural primitivism and modern nationalism came with publicity given to European peasant art. European peasant costumes, houses, furnishings, and paintings suggested the historic romance and natural rootedness of the ethnic stock that made up a nation. The Studio, a prominent London publisher, put out a heralded series of books on peasant art of Sweden and Iceland (1910), Austria and England (1911), Russia (1912), Italy (1913), the Netherlands (1913), and Switzerland (1914).

In America, ethnological publications on the American Indian served to give the image of a romantic past close to the land, but Americans could not connect their roots to a different racial stock. In Pennsylvania, collectors Henry Mercer and Edwin Barber wrote on their finds of fractur, pottery, and ironwork of German immigrants during the colonial period. The Germans gave the state much of its distinctiveness on the landscape and in politics, the collectors argued. The art was crude but important to these Pennsylvanians for its romantic roots. This was fine for Pennsylvania, but the reflection of America's heritage, especially after World War I, could not be German.[30]

Barber influenced Albert Hastings Pitkin of Connecticut, curator of the Wadsworth Atheneum and a member of the Society of Mayflower Descendants. Pitkin wrote *Early American Folk Pottery* (1918), borrowing "folk" from Barber and Mercer's use of it for artistic products of the Pennsylvania-German culture. There were lines to be drawn: "I shall confine my attention to the fictile productions of the American Folk, and used by American Folk, as exemplified in the work of our English and European ancestors who were among the early settlers in this country. The Pottery made by the aborigines will have no consideration, because it was an un-glazed ware and because it belongs essentially to Ethnological study."[31] The pottery was America's nativist primitive art. Its makers were not peasants but hard-working ancestors.

Allen Eaton, working for the reformist Russell Sage Foundation, called for a different view of folk art. In exhibits such as "Arts and Crafts of the Homelands" first put up in Buffalo in 1919 and "America's Making Exposition" in New York City in 1921, Eaton displayed immigrant arts such as woodcarving, embroidery, and egg decorating and promoted performances by immigrant groups to place the objects in their vital cultural surroundings. The exhibits confirmed the value, not threat, of immigration to American life. Both shows traveled widely and resulted in a book, *Immigrant Gifts to American Life* (1932). Other organizations and exhibits of immigrant folk art sprang up in Omaha, Minneapolis, Cleveland, and New York

City during the 1920s. This folk art celebrated a pluralistic social mosaic in America, not a dominant stock. Eaton's folk art was influenced by ideas of anthropologists and folklorists, especially Stewart Culin, for the purpose of social work.[32] His folk art was not a commodity but a living tradition. It did not attract approval from fine arts centers or commercial interests. It would not be the use of folk art that came to the fore.

The folk art that came to be prominent honored the common man, a figure drawn from a vision of a dominant American stock and consensus history. It was collected with other domestic antiques and written up in antiques guides and magazines. The guides encouraged those with new money and leisure time to engage in collecting. Dyer added its value for providing intensity to middle-class life: "Your collector is usually an amiable person, sometimes a bore, but more often interesting. Too much enthusiasm is better than too little. And the collecting of antiques begets something not unlike learning." The era of folk art growing out of the antiques craze witnessed the move from the City Beautiful to the City Practical, a concern for machined practicality and productivity. Guides in the 1920s turned their attention to showing how the intensity and learning of antique hunting was practical and productive. One made history by consuming it. The hunter could be advised by *The Practical Book of Chinaware, The Practical Book of Period Furniture,* and *The Practical Book of American Antiques* (formerly *The Practical Book of Early American Arts and Crafts*). Francis Lichten observed the self-justification of something not unlike productivity: "But in fairness to that complex called human nature, it must be admitted that several other less worthy characteristics also brought accessions to the world of 'antiques.' Though shiftlessness, sentimentality, and laziness may be negative traits, the *end-product* of their operation is the survival of the handwork of our forebears. This folk material, ignored for the most part until recently, has been worthy of the study given to it, for it quietly teaches the beauty inherent in sound craftsmanship and stresses the virtues that were needed for its fashioning—patience and application, two things which we of the machine world are prone to overlook."[33]

Rich Americans such as John Pierpont Morgan, Henry Clay Frick, and William Randolph Hearst were meanwhile making news with their collections of European fine art. Many upwardly aspiring middle-class socialites in America could share in the thrills of collecting by buying American antiques. The Walpole Society, the first club for collectors of American decorative arts, had formed in 1910, and established an exclusive "guild of workers in the collector's noble craft," but the popular guides were encouraging people of lesser note to collect silver, china, furniture, and painting.

It was this boom of collecting during the early twentieth century that drew satire from Stewart Culin, an ethnologist from Pennsylvania who turned to fiction to comment on those who debased his "scientific" folk art collecting at the Brooklyn Museum. In "The Perfect Collector," written in the twenties, Culin introduces Mr. Greatrox, who says,

> I started in a small way and grew up much like other people until I became a collector . . . There are collectors of cups and saucers and even tureens, but I confine myself to plates. . . . My only difficulty now is lack of room. Every day my agents report a new find. If only I had not sold the land adjacent to my house, what a collection I might have had. As it is all the servants sleep out, and I am thinking of doing over one of the cellars as a bed room, for of course even the most enthusiastic collector must have a place to sleep. I know you are going to ask if Mrs. Greatrox likes porcelain and I must tell you she dotes on it. She thinks of nothing else. Now as for myself I have such a diversity of interests! There is the church. Of course I don't have the same occasion for it as most people for I feel my life is consecrated. There are so many ways we can do good. My object is to aid and instruct. Every step I take toward completing my collection I feel that I am gaining in grace.

Later at breakfast, the separation of collecting from practical life comes out:

> I have a different set for every day in the year. Not from my collection, for that I never think of using. Nothing that is put to practical use belongs to art. I might even say nothing that could be used practically is art. Our best houses prove that. Only the other day I read some anarchist spoke of art as a byproduct of industry. Or was it a socialist? I am glad the law is to take its course with those fellows. They attack the very foundations of society. A china collector is in a peculiarly delicate position. Imagine the harm a bomb would do in this house.

Culin saw in the collecting of these utilitarian items as art a defense of the foundations of the "best" society. It was consumption revolving around consumption. The genteel products they sought—china, silver, and furniture—created an image of domestic harmony.[34]

Even more than the hunt for the old, sighting of the new came into the limelight after the *International Exhibition of Modern Art* in New

York City in 1913. *"The Armory Show"* as it is now called, ushered Americans into "modernism." The show was international in scope, but considerable attention was paid to the budding of American modernism. Works by artists such as Bernard Karfiol, John Sloan, and Stuart Davis were on display with Picasso and Kandinsky. The art was modern and yet it was primitive. Critic W.D. MacColl commented that the modern painters "achieve the first place by the force of a pure native power that is in them." Artist Kenyon Cox wrote in *Harper's Weekly,*

> In the wildest productions of Picabia or Picasso there is usually discernible, upon sufficiently painstaking investigation, some faint trace of the natural objects which are supposed to have inspired them; and even when this disappears the title remains to show that such objects have existed. It has remained for Mr. Marsden Hartley to take the final step and to arrange his lines and spots purely for their own sake, abandoning all pretense of representation or even of suggestion. He exhibits certain rectangles of paper covered with a maze of charcoal lines which are catalogued simply as Drawing No. 1, Drawing No. 2, etc.. . . . Deliberately and determinedly these men have stepped over the edge. Now the total destruction of painting as a representative art is a thing which a lover of painting could hardly envisage with entire equanimity, yet one may admit that such a thing might take place and yet an art remain that should have its own value.

Others were less generous. Art critic Royal Cortissoz writing in the New York *Tribune* and *Century* equated the modern art with the invidious influences of immigration, which introduced alien elements shaking the foundation of the nation. "The thinking they have done," he said, "has been invertebrate and confusing. Steadily, too, it has led them to produce work not only incompetent, but grotesque. It has led them from complacency to what I can only describe as insolence."[35]

Some American modernists returned that their designs had roots in the American soil. It was inspired by American primitives such as the "naive" painting and sculpture of the eighteenth century which showed abstraction of line, disregard for perspective, boldness in color. "Modernism" called attention to the blandness of modernity. It sought roots and inspiration in the reality of the primitive. Charles Messer Stow, writing in the *Antiquarian* in 1927 on "Primitive Art in America," reported, "Indeed, certain of the ultra-modern painters, whose work now and then comes to the attention of bewildered lookers, confide that they are endeavoring to return to the primitive in their art. That some of those who see these efforts whisper that they too would like to return for a space to the primitive—a primitive stone hatchet preferred—is beside the point. And yet there are American primitives." The Whitney Studio Club exhibit of early American art arranged by painter Henry Schnackenberg in 1924 showed some of the primitives and their relation to modernism. There were theorems, many naive paintings and watercolors, pieces of pewter, woodcarvings, a brass bootjack, and a plaster cat. Stow wrote of the show, "In the midst of a sophisticated existence it is refreshing to turn to something that totally lacks sophistication. And these early paintings give that refreshment. Seeing them is like getting all at once a new outlook, a new viewpoint, a new approach to the world. By contrast their realism seems most attractive to us, even though it be crude." Wealthy New Yorkers, he said, were impressed, and they drew connections of their present condition to that of the paintings. "They may truly be said to have retained their 'primitive' feeling. Many of them are products of that time of stress of the early nineteenth century, that time when the people of the new nation were forced, whether they like it or not, to take one of the forward steps in civilization."[36]

Modern artists such as Elie Nadelman, Robert Laurent, Bernard Karfiol, and Charles Demuth decorated their houses with the American primitives gathered from local auctions and junk shops. Weathervanes and decoys, rag rugs and quilts, once utilitarian, became fashionable decorations. But the paintings and sculpture, fitting into existing fine arts categories and therefore more visual, leisurely, and high-status, were demanded for exhibit.

This modernist taste for folk art was an aesthetic and nativist movement. The aesthetic was influenced by a middle-class taste for the domestic and colonial brought on by the Colonial Revival. New York celebrated its colonialism with the discovery of the "Van Bergen Overmantel" (c. 1735); Pennsylvania celebrated its sense of colonial harmony with Edward Hicks's many paintings of the "Peaceable Kingdom" (c. 1820-1840). America's growing national mercantile and economic power was hailed with exhibited weathervanes and ship figureheads brandishing patriotic symbols. Prized items, for instance, were the "Goddess of Liberty" weathervane (c.1865) and the Columbia ship figurehead (c. 1850-80) in the Eleanor and Mable Van Alstyne folk art collection, now housed in the Smithsonian Institution. Individually, the objects were admired for their reality, their boldness of design. Assembled together, the objects were converted into Americana, standing for an American tradition drawn from the

"Van Bergen Overmantel," attributed to John Heaten, 1732-33 (New York State Historical Association, Cooperstown)

"Peaceable Kingdom" by Edward Hicks, 1840-45 (New York State Historical Association, Cooperstown)

Goddess of Liberty weathervane (Eleanor and Mabel Van Alstyne Folk Art
Collection, Smithsonian Institution)

Figure from a Hudson River sidewheeler (Eleanor and Mabel Van Alstyne Folk Art Collection, Smithsonian Institution)

East's predominantly small-town, white Anglo-Saxon Protestant past. While acknowledging ethnic and racial contributions, collectors preferred to emphasize the mythologized New England roots of the newly dubbed primitive imagery.

The boom of Americana drew front-page attention from the *Saturday Review* in July 1926. The article led with the announcement, "The American Past has become a national industry." It continued, "There are almost as many 'antique' signs in Connecticut as gas stations, and it is impossible to guess at the millions which have been spent in refurnishing ornate Louis XIV houses and apartments with plain but far more costly American pine and maple." The cause, the anonymous author declared, "is a change in the country itself." The author failed to give specifics, but summarized the feeling by saying, "An era ended in the decade that included the war, so that 1910 seems more archaic to our children than did 1870 to us." The celebration of Americana projected into the complex twentieth century the desired stable image of nineteenth-century "Americanization," the author opined. Thus "vanity and an acuter sense of our history as a great common people are partly responsible for the vogue of Americana." To underscore the theme, the front page was balanced with an article on "American Folk-Lore" by Ernest Sutherland Bates. "One of the few indubitably good results of our recent patriotic movement," he observed, has been the increased interest in days 'when America was young'—twenty, fifty, or one hundred years ago, according to locality. We have begun to realize . . . that we are just emerging from a most romantic and picturesque phase, rich in many of the raw materials of art." The exhibits of folk art in the 1920s responded to the vogue reported by the *Saturday Review,* based, as were most of the exhibits, in New York.

In his article on "Primitive Art in America," Charles Messer Stow mentioned that antique dealer Isabel Carleton Wilde of Boston was impressed with the Whitney exhibit in New York, and it moved her to collect and sell such primitives. In November 1926, she advertised in the magazine *Antiques,* "Beginning November 1st Isabel Carleton Wilde announces an important exhibition of American Primitives including paintings on velvet and glass, portraits in oil, water colors, pastels, and tinsels. Many of these are in their original old frames." Among her customers was Abby Aldrich Rockefeller, wife of John D. Rockefeller, Jr. Abby Rockefeller had already been active in the "Americanization of immigrants." She was involved, for example, in the operation of International House near Columbia University, a facility for international students. She had the house designed and furnished in colonial styles, which, she believed, would force a sympathetic impression of America. Eventually one of the largest folk art collections, Abby Aldrich Rockefeller's purchases now fill a building bearing her name at Colonial Williamsburg.

In 1927 some of Wilde's collection came to an exhibit at the Whitney Studio Club. Coming to the attention of art dealers and collectors in New York, the primitives received more coverage in the popular press. Abby Aldrich Rockefeller and other wealthy eastern socialites such as Mrs. Henry T. Curtiss and Electra Havemeyer Webb, turned their resources to acquiring the primitives, and they in turn influenced the appearance of femininity in primitives collected and displayed by others. Although "crude," many scenes were landscapes and sentimental portraits, decorative objects and textile paintings. Stow pointed out, "It is quite probable that . . . most of the pictures in this collection were done by young ladies as part of their education. They took the place formerly occupied by samplers, though these examples of feminine handicraft were not entirely displaced till well towards the middle of the nineteenth century." The primitives dramatized the still-lingering paradox of Victorian Protestant middle-class women: they were the steadfast, industrious nurturers of children, home, and nation, yet they were considered fragile, leisurely, and primitive.

Edith Halpert answered the call for a New York center for purchasing primitives by collecting them in her Downtown Gallery in 1929, and later in the American Folk Art Gallery. The folk art objects she offered, she said, were chosen "not because of . . . antiquity, historical association, utilitarian value, or the frame of their makers, but because of their definite relationship to vital elements in contemporary American art."[37]

Folk was a market term to separate a commodity from the fine arts above and antiques below. It was an art that challenged the assumptions of art schools and epicurean control of taste, yet it supported the system by using the fine arts as the standard of judgment. Peasant and primitive art was being used similarly for New York manufacturers and designers, especially after 1914, when designs from Paris were no longer available. Marion Nicholl Rawson reported what happened: "Up at the Museum of Natural History the situation was being welcomed and gladly met by some of the curators who saw at last a chance to air the ancient weavings and pottery of the South Americans, and red Indians of both our continents, which had so long been shut up under glass. Cases were thrown open and art students spent their Saturday mornings copying the priceless designs of the primitive Americas. With eyes suddenly opened, the manufacturers began to offer prizes for the best designs from our art schools, and now went to the other extreme and not only urged purely native motifs but said to the young designers: 'When you design a silk pattern for a coat be sure that it is the kind that you yourself would love to wear,'—and American designing was off on its belated start, at least partially divorced from foreign influence."[38] Folk art, too, was native and new, populist and elitist, commercial and trendy. It fit the post-World War I bill.

What made the aesthetic modernist use of folk stick, though, when it had challenges from ethnological folklorists, especially in Pennsylvania? In 1926 at the American Sesquicentennial celebration in Philadelphia eyes were turned toward Hattie Brunner's exhibit of Pennsylvania folk art, items such as fractur, papercuts, ironwork, pottery, and textiles. The techniques of handwork, the cultural context of the objects, the basis in local tradition, took precedence over the aesthetics of the objects. *The Annual of the Pennsylvania German Folklore Society* ridiculed the rage for folk art coming out of New York as "antiquarian" and "unscientific." The Pennsylvanian interest was inclined less toward the visual, leisurely, decorative products, and more toward those of labor in communal societies, as existed in the Pennsylvania-German settlements. John Baer Stoudt published *The Shenandoah Pottery* in 1929, and his son John Joseph carried on with general studies of fractur and iconography in *Consider the Lilies* (1937) and *Pennsylvania Folk Art: An Interpretation* (1948). Preston Barba wrote in the *Annual* that folk art should be tied to a social world of folklore, not to the "individual achievement" of the artworld. Folk art is a "result," not a "product," he argued. "It s a living link in the long chain of a people's social existence."[39]

The word *folk* did not speak for itself. The argument over it went beyond semantics. The battle involved different social worlds and visions of America. For those stressing the art, folk represented an appealing romantic, nativist qualifier used in the marketplace. For those stressing the folk, it represented a sense of community and informal learning examined in academe. Participants in the battle staked their claim through use and publicity. The prize was ownership and public acceptance. Folk art, as an aesthetic term that was stirred by Holger Cahill's widely publicized New York and Newark exhibits in the 1930s, won out for a time. On staff at the Newark Museum, Holger Cahill had been exposed to the presentation of European peasant arts, and expressed an interest to director Beatrice Winser for the presentation of an analogous nativist collection for America. Cahill had visited the collection of modernist Robert Laurent with Edith Halpert, and, with contributions of sculptor Elie Nadelman and collectors Abby Aldrich Rockefeller and Isabel Wilde, he prepared an exhibit in 1930 of American primitive painting done, he said, by folk artists. "The word primitive is used as a term of convenience, not to designate any particular school of American art, or any particular period. It is used to describe the work of a simple people with no academic training and little book learning in art. . . . Contemporary interest in the native American expression has been stimulated by the modern artists who have rescued the pictures from antique dealers' basements and farmhouse attics. Of recent years, private collectors and museums have been hunting them."

The primitive painting show received critical acclaim in New York and a second show on sculpture followed in 1931. This time Cahill used the term *folk* to describe the art. "In grouping together these carven images which have previously been little known or studied other than for their interest as pleasant mementos of the past, the exhibit offers testimony that there has always existed in this country a robust native talent for sculpture, which has been capable of expressing itself spontaneously and with characteristics of its own." The show included cigar store Indians, decoys, weathervanes, ship figureheads, and stove plates.[40]

Cahill officially canonized folk art with an exhibit called "American Folk Art: The Art of the Common Man in America, 1750-1900" a year later at the Museum of Modern Art in New York City. "This exhibition," he flatly stated, "represents the unconventional side of the American traditon in the fine arts." In the catalogue, Cahill was still tentative about what to call the material, vacillating between provincial, primitive, popular, and folk. He settled on *folk art,* because it is the "expression of the common people, made by them and intended for their use and enjoyment. It is not the expression of professional artists made for a small cultured class, and it has little to do with the fashionable art of its period." Realizing the vagueness of the term, he turned the defining process around and used the exhibition to establish a definition. "Folk art," thus "as it is defined by the objects in this exhibition, is the work of people with little book learning in art techniques, and no academic training."[41] The objects are part of a dichotomy, between academic and nonacademic, educated and noneducated, and, by extension, between upper and lower classes. In effect, Cahill suggested that upper-class collectors use a definition based on their taste to select appropriate objects and then allow the objects to establish a folk art canon. Despite his circular reasoning, Cahill's definition, as Beatrix Rumford, former director of the Abby Aldrich Rockefeller Folk Art Collection at Williamsburg, noted, "is still being quoted, and curators and collectors continue to regard the 1932 catalogue as an indispensable reference."[42]

Cahill's definition was convenient. It allowed collectors to gather a great variety of objects into the net of folk art based on their relation to the exhibit, and it thus helped give a coherence to the diverse objects. The collectors and dealers became the specialist hunters; museums and galleries displayed the work for public consumption. For the collector troubled by the assumption that, as William Ketchum has stated, "where academic art required the learning of and adherence to certain techniques which were universally recognized and applied in the field, folk art required and requires only an open eye and an open mind," folk art could be categorized and given order by using the organization of academic arts categories, such as painting and sculpture, and the periodization of academic arts.[43] The categorization established folk art as a tradable commodity, with evidence of the trading especially prevalent in the pages of the magazines *Antiques* and *Art in America,* based in New York. With New York at its center, a web of urban consumption and artistic display was spun from extinct rural production.

For many years the web went virtually undisturbed. A protective concern in the 1960s for the viability of traditional societies and a concomitant democratization of art raised doubts about the rights of collectors to remove such objects from locales and make nativist claims for them. Henry Glassie's sweeping *Pattern in the Material Folk Culture of the Eastern United States* (1968) and his essay "Folk Art" in *Folklore and Folklife* (1972) highlighted folk art as an index of local traditions, and pointed out that folk art production continues into the present day. Glassie used the criteria, common to the Pennsylvania folklorists, of informal learning and community context. Cahill's popular use of *folk* to describe a crude surface quality and earthy innocence implied a social dominance and upper-class standard. Instead, Glassie called for a cultural relativism by which societies are analyzed not as better than one another, just as different. Societies are based on different norms; they cannot be assumed to be backward or inferior because they are not mechanized, urban, and commercial.

In 1974, the aesthetic approach had a resurgence of popular interest with an exhibit at the Whitney Museum of American Art, "The Flowering of American Folk Art." The catalogue glittered with photographs and documentation that reified the fine arts categories of folk art, yet authors Alice Winchester and Jean Lipman admitted that much of the material could not accurately be called folk. Although the aesthetic approach enjoyed popular attention, the barrage on the approach kept up.[44] Still, the aesthetic approach held its ground because its proponents held prominent positions in museums and in the market. The fires of an aesthetic approach to folk art were fanned by a desire for romanticized alternatives to mass society and its products, and the avowed purpose of many museums to promote appreciation of objects for their own sake. One could not just "live and let live," allowing one side to "do their thing" and the other to "do theirs," in the lingo of the day, because the approach taken implied different political ideologies about control of national culture and the attitudes taken toward alternative ways of living. Proponents of the aesthetic approach did battle because its well-established, lucrative system of consumption was threatened. The folklorists retaliated because of worries about the effect on traditional production which the aesthetic approach made, and about the integrity of professional folk studies.

As an example of how things are maintained for consumption and take on a political character, the battle is revealing. It is reminiscent of Veblen's conflict between "pecuniary" and "industrial" economic institutions. The pecuniary has to do with ownership or acquisition, while the industrial has to do with workmanship or production. Since they have separate institutions supporting them—in the case of the aesthetic approach, museums and galleries, and in the case of the folkloristic challenge, universities and professional societies—the conflict became institutional. The argument was at bottom over the use of an invention—the work *folk*. It was a labor-saving device designed to interpret for the viewer. With its standardization could come a mechanical control. Like the arguments over machinery in the last chapter, this one too ran between producers and managers. Yet unlike earlier arguments this one did not cut across a layer cake of classes but split into different professional interests. It was a mark of cultural boundaries in flux. As culture was named, so too would the roles of namers and named be spelled out. So too would their visions be objectified.

I pick up the action with a major conference intended to air out the issues and identify the sides. Sponsored by the folkloristic American Folklife Center and the aesthetic Museum of American Folk Art, the conference took place at the Library of Congress in Washington, D.C., in December 1983. Representing the aesthetic approach, Robert Bishop of the Museum of American Folk Art, said, "The conference succeeded in its purpose of bringing together those who view the folk art object primarily as art and those who emphasize its artifactual content within a cultural context."[45]

Bishop's address rephrased what he had written in the foreword to the ballyhooed publication *American Folk Art of the Twentieth Century* (1983) by Jay Johnson and William S. Ketchum. The book draws on the judgments of New York gallery expertise to select the "star" folk artists of the twentieth century. Brief biographies detail where the creation of the makers have been exhibited and honored. Brilliant color photographs of their titled works, all falling into the studio categories of painting and sculpture, accompanied by the names of the works' owners, proclaimed a continuity of a "folk art" style embodying the "native" and "primitive." The foreword proclaims the tack taken as different from that of "folklorists and folk culturists" who, "in their zeal for the 'folk,' occasionally ignore the 'art' part of the term. So few cultural and social artifacts constitute art that it becomes imperative to separate the cultural artifact from the folk art object."[46]

But if the folk art object in the aesthetic view is not social and cultural, then what is it? It is a thinly veiled commodity—a commodity not necessarily, although often, to make money, but one to offer or suggest excitement, reality, and taste for a distinct social world. It is a cultural statement by its owners rather than its makers. Quoting collectors and holding up studio categories from their collection, Bishop's folk art has been shaped by consumers more than by producers. Folk art here is a matter of economics, of education, and of social status.

Let me begin with economics. Defending the acultural use of folk art, Bishop relies on an intellectual geneaology beginning with Cahill and its connection to the language of vested things and institutions. Bishop quotes Louis C. Jones, former director of the New York State Historical Association, who invokes Holger Cahill: "Problems arise . . . over such items as factory-made weathervanes, trade signs which come off an assembly line (e.g. the later wooden Indian), school-taught arts such as theorems, memorials, calligraphy, landscapes after prints, and portraits which show an acquaintance with academic portraiture, all of which have been called folk art for fifty years. The fact is that neither dealers, nor museums, nor collectors, nor magazine writers, nor the general public have made the distinction between the two groups. They have lumped it all together and have called it American folk art. And it is too late I think to change."[47] The argument here is that objects not conforming to the tests of folkness are acceptable nonetheless because of previous linguistic use. Those groups with vested interests in the objects—dealers, collectors, and magazine writers—find it practical to continue this use.

Illustrating this standpoint is *Folk Art: Paintings, Sculpture & Country Objects* (1983) by Robert Bishop, Judith Reiter Weissman, Michael McManus, and Henry Niemann for the Knopf Collectors' Guides to American Antiques. Outlining in the preface the audience for folk art consumption, Bishop lists "connoisseurs who shop at elegant galleries, experts tracking down the identities of anonymous artists, and amateur collectors decorating their homes in a country style with the household objects that are often called 'primitives' today."[48] Bishop defines folk art by what collectors tied to a dealer-art gallery network found: portraits and other paintings, gravestones and shop signs, figureheads, and decoys. Category is shaped by the consummable object, art by the urban collector, folk by "primitive" design. The approach is inherently visual. A "visual key" is included to match objects to a shadowed outline of the object's surface characteristics.

Worked into the treatment of folk art as a commodity is a hierarchy. First comes the separation from fine art, representing a genteel, academic tradition. Folk is a negative entity, characterized as *non*-academic, *un*sophisticated. Although vying for acceptance as legitimate art, folk art is on the defensive. It is below fine, but above utility. It characterizes ownership by a rising middle class. For Cahill, "Folk art cannot be valued as highly as the work of our greatest painters and sculptors, but it is certainly entitled to a place in the history of American art." For Bishop, "while much folk art is clearly derivative, it is often original and exciting, and as powerful as the finest academic art."[49] Identified as art, however, the utilitarian and decorative objects become elevated above the everyday. As art, it is open to judgment by its owners, not its producers. William Ketchum, for example, in an article appropriately entitled "American Folk Art: The View from New York," states, "There is good and bad folk art. Some 'works' and some does not. Trained as we are to appreciate the illusion of reality created by the academic artist, the simplicity and openness of folk art may escape us."[50]

Another hierarchy codifies the judgment of taste into "Good, Better, and Best." Six pages of the collector's guide are divided into three strata to illustrate the difference. The "best" painting is distinguished by being made by a "well-known" artist, "its impressive provenance and record of exhibitions," and "design, palette, and characterization." The "good" painting is "charming" and "attractive," but lacks information and is generally "too primitive for many collectors." "Interesting accessories and rich scenery" would make the painting more highly "prized." "Good, Better, and Best" shows the proclivity for stratification in the social world from which it springs, and is a projection, manifestly, of financial worth. The "Good, Better, and Best" household objects, for example, divide into, at the bottom "utilitarian," "primitive," and "graceless" objects. In the middle, the "stylishness" of the object stands out. At the top, the chandelier is "unique," "beautiful," and "highly functional." Parallels can be made to the "primitive" groups in society at the bottom, the stylish, popular groups in the middle, and the beautiful, "unique" and "exceptional" people at the top. The "prized" objects, those that bring status and money, parallel the socioeconomic scale. In offering "what to look for and what to avoid, what factors affect value," the authors of the collector's guide prescribe how to be right and how to do it right, much in the style of the manner advisers.

For art critic Roger Fry, the "best" art also meant the "right" art and aligned him with the "right" people. It marked him with a snobbish adherence to aesthetic and intellectual values. As he put it, "The snobbist, by his pilgrimage to the 'right' picture gallery at the 'right' moment, and his display there of the 'right' enthusiasm before the 'right' works of art is really upheld by the consciousness that those acts bring him into close communion with a certain group of people, and it is not altogether remote from his consciousness, although, perhaps, kept below its surface, that those people are socially influential."[51] The visual characteristic of a taste for painting and sculpture lent an air of rational objectivity, even though it was a subjective social world being projected.

Judgments of taste in the aesthetic view invoke education. In the preface to the collector's guide, Bishop maintains that "a taste for the primitive is often a product of sophistication." Again, this sentiment is taken from late nineteenth-century Victorian attitudes. For example, when Stewart Culin in 1900 reviewed the origin of primitive ornamentation, he noted the Victorian fascination with the "rudest effort of the existing savage," which is mostly decorative, because, he surmised, "The general trend of our education is to encourage and foster what is regarded as the 'art' instinct, and we have been led to view development of the so-called decorative arts as concomitant with the highest culture."[52] The bold, unrestrained primitive art provided a contrast with civilized culture—an urban, industrial culture. The taste for the primitive allowed an outlet for patterns restrained by highest culture, and underscored, as Culin said, the "undisguised superiority" by which high culture expresses its station above the primitive, while it also expresses a longing for the tactile depth, closeness to nature, and emotional reality, of the primitive. Arnold Hauser in *The Philosophy of Art History* (1959) underscored differences in viewing folk art: "Today the art of the urban masses is impossible to confuse with folk art, being utterly incompatible with it. Indeed, nothing is less attractive than folk art to the modern half-educated crowd that apes the ways of life and modes of culture of the upper class; what the educated value and enjoy in folk art escapes the half-educated altogether."[53]

Hence, the modernists looked to pristine abstraction, a combination of old and new, to mediate the dilemmas of modernization. The fascination with pristine abstraction extends to the fashionable demand for the work of living folk artists. Cahill noted in 1931 that their work "finds its way into the big annual no-jury shows, the New York dealers' galleries, and even into the Carnegie International."[54] It was not the life of the work being sought, but the visibility, Johnson and Ketchum say of painter Inez Nathaniel Walker, for example, "Like many folk artists her work was influenced by the needs and demands of her collectors." Bishop adds in the collector's guide that "since there are dealers who specialize in virtually every kind of folk art and in every price range, you are sure to find one who suits your taste and budget." Invoking aesthetics can be a way of intellectualizing economics.

For consideration of cultural politics, let me summarize the visual rhetoric of the "aesthetic" books, using *American Folk Art of the Twentieth Century* as an example. The book uses a similar script and features many of the same actors found in gallery books that preceded it, and the set is laid out similarly too. Taken together, the books have four noticeable characteristics: (1) surprise at finding a "naive" and "primitive" mode of production in modernized America; (2) citing objects out of cultural context, coupled, however, with attributing names of the maker and titles for the works; (3) emphasizing the regularity of "unusual" and "bold" aesthetic qualities; and (4) stressing the appeal of the objects in the marketplace, gallery, and museum.

First is the reference to the "unconventional" side of life expressed by the art. Bishop, for example, quotes Cahill's "folk art is the unconventional side of the American tradition in the fine arts." The convention of life, of art, is the "fine," a pinnacle of urban, modern existence. From this vantage of a controlled fine arts market system and an urban, elite center, collectors find unexpected objects. They are creative, colorful, manually executed, and public. They are not judged from the vantage of traditional communities, but for their contrast of, or appeal to, the experience of an upper-class urban network. Being done outside the fine arts system, they are pulled into it. Alice Winchester, editor of *Antiques* and co-author of the *Flowering of American Folk Art* wrote, for example, in 1979, "Produced apart from the main currents of urban culture, by and for people unversed in the conventions of academic art, these works often lack technical proficiency. Their quality as art depends basically on design and color, handled with vigor, honesty, and individuality. Folk art is, then the nonacademic counterpart of the fine arts and the formal decorative arts. It does not include objects produced for a popular market or the arts of the American Indians produced prior to or apart from European influence."[55]

For Louis C. Jones, the important question is, "Is there an aesthetic quality that delights the eye, that stirs the imagination?" Whose eye? His, as he explains. "I am more concerned with whether an object is art than I am with whether or not it is 'folk.' "[56] Such a position typically obscures class difference. When New York's John Gordon, curator of "Masterpieces of American Folk Art" (1975), put together his exhibit, he claimed that the art represented a classless society, one in which no aristocracy dictated what to make, yet he drew the objects from "private collections that seldom lend, and items from museums, including their storerooms, that have infrequently if ever been exhibited." The gauge of folk art's appreciation, according to Gordon, was "record breaking attendance at exhibitions, the large number and variety of books published, the escalating prices of the objects."[57]

The folk art displayed by the aesthetic approach is, as Cahill asserted, "art of the common people." Yet *common* is not a synonym for *typical*. Common here stands for unlikely work coming from unlikely groups outside the formal artistic training and market hierarchy, yet tied to a dominant racial stock. Early in his description of American folk art, Holger Cahill pointed out that "many writers appear to have taken it for granted that the American people is not given to esthetic expression and that Puritanism is to blame for this national deficiency."[58] Thus the art is described by the relative terms "bold," "striking," and "strong." More than aesthetic descriptions, they also suggest threatening social characteristics, especially when Cahill describes a Puritan American standard connected to a high art standard. For New York gallery director Jane Kallir, "The concept of folk art is one of negation. It is a catchall category for misfits— wallflowers at the dance of Western civilization. Like all things defined in the negative, the concept remains strongly dependent on the thing negated."[59]

The "unlikely" groups and "misfit" individuals producing folk art in the aesthetic view, however, are not usually characterized by ethnicity or race. The folk artist, William Ketchum states, "is more likely to be a social isolate, living alone or in a group in some way out off from the mainstream." For Robert Bishop, an American folk art arose when "European traditions gradually began to fade and were replaced by an ever-increasing American consciousness and artistic sensibility."[60] Such statements of modern nativism are underscored by gallery presentations. The folk art presented by galleries is not bound by groups but by theme, by aesthetic pattern, by the collection from which it came. Indeed, the art's location in America as an assumption of an Americanized art sidesteps the social circulation of the object, as the following recent "aesthetic" exhibit and book titles show: *Folk Painters of America, American Folk Art: Expressions of a New Spirit, Folk Art in America,* and *Folk Art: The Heart of America.* Domesticity and sentimentality carry over from the antiques craze in concerns for exhibits on the dog, the cat, the heart, and the child in folk art, all produced at the Museum of American Folk Art in New York City. More than any genre of material culture, art celebrates the conspicuous consumer. The "great" collectors overshadow their objects. Having the unique and rare in their collections gives them distinction. Having reached an impressive size, the collection becomes the artifact, an extension of a collector's exceptional eye and purse.

When a racial or ethnic connection is made in an aesthetic approach, the latent effect of maintaining social control is laid bare. Eugene Metcalf's criticism of the exhibit *Black Folk Art in America* (1982) points out that utilitarian objects are neglected in favor of those fitting into high art standards because "utilitarian black folk objects represent useful work that has not been performed at the behest and for the benefit of the leisure class. Furthermore, these objects generally exhibit close kinship to their African origins and proclaim a black identity independent of white domination."[61] Following Veblen, Metcalf argues that control of the art was important to maintain the hegemony of the leisure class and their consuming economic system. Yet Metcalf does not pursue the motivations for consumption further with other groups. Because art by minority groups is generally not represented in national folk art, the political and economic implications of judging folk art according to high art aesthetic values may appear benign. I will argue, however, that because of its subtlety, its masking of latent motives, and its unintended effects, the judging of folk art in terms of high art standards can become highly charged with cultural politics.

Downplaying the "folk" of folk art, as the aesthetic approach is wont to do, suggests social forces made more latent. Recognizing this possibility, art historian Daniel Robbins wrote in a catalogue devoted to the aesthetic appreciation of folk sculpture:

> The strange marriages of high art themes with hobbiest techniques appeal to a sophisticated jaded taste in a way that may or may not have been intended by the artist. (The more intentional the strange union, the less Folk the artist.) Among the many influences and relationships that have contributed to the formation of American folk art, we—collectors, dealers, curators, or

historians—must add our own influence. Its cumulative effect all too frequently crosses the thin line separating patronage from corruption in modern society. It governs by both selection (which is remedial), and by influencing production (which is not), subsuming the folk roots of a tradition.[62]

In the name of aesthetics, class and occupational relationships are obscured. In the name of taste, shrines are built to perpetuate patronizing attitudes toward "folk" and to project the social world of owners.

Let me offer one analysis of what is occurring latently. It may be surprising to find references to creativity in the aesthetic books because such creativity is being presented from an educated, urban vantage. However, from the economic vantage of art consumers, the creativity of Ketchum's "practitioner [who is] . . . likely to be a social isolate, living alone or in a group in some way cut off from the mainstream" is considered a leisurely creativity that is surplus, that comes from those not supposed to be able to produce such in a hierarchical market economy in which agents siphon off valued decorative, leisurely products. Having surplus gives a producer the power to express control, possibly freeing the producer from the pressure of an agent who takes on importance because of access to special information and privileged networks. In the case of folk artists, who often do not intend their products for the market, the intervention of the agent or dealer can be considerable. The dealers contribute to what one author calls "country chic." For example, Karl Meyer writes in *The Art Museum* (1979) of a folk quilt show at the Whitney Museum of American Art in New York City drawn from the collections of Jonathan Holstein. "But Holstein is a dealer as well as a collector, and the Whitney show was therefore of inestimable importance in establishing folk quilts as a desirable art form to collect."[63] Mention of the artists is absent. A flow of goods upward, instead of laterally, is established.

Much of the folk art literature has dwelled on the "problem" of twentieth-century folk art because in the twentieth century the practicality of handcrafted objects has supposedly dwindled. Ketchum states of the typical nineteenth-century folk artist, for example, "He made furniture, drew maps and diagrams of new buildings, recorded births and deaths, baked pottery, or carved the figureheads that were an essential part of every sailing ship. As the 20th century dawned, however, this social utilitarianism diminished. . . . By right, folk art should have died then; indeed, for some collectors and authorities who recognize no 20th-century folk art, it did."[64]

To accept twentieth-century folk art meant to alter the view of artists, since they were now living close by instead of being relegated to an idealized past. The contemporary folk artist was assigned a role subordinate to that of other present-day artists. As subordinates rather than ancestors, folk artists could be marked by their removal from centers of community, modernity, and therefore power. The so-called surplus art ceases to be functional for communities when treated as tradable commodities. The flow of surplus is redirected upward by creating an art hierarchy for material that did not have such a system in place. In scholarship, the production of the art is identified by its desirable goods rather than by its social processes. This redirection patronizes makers while controlling their products, often making them work for hire. The Fall 1983 issue of the *Clarion*, organ of the Museum of American Folk Art, included advertisements from over sixty dealers or agents with copy such as "Provenance available to purchaser," "will feature the work of master craftsmen, each skilled in the individualized hand production of only the finest traditional Americana," and "Dealing in Investment Quality American Folk Art."

Highlighting and framing the object out of its cultural context sidesteps social process again. The object is no longer integral to a social or historical environment. It is decorative and solely visual, and ultimately trivial. Put in a case or put behind a barrier, social distance is created between the viewer and the object, and between the community and the object. The folk art object is converted into the fine arts system of painting and sculpture, patronage and appraisal, dominance and control. If folk really is unimportant, as proponents of the aesthetic approach claim, then its use is simply to label it apart from yet akin to fine arts. Like decorative art, folk art is labeled apart so as to site it below the top shelves of the hierarchy. The symbolism that emerges is elitist, not subordinate; capitalist and materialist, not social and tactually expressive. Visitors to accommodating galleries and viewers of supportive books are given a controlled, shielded view of "primitive" objects from exotic people. They are of this time, but not of its center. Further, painters may be described as John William Dey is by Johnson and Ketchum: "The almost childlike pictures of John William Dey . . . have an immediate appeal for most collectors of American folk art." The frequent choice of "childlike" to describe folk art suggests an embodiment of the undisciplined and youthful watched over by superiors. Such references are made objective, by the justification that "the objects speak for themselves," as Robert Bishop states in the foreword to Johnson and Ketchum's book. The hidden meaning is that the social and economic challenges have been made mute. The objects speak for their owners.

Proponents of the aesthetic approach defend themselves by noting their attention to the identities of artists. But this is often to uncover names rather than life histories, names akin to Sister Carrie's Tiffany, Sherry, and Haviland. A biography in Johnson and Ketchum's book, to give an illustration, describes most frequently the quality of the work, where it has been exhibited, and experiences as they bear on the production of consumable art. It is recognition of the signature and its attachment to a known style that provides a value, as Bishop pointed out in the collector's guide. Such figurative signatures, known in a traditional community orally but usually not on the piece itself, provide what anthropologist Mary Douglas calls "marking services." Goods named materially, she points out, "can equally be perceived as a mere installment, just part of a flow of marking tape or paint that goes into the construction of a classification system. The stream of consumable goods leaves a sediment that builds up the structure of culture like coral islands. The sediment is the learned set of names and names of sets, operations to be performed upon names, a means of thinking."[65] Identifying names of makers builds a system of consumption. As an illustration, I can cite the case of folklorist Robert Teske, who challenged the claim of an Ammi Phillips painting as folk art because it did not represent a communal aesthetic and a long-standing tradition.[66] Bishop reacted by invoking a fine arts classification of masters and masterpieces: "This painting by one of the acknowledged folk masters, is not folk art in his opinion." The key here is to note "acknowledged," for it points to the social agreement of dealers and collectors for marking services. Other complaints were more strongly voiced and made earlier than Teske's. Teske drew immediate reaction because he challenged the classification system built upon names.

The classification system calls for control of the items through consumption. Aiding this is the scale of the objects. They are separate from and as large as, or smaller than, the size of the human body. They can be grasped and carried by the owner. They cannot tower over the owner. Being visual, however, means that one has to compensate for lack of depth by enlarging their scope. One has to compile many to make up for the direct experience of one, since much more is needed to occupy the eye than the hand. Being inherently amassable, their importance can be heightened by repetition and variation, on a wall, on the floor. Being separate, they suggest singular consumer ownership and a separate individual producer. The objects are framed by countable, consistent, and hence consumable shapes—rectangular pictures, rectangular sculpture stands, rectangular cases. Folk art, Louis C. Jones insists, "exists item by item and should be enjoyed for its own sake."[67]

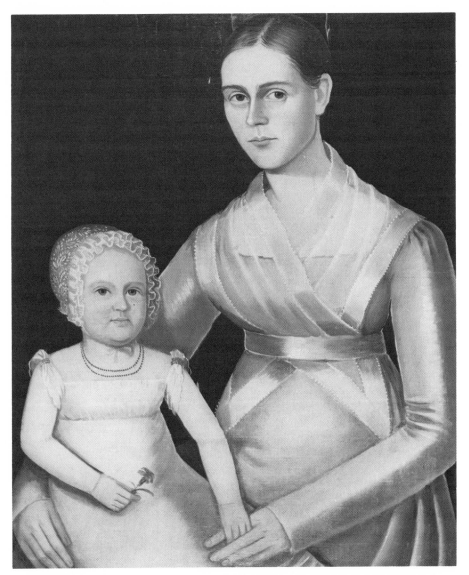

"Mother and Child in White" by Ammi Phillips, ca. 1820 (New York State Historical Association, Cooperstown)

Marking services provided by signatures in a web of consumption, as opposed to the social services in a system of community experience called for by critics of the aesthetic view, set apart the work from its use and surroundings. Thus the maker's social ties to a cohesive group are reduced. Such social ties can threaten agent roles in the market system. The community is not allowed to appear organized. It is anachronistic compared to modern urban bourgeois culture. In books and galleries, folk art objects are presented as scattered, atypical, and static. In the "Masterpieces of American Folk Art" show, "the emphasis . . . is upon the artistic merit of the individual pieces rather than upon their historical associations. Our intention is to allow each object to make its appeal directly and intimately to the viewer, even to people uninitiated in the arts." Denied continuity and wholeness, the object's world is broken down into manageable bits lacking volition. The objects stand still, while viewers are on the move. The object is art and its surrogate sterile environment influences the valuation of it as an isolated instance meant for consumption. The repetition of a nonutilitarian, unusual aesthetic suggests a commonness not characteristic of subcultures. The strong lines and bold colors, attributed to eccentrics and outsiders presented as the "folk" distort existing traditional value systems based on class, ethnicity, and race.

Doing so reinforces the legitimacy of a fine arts standard and by extension a cultural standard. Harry Lieberman is "extremely" old; Carlton Garrett is "extremely" illiterate; Charlie Dieter is "extremely" isolated. Recall Kallir's description of them as "wallflowers in the dance of Western civilization" and their work as "social misfits." Alternative systems, often conflicting with the dominant one, are kept illegitimate by calling attention to the exoticness of objects taken from the fringe of those systems (and therefore mistaken for the center of alternative systems of community), and by calling attention to unself-conscious makers chosen for their social vertigo and often passivity. Even granted that the folk art exhibitions done in this way serve and reflect one network in the world of the urban educated, and do not necessarily claim to show the social patterns of the folk, they make subtle and lasting statements about upper-class attitudes toward work and people "out of the mainstream."

Although ostensibly describing someone else, the attitudes shown often project the social world in which the collector lives. The upper-class taste for folk art often was latently a sympathy for those "out of the mainstream," a quiet vicarious rebellion, since early collectors of folk art, such as Henry Francis du Pont and Electra Havemeyer Webb, were themselves reacting to the older dominant upper-class taste for European fine art and genteel European standards. Webb recalls the reaction of her mother to her American folk art collection as, "How can *you, Electra, you* who have been brought up with Rembrandts and Manets, live with this American trash?" Even today, mention is made of folk art as an American alternative to the more elite fine arts for collection and appreciation.[68] To achieve legitimacy for the reaction in this social world was to establish its economic value and its status value, through the existing fine arts market system.

The rival use of folk outside the market projects a different political message. Describing folk as an integral type of learning and social exchange, viewing folk as a constant, dynamic process, and characterizing folk as part of vitally functioning communities which often downplay individual capitalist competition stress the legitimacy of productive activity's utility for the community itself, not for an urban consumer. Standards for judgment come from within, not from without. Folk is local. It is typical, not unusual. Rather than hierarchy, relativism is stressed. The communities and their ways of life, stressing social rather than pecuniary purposes, are viable. America is pluralistic, made of many groups vying for space in the social structure. Even if the groups do not appear organized, there are informal situations in which subcultural values are expressed and maintained. The spirit of folk production is steeped in labor and "mainstream" in its own social setting.

The image of "out of the mainstream" comes from flipping through pages of aesthetic folk art picture books or walking through sterile galleries. A regularity of unusual aesthetic qualities appears. Tightly framed paintings display "loud" colors, "sharp" lines, and "striking" imagery. "Rugged" sculpture boasts "strong" textures, "bold" dimensions, and "imposing" stances. The objects, having little to do with one another, are supported by one another. For Louis C. Jones, speaking from the viewpoint of a museum director, a "common characteristic of these heterogeneous objects is a tendency toward strong design; indeed, this is one of the criteria by which folk art is to be judged." "And the key," he adds, "tends to be simplicity rather than sophistication, directness rather than subtlety."[69] The gallery setting provides a metaphor for alienation of controlled objects, of artificiality within mass society. Blank spaces and visual objects put in cases and frames emphasize sharp technological lines and social isolation and enclosure. The gallery reflects and creates "fashion" for an urban-bourgeois social world. Alice Winchester's article in *Art in America,* "Antiques for the Avante Garde," for example, described folk art as a desirable fashion for trendsetters. "Living with Antiques" is a regular feature of the magazine *Antiques,* which displays fashionable houses decorated with folk art. Collector Henry Francis du Pont, writes Scott Swank, "was always strongly influenced by other important collectors, interior designers, and professionals. He, like the other great collectors of American decorative arts of the twenties and thirties, sought the most aesthetically pleasing antiques, the most firmly documented objects, and those also deemed collectible by his peers."[70]

"The more you see of the objects themselves, the more they fall into their levels of quality," Louis C. Jones observes, and this proclivity for stratification has made folk art appealing to the consumption by an upwardly aspiring bourgeoisie prone to relying on material accumulation for status.[71] Robbed of their intrinsic content and social intent, the quality of the works becomes extrinsic surfaces to be selected, arranged, and manipulated. They are thus counted (number produced, price paid, and number of times exhibited) and fall in line with other material possessions. The visual key in the Knopf collector's guide thus provides the desirable makes and models. Museums offer catalogues and shows of folk art. The metaphors stem from fashion and commerce. Chuck and Jan Rosenak, a prominent collecting couple I interviewed, mark in their catalogues and picture books items or styles that they want to acquire. The catalogues are the pattern books, the trade catalogues of consumption.[72]

The rhetoric of folk art has become such a bone of contention between the rival social worlds, because, as Alan Trachtenberg has noted, rhetoric constitutes "vehicles of self-knowledge, of the concepts upon which people act. They are also, especially in the public domain, forces in their own right, often coloring perceptions in a certain way even against all evidence. At the same time, figurative representations occupy the same social world as other forces, material and political."[73] The language and the material are indeed political, for they describe art and thus confer a hierarchy of taste and of goods. Eugene Metcalf, for example, makes the point, "Art represents and sanctifies what is valued in a society; the ability to create and appreciate art implies heightened human sensibility and confers social status and prestige."[74] The descriptive words *folk, art, naive, strong design, exhibit,* and *collection* in the aesthetic view extend the persuasiveness of a behavioral grammer for choosing, displaying, viewing, and consuming the material. When Robert Teske did dare criticize the gallery-honored work of Ammi Philips, for example, Robert Bishop retaliated by accusing him of being academic and unaware of art collecting. Why should this be a detriment? One can argue that the academic sector (actually Teske works in the public sector) can be construed as a threat to the dealer-agent system, for it has traditionally supported liberal intellectual values and critical lines of questioning. Indeed, selling as folk art, a painting by Ammi Phillips of a girl in a red dress set an auction record of $682,000 on 26 January 1985. Through a dealer, the Museum of American Folk Art received a similar Phillips painting valued at one million dollars.

The origins of the dealer system can be traced back to a successful resistance to academic dominance in mid-nineteenth-century Paris. European dealers spread the system to New York. Based on competition, advertisement and exclusive representation became techniques to promote trade and control artists and information. The system brought more financial reward to artists than they had enjoyed previously, but the system also dictated production and geared it to consumption.[75] Such is the case today with aesthetic folk art collection. Seeking to expand into the academy, the Museum of American Folk Art in 1982 spawned a degree program with New York University in Folk Art Studies. Marilynn Karp, describing the program in the *Clarion,* confessed that the growing acceptance of folk art within the fine arts tradition was "more evident in the market than its impact on art criticism." But boasting the program's station in New York, "the art capital of the world," Robert Bishop envisioned graduates joining the "ranks of museum administrators and curators, art collectors, writers and professionals." Supported by bourgeois institutions and an urban social world, appropriate roles for perpetuating a commodity aesthetic and its intellectual genealogy were being assigned. Bishop's "folk art historians," rely, he asserted, on "taste and instincts."[76]

Folklorists, typically caught between the muses and the masses, have responded. Their academic claim to folk art is an old story, but their entrance in the public arena is new. A network of state folk art coordinators now try to defend folk as process, folk as a vehicle of social meaning. Folkloristic literature, now circulating widely, stresses life histories, community studies, and labor studies. A session on folk arts and marketing at the 1983 American Folklore Society raised discussion of the folklorist's obligation to correct "misconceptions" of folk art in the marketplace. The lines drawn were for folklorists to dwell on production, as Michael Owen Jones did in "Folk Art Production and the Folklorist's Obligation" (1970). He stated, "Folklorists who conduct field research among contemporary craftsmen have a two-fold obligation: To assist individual craftsmen market their products . . . and to . . . educate museum personnel and the general public who are so ill-informed about American folk art production."[77] The public arena is ultimately where decisions will be made. Most likely both views will continue, since they represent institutionalized expressions of established social worlds, but the main decision is one of legitimacy, a claim to the center.

Art, more than other terms, is one likely to draw mixed feelings. Art, with its assumptions of superiority and its built-in subjectivity, like turtling, can evoke pride or loathing. "Art collecting," Maurice Rheims wrote in *The Strange Life of Objects,* "involves a permanent conflict between what the eye sees and what it reads, between instinct and scientific research."[78] Art can provide psychic distance and social maintenance for a consuming community, just as turtle soup does. Art, too, is a matter of distinctiveness, a reflection of attitudes toward the structure of society, of personal surroundings and productive activity. Folk art attracts extra notice because it mixes apparently opposed categories. Then again, so does turtle soup. Folk art and turtle soup are both socially important goods, but they operate under different conditions and with different purposes. Both generate mixed feelings among their producers and consumers and those who study such things.

It has been stated that America is a consumer society, just as it is a mechanized society, an urbanized society, and a visual society. These are frames for public pictures of national homogeneity, but lest the sterile gallery be mistaken for real life, the varied textures of private experience, the patterns of production and consumption, and the dimensions of face-to-face encounter call for uncovering. In informal settings and situations, tactual private experience gives depth, gives wholeness, to the imagery of living and learning. The small worlds vie with the larger social order for meaning. Objects held and entered, produced and consumed, tangibly relate sides of the body politic. Americans will consume, but whether they are consumed will depend on how well they grasp things.

Epilogue

I MADE my observations, wrote my stories, and wondered if events that followed would change things. Turtle soup still sells briskly at church picnics in southern Indiana. Meanwhile consumption of folk art adds plates to its feast. *Americana* (January-February 1985) spreads on its pages an advertisement of a porcelain plate collection of Mattie Lou O'Kelley, "the South's greatest folk artist." The first issue is entitled "Down Home Memories" and the advertisers note, "You will be assigned your personal registered number so every plate will be matched, enhancing the value of the series." Anna Bock writes to tell me that she has finished her 441st painting of 1984, just enough to fill her "orders." The family continues to live and pray together, but Anna's sister, who has worked at the recreation-vehicle factory, has cancer and her father at ninety-one manages little more than tending the horse. Anna is more on her guard for exploitation after finding that a local store was selling cards of her work without her knowledge.

A calm settles over Penn Street in the spring of 1985. Cal paints the porch and trim on Fred Raleigh's house. A loud red announces Cal's hand. Fred kids Cal. "Remember, Cal, no bricks." Cal smirks "sheeet." He gives Fred a break on the price because, he says, "You're part of the neighborhood." Fred returns with a tip above the charged price. In early summer, another house on Penn Street is taken over by professional renovators. Repainting his three-tone front, Cal draws complaints once more. Again the shutters become white and Cal paints over the red and black on the sidewalk with a dull gray. He works on his bulwark of sidewalk structures (plate 6). Strips of wood encase the portico and a door goes up (plate 5).

Meanwhile Ross Butler's Agate Street is uneasy. It has become more run-down. He paints the empty shells across the street from his house. Now on this tattered facade one can make out the door of the post office next to the newspaper headquarters and follow down the line with other downtown commercial sights (plate 16). He is unaware that the National Municipal League and *USA Today* have selected Harrisburg an "All-America City." The key, a brochure announces, is "business development."

The degree of influence people bring to objects or that objects hold over people in these scenes may be less the issue than the meanings that adhere to them. With this realization, one is tempted to draw universals, to compose a theory of materialism. What we are left with when we do so, however, is a set of abstracted propositions of uncertain application to real-life situations. Rather, theory gives way in practice to parables which objects provide. This is not to say that objects are judged case by case, or that they all carry meaning equally. Folk objects and traditional manual labor have taken on more significance in the last century because they appear unusual when compared to the norms of a rising mass society. Involving communal participation and tactual compassion, the coloring of folk objects lies outside the lines, and thus it forces on mass standards and structures questions of organizing and doing things. Is a cybernated, bureaucratic social system and a consumer-oriented service economy inevitable and all-powerful? Is it always progress? Can we demand the compassion of craftsworkers while subordinating the social structure on which they are based? Has the recent raising of folk crafts to the level of folk art, and of folk housing to the level of architecture, been a sign of heightened appreciation or of cultural weakening?

Objects do not speak for themselves. They are interpreted. Folk objects appear more evocative than others because they are part of, yet apart from, the run of society, thus providing imaginative ingredients for parable. In a visual society, the tendency is to give attention to the surface connection of a mass of objects. Tactile involvement typical of folk objects invites deeper explorations of those few things attached intimately to group and locale. As parables, objects made and used are not meant to be understood by all. They have hidden messages waiting for explanation, a fact that in itself holds a story. That story may come from connection to other objects and persons or from the perspective brought by stepping away from the situation. The explanation is set, however, in the terms of the teller. Thus, for instance, folk art holds separate meanings—separate often from the objects themselves—for the New York gallery, the state arts council, the university department, and the Indiana village. It is in this way, too, that language becomes entwined with objects, drawing on them for metaphor, describing them in symbol, and wrestling with them for meaning. The object is artificial, fictional and true like the parable, and equally designed to persuade and hold moral as well as practical meaning.

Parable becomes more subtle and thus more important as the gulf between nature and man grows. Signaling this dilemma for Western thought was Goethe in his famous last chorus of *Faust* (Part Two), 1932: "Alles Vergangliche / Ist nur ein Gleichnis" (All things fleeting / Are but a parable). The paradox is that those things we believe to be most lasting are those we construct. Yet in parabolic terms, they are the most fleeting because their utilities and meanings change. Indeed, some translate *Vergangliche* as "destructible," which emphasizes change and contradiction even more.

Not just a literary sentiment, the parabolic meaning of traditional things at moments of deeply felt social and cultural change drew editorial comment in the *New York Mirror* as early as 1827. Those step-gabled Dutch houses of previous settlement, those "time honoured edifices," the editorial ran, stand "like the small remnant of the revolutionary band, on a military holiday, in the midst of the gold-bedizened troops of the present period." The edifices, these "good secret-keepers," indeed, awaken "strange thoughts and associations." Because they are old, must they give way? The writer continues, "It grieves us whenever we see one of these relics of the olden time demolished. But fashion and business care little for antiquarian lumber; and in a few years more, not one of them will be left to speak its 'moral to the heart.' " The honor of time thus turns into the shame of age standing in the way of "progress." To others, the things are not old but social, not relics but reinforcements of alternative social and ecological order. "Whenever the spirit of innovation and improvement which is abroad among us is stirring energy, levels one of them to the ground, the noise of the trembling structure falls upon the ear of the sensitive man with a sound somewhat akin to that of the earth, as it rattles on the coffin of an old and long-known friend."[1]

Although Franz Kafka and W.H. Auden also used the term *parable*, it has not been much used in twentieth-century literary discourse, but it can be applied directly to the social discourse of folk material culture in a technologizing society. A literary harbinger of such application is H.G. Wells, who in the crucible of the late nineteenth century wrote *The War of the Worlds* (1898) as a parabolic battle of the brainy (but not brawny) Martians dependent on a bodily-based technology against "progressive" Victorian society. Yet the technological Martians take on attributes of colonized, traditional society appearing close to home, eventually taking on urban London at its height. The Martians are "strange" and brown, come from the south, emanate from the villages, are likened to the "primitive" Tasmanians near Australia, and are associated with the words of American Indian Chief Joseph of the Nez Percé. Their downfall comes from minute, natural causes—bacteria to which they are not immune—much as

French canal engineers failed in Panama in 1889. Wells turned evolutionary and technological assumptions on their heads.[2] In modern folklore, bureaucratic and corporate assumptions are turned on their heads in photocopied folklore passed around the office, legends rapidly circulating on the dangers of large corporate products, and folk crafts given notoriety in the face of mass produced goods.[3] They are typically parables rather than challenges, expressions rather than utilities.

Such expressions reveal for culture "real" conditions and relations, just as "real" wages measure not only dollars but also rent and the prices of basic commodities. A temptation in describing the "real" terms of materialism is to draw a model of evolution from folk to technological, tactual to visual, communal to the bureaucratic. Doing so, however, commonly obscures changes of power relations and social structures, and the dynamics of history. Real history is not the life cycle of the moth, where once transformed past forms are never seen again. Folk and technological, communal and bureaucratic systems commonly exist simultaneously, but their practicality and integrity commonly appear in disproportion. Anthropologist Maurice Bloch writes. "In each historical case, the particular situation, 'the social formation,' is to be understood not by just one 'mode of production' but by an articulation of several. For example, in a colonial situation a communal mode of production may coexist with a capitalist one but the capitalist one will dominate the communal mode of production; in other words, the structural relationship of the two modes of production will not be an equal one, but rather the dominant mode will be more powerful, and it is in the constructing of these many different structures both within individual modes of production and between modes of production that the actual process of history is to be understood."[4] Thus it is essential to understand society through history in real terms, Bloch asserts, by looking behind what people say and what people do.

Of course *folk* and *technological, communal* and *bureaucratic* are not as separate or adversarial as common diction would imply. They commonly emerge as abstractions for dominant and subordinate power relations and social structures. "The whole nation is a chocolate chip cookie," political scientist H.L. Nieburg offers as a possible clarification. No longer conforming to the older metaphor of a layer cake of classes, an entrapping batter of mainstream culture holds varieties of chips scattered haphazardly about. "An entirely new class system has emerged," he explains, "based on the current alignments of people into value systems which reflect the active organizational principles of their lives, and reflect the active structuring process of mass societies." What people do voluntarily, what they need to see and show others, what they do with their friends, "these are the significant things in people's lives."[5] Folk experience is an informal organizational principle. The things that come out of it are the symbolic chips in a marketed batter.

As the scenes in this book indicate, folk ideas continue even after some folk experience may no longer be apparent. They move to a different sphere of existence, but they still provide crucial parables, although out of sight or understanding of the historical record. Although relocated, they nonetheless depend, as folk systems, on larger formal structures for benchmarks. They rarely, if ever, exist in isolation. In that role, however, they have great parabolic meaning, for they dwell typically in shadowy, imaginative realms of family, community, and spirit. Such realms are often imagined to be harmoniously stable, but they erode, at times of rapid social, economic, and cultural change, and, commonly, of social conflict. To be sure, the process in America has been continuous, but the channeling and idealizing of the traditional in a system of modernization and commercialization appears heightened, as many of my examples show, in the 1850s, 1890s, 1920s and 1980s. The parabolic meaning of folk things is also heightened by the tendency of folk expressions to deal poignantly, and in the case of material culture tangibly, with ambivalent feelings toward nature, machine, and society.

In America, it is common to mythologize the virtues of community, spirituality, and austerity, while goals of obtaining individuality, property, and wealth seem greater than ever. This is subject to historical variance, as shown by the experience of the last twenty years. American opinion polls report a swing from nonmaterialist criteria of life-satisfaction in the 1960s to a materialist requisite of such satisfaction in the 1980s. By "materialist," Americans mean accumulation of wealth and goods rather than the means to produce goods, as the term once implied. A telling sign, for instance, was the recommendation in 1985 to abolish Boston University's artisan program. "The program got started in the '70s when there was a 'back to nature movement' and lots of people wanted to be self-sufficient artisans," the university's president commented. "The appeal of this has waned in the '80s," he continued, "The rat race is more appealing to students now."[6] Or, even more popularly put, Madonna hit the top of the record charts in 1985 singing the message, "We are living in a material world, and I am a material girl."

Still, the viewing of artisans' works is gaining ground as state folk art exhibits and connoisseur magazines increase by leaps and bounds. Among the most popular films of 1985 were those depicting the conflict of traditional and modern values: *Country, Witness, Places in the Heart, The River.* and still strong in the history of ideas is Richard Hofstadter's thesis that the more commercial American society became, the more reason it found to cling in imagination to noncommercial agrarian values. Becoming a visual mass society, Americans sought the feeling of separate identities, many inspired by folk culture.

What lies ahead? We can find signs in what Americans do in today's commercial society. They work predominantly in service and information fields. Although these fields do not result in the production of goods, by encouraging consumption they feed into the most materialist of attitudes and the further mythologizing of folk culture and its tactile things. Service and information arrange and perform things. They remove responsibility from our grasp.[7] For a mass society ready to serve, folk material culture gives tangible reminders of involvement. It involves us with our fundamental parables. The question is, what moral will we draw from them?

Notes

Chapter 1: Grasping Things

1. Alan Dundes, "Seeing is Believing," in *Interpreting Folklore* (Bloomington: Indiana Univ. Press, 1980), 86-92.
2. Erasmus Darwin, *Zoonomia; or, the Laws of Organic Life*, 2 vols. (London: J. Johnson, 1794), 1: 109-11; Sigmund Freud, *Three Essays on the Theory of Sexuality* (1905; reprint, London: Imago, 1949), 60.
3. Harriet L. Rheingold and Carol O. Eckerman, "The Infant Separates Himself from His Mother," *Science* 168 (1970): 78-83.
4. Frank Hamilton Cushing, "Manual Concepts: A Study of the Influence of Hand-Usage on Culture-Growth," *American Anthropologist* 5 (1892): 308.
5. Ashley Montagu, *Touching: The Human Significance of the Skin* (New York: Columbia Univ. Press, 1971), 286-87.
6. Mihaly Csikszentmihalyi and Eugene Rochberg-Halton, *The Meaning of Things: Domestic Symbols and the Self* (Cambridge: Cambridge Univ. Press, 1980), 16.
7. Theodora Kroeber, *Alfred Kroeber: A Personal Configuration* (Berkeley: Univ. of California Press, 1970), 267-68.
8. Cushing, "Manual Concepts," 290.
9. Simon J. Bronner, *Chain Carvers: Old Men Crafting Meaning* (Lexington: Univ. Press of Kentucky, 1985).
10. Susan E. Hirsch, *Roots of the American Working Class: The Industrialization of Crafts in Newark, 1800-1860* (Philadelphia: Univ. of Pennsylvania Press, 1978), 137. For the occupational humor of memos and cartoons, see Alan Dundes and Carl R. Pagter, *Work Hard and You Shall Be Rewarded: Urban Folklore from the Paperwork Empire* (Bloomington: Indiana Univ. Press, 1978); Alan Dundes, "Office Folklore," in *Handbook of American Folklore*, ed. Richard M. Dorson (Bloomington: Indiana Univ. Press, 1983),

115-20; Simon J. Bronner, "Folklore in the Bureaucracy," in *Tools for Management,* ed. Frederick Richmond and Kathy Nazar (Harrisburg: Pennsylvania Evaluation Network, 1984), 45-57.

11. Richard Nelson Bolles, *The Three Boxes of Life* (Berkeley: Ten Speed Press, 1978), 209.

12. Sue Samuelson, "The Cooties Complex," *Western Folklore* 39 (1980): 198-210.

13. Jan Harold Brunvand, *The Vanishing Hitchhiker: American Urban Legends and Their Meanings* (New York: W. W. Norton, 1981); Ronald L. Baker, "The Influence of Mass Culture on Modern Legends," *Southern Folklore Quarterly* 40 (1976): 367-76; Gary Alan Fine, "The Kentucky Fried Rat: Legends and Modern Society," *Journal of the Folklore Institute* 17 (1980): 222-43.

14. Samuel Eliot Morison, *The Oxford History of the American People: Volume Three, 1869-1963* (New York: New American Library, 1972), 488; Marvin Harris, *America Now: The Anthropology of a Changing Culture* (New York: Simon and Schuster, 1981); Richard Wightman Fox and T. J. Jackson Lears, eds., *The Culture of Consumption: Critical Essays in American History, 1880-1980* (New York: Pantheon, 1983); Chandra Mukerjii, *From Graven Images: Patterns of Modern Materialism* (New York: Columbia Univ. Press, 1983).

15. Quoted in Edward P. Alexander, *Museums in Motion: An Introduction to the History and Functions of Museums* (Nashville: American Association for State and Local History, 1979), 73, 92.

16. Montagu, *Touching,* 212; Marshall McLuhan, *Understanding Media: The Extensions of Man,* 2d ed. (New York: New American Library, 1964); Ray Browne, ed., *Children and Television* (Beverly Hills: Sage Publications, 1976); Stephen B. Withey and Ronald P. Abeles, eds., *Television and Social Behavior* (Hillsdale, N.J.: Lawrence Erlbaum Associates, 1980).

17. George Herbert Mead, "The Physical Thing," in *The Philosophy of the Present,* ed. Arthur E. Murphy (1932; reprint, Chicago: Univ. of Chicago Press, 1980), 138.

18. See Robert S. Lynd and Helen Merrell Lynd, *Middletown: A Study in American Culture* (New York: Harcourt, Brace, & World, 1929). For other examples see the discussion of the lure of centeredness offered by cities in Blake McKelvey, *The Urbanization of America, 1860-1915* (New Brunswick, N.J.: Rutgers Univ. Press, 1963); centeredness in manners is discussed in Karen Halttunen, *Confidence Men and Painted Women: A Study of Middle-Class Culture in America, 1830-1870* (New Haven: Yale Univ. Press, 1982); see also relevant comments in Edward Pessen, "The

Egalitarian Myth and the American Social Reality: Wealth, Mobility, and Equality in the 'Era of the Common Man,' " *American Historical Review* 76 (1971): 989-1034.

19. The broadcast was made 12 July 1984. The reference to "over the counter culture" comes from H.L. Nieburg, *Culture Storm: Politics and the Ritual Order* (New York: St. Martin's Press, 1973), 1-2. The chocolate chip metaphor is discussed in H.L. Nieburg, "Structure of the American Public," *Journal of American Culture* 7 (1984): 49-56. For the importance of culture to modern politics, see Byron E. Shafer, "The New *Cultural* Politics," *PS* 18 (1985): 221-31.

20. Richard Parker, *The Myth of the Middle Class: Notes on Affluence and Equality* (New York: Liveright, 1972); Bernard Sternsher, *Consensus, Conflict, and American Historians* (Bloomington: Indiana Univ. Press, 1975), 235.

21. Michael Zuckerman. "Myth and Method: The Current Crises in American Historical Writing," *History Teacher* 17 (1984): 219-45.

22. Henry Glassie, "Folkloristic Study of the American Artifact: Objects and Objectives," in *Handbook of American Folklore,* ed. Richard M. Dorson (Bloomington: Indiana Univ. Press, 1983), 381.

23. Alan Dundes, "The Number Three in American Culture," in *Interpreting Folklore* (Bloomington: Indiana Univ. Press, 1980), 134-59.

24. Alan Dundes, "Thinking Ahead: A Folkloristic Reflection of the Future Orientation in American Worldview," in *Interpreting Folklore,* 69-85; Louis C. Gawthrop, *Administrative Politics and Social Change* (New York: St. Martin's Press, 1971). Incrementalism in small groups is discussed in Simon J. Bronner, " 'Who Says?': A Further Investigation of Ritual Insults Among White American Adolescents," *Midwestern Journal of Language and Folklore* 4 (1978): 53-69.

25. Charles Kay Ogden, *Opposition: A Linguistic and Psychological Analysis* (Bloomington: Indiana Univ. Press, 1967); Henry Glassie, "Folk Art," in *Folklore and Folklife: An Introduction,* ed. Richard M. Dorson (Chicago: Univ. of Chicago Press, 1972), 272-74.

26. Alexander, *Museums in Motion,* 189; Amos Rapoport, *House Form and Culture* (Englewood Cliffs, N.J.: Prentice-Hall, 1969); Colin Duly, *The Houses of Mankind* (New York: Thames & Hudson, 1979).

27. Archie Green, "Interpreting Folklore Ideologically," in *Handbook of American Folklore,* ed. Richard M. Dorson (Bloomington: Indiana Univ. Press, 1983), 351-58; J.L. Dillard, *Black English: Its History and Usage in the United States* (New York: Random House, 1973); Michael Owen Jones, "A Feeling for Form, as Illustrated by People at Work," in *Folklore on Two Continents,* ed. Nikolai Bur-

lakoff and Carl Lindahl (Bloomington, Ind.: Trickster Press, 1980), 260-69; Shafer, "The New *Cultural* Politics," 221-31; David E. Whisnant, *All That Is Native and Fine: The Politics of Culture in an American Region* (Chapel Hill: Univ. of North Carolina Press, 1983).

28. Nicholas Lobkowicz, *Theory and Practice: History of a Concept from Aristotle to Marx* (Notre Dame: Univ. of Notre Dame Press, 1967); Gunnar Skirbekk, ed., *Praxeology* (Bergen: Universitetsforlaget, 1983); Robert S. Cohen and Marx W. Wartofsky, eds., *Praxis* (Boston: D. Reidel, 1979); Richard Kilminster, *Praxis and Method* (London: Routledge & Kegan Paul, 1979); Marshall Sahlins, *Culture and Practical Reason* (Chicago: Univ. of Chicago Press, 1976);

29. Richard Bernstein, *Praxis and Action: Contemporary Philosophies of Human Activity* (Philadelphia: Univ. of Pennsylvania Press, 1971), 306.

30. Mary Douglas and Baron Isherwood, *The World of Goods: Towards an Anthropology of Consumption* (New York: W.W. Norton, 1979), 4; William Burnell Waits, Jr., "The Many-Faced Custom: Christmas Gift-Giving in America, 1900-1940" (Ph.D. diss., Rutgers University, 1978); Alan Dundes, "Christmas as a Reflection of American Culture," *California Monthly* 78 (1967): 9-15; Sue Samuelson, "Festive Malaise and Festive Participation: A Case Study of Christmas Celebrations in America" (Ph.D. diss., University of Pennsylvania, 1983).

31. Glassie, "Folkloristic Study of the American Artifact," 381.

32. George Herbert Mead, "Mind Approached through Behavior— Can Its Study Be Made Scientific?" in *George Herbert Mead on Social Psychology,* ed. Anselm Strauss (Chicago: Univ. of Chicago Press, 1964), 81.

33. Sahlins, *Culture and Practical Reason,* viii.

Chapter 2: Entering Things

1. *Ellettsville Farm,* 12 September 1896.

2. Erving Goffman, *The Presentation of Self in Everyday Life* (Garden City, N.Y.: Doubleday Anchor Books, 1959).

3. Yi-Fu Tuan, "Moral Ambiguity in Architecture," *Landscape* 27 (1983): 15.

4. Henry Glassie, *Pattern in the Material Folk Culture of the Eastern United States* (Philadelphia: Univ. of Pennsylvania Press, 1968), 78-79.

5. William Lynwood Montell and Michael Lynn Morse, *Kentucky Folk*

Architecture (Lexington: Univ. Press of Kentucky, 1976), 37. By contrast, the hollows of Knott County, for example, never witnessed much building beyond the double-pen. See Charles E. Martin, *Hollybush: Folk Building and Social Change in an Appalachian Community* (Knoxville: Univ. of Tennessee Press, 1984).

6. Henry Glassie, *Folk Housing in Middle Virginia* (Knoxville: Univ. of Tennessee Press, 1975), 134.

7. Grace Heffelfinger, "The I House: An Architectural Form in Rockbridge County, Virginia" (M.A. thesis, Cooperstown Graduate Programs of the State University of New York, 1972).

8. *Ellettsville Farm,* 7 March 1929.

9. See Daniel T. Rodgers, *The Work Ethic in Industrial America, 1850-1920* (Chicago: Univ. of Chicago Press, 1974), 65-93; Alan Trachtenberg, *The Incorporation of America: Culture and Society in the Gilded Age* (New York: Hill & Wang, 1982), 38-69; Thorstein Veblen, *The Instinct of Workmanship; and the State of the Industrial Arts* (1914; reprint, New York: Augustus M. Kelley, 1964); Herbert Guitman, "Work, Culture, and Society in Industrializing America, 1815-1919," *American Historical Review* 78 (1973): 531-88; Hagley Museum and the Henry Francis du Pont Winterthur Museum, *Technological Innovation and the Decorative Arts* (Wilmington Del.: Eleutherian Mills-Hagley Foundation, 1973).

10. Jack Goody, *The Domestication of the Savage Mind* (Cambridge: Cambridge Univ. Press, 1977), 111.

11. Blake McKelvey, *The Urbanization of America, 1860-1915* (New Brunswick, N.J.: Rutgers Univ. Press, 1963), 19.

12. Maud C. Cooke, *Social Culture; or, Our Manners, Conversation and Dress* (Philadelphia: World Bible House, 1896), 19-20.

13. See Karen Halttunen, *Confidence Men and Painted Women: A Study of Middle-Class Culture in America, 1830-1870* (New Haven: Yale Univ. Press, 1982).

14. Tuan, "Moral Ambiguity in Architecture," 15.

15. *Our Manners at Home and Abroad* (Harrisburg: Pennsylvania Publishing Co., 1883), 3.

16. Ibid., 4.

17. Arthur M. Schlesinger, *Learning How to Behave: A Historical Study of American Etiquette Books* (1946; reprint, New York: Cooper Square Publishers, 1968), 51. See also Arthur M. Schlesinger, *The Rise of the City* (New York: Macmillan, Co. 1933); Gerald Carson, *The Polite Americans* (New York: William Morrow, 1966), 166-200; Esther B. Aresty, *The Best Behavior: The Course of Good Manners* (New York: Simon and Schuster, 1970); Yi-Fu Tuan, *Segmented Worlds and Self: Group Life and Individual Con-*

sciousness (Minneapolis: Univ. of Minnesota Press, 1982), 35-51; Russell Lynes, *The Domesticated Americans* (New York: Harper & Row, 1963).

18. Sarah Josepha Hale, *Manners; or, Happy Homes and Good Society* (Boston: J.E. Tilton, 1868), 5. Another preceptor, George W. Hervey, wrote: "And these who are not to be recalled to duty by witnessing the sad effects of disorder, ought at least to feel some respect for the divine command" and "Disorder, being a mark of insanity, those professors, who are addicted to it in their devotional exercises, expose themselves to the imputation of mental derangement" in *The Principles of Courtesy: With Hints and Observations of Manners and Habits* (New York: Harper & Brothers, 1852), 107, 114.

19. Schlesinger, *Learning How to Behave,* 65.

20. Examples of popular folklore collections are Lillian Eichler, *The Customs of Mankind: With Notes on Modern Etiquette and the Newest Trend in Entertainment* (Garden City, N.Y.: Doubleday, 1924); Leopold Wagner, *Manners, Customs, and Observances: Their Origin and Signification* (London: William Heinemann, 1894); William S. Walsh, *Curiosities of Popular Customs and of Rites, Ceremonies, Observances, and Miscellaneous Antiquities* (Philadelphia: J.B. Lippincott, 1898); James A. Farrer, *Primitive Manners and Customs* (London: Chatto & Windus, 1879).

21. Harriet Goldstein and Vetta Goldstein, *Art in Every Day Life* (1925; rev. ed., New York: Macillan, 1932), 1; Joseph Hudnut, "The Post-Modern House," in *Roots of Contemporary American Architecture,* ed. Lewis Mumford (New York: Grove Press, 1959), 309-10.

22. Clifford Geertz, "Art as a Cultural System," *Modern Language Notes* 91 (1976): 1499. For further discussion of how designing within a system entails change, see Herbert A. Simon, *The Sciences of the Artificial* (Cambridge: MIT Press, 1966), 55; George Kubler, *The Shape of Time: Remarks on the History of Things* (New Haven: Yale Univ. Press, 1962), 62-82.

23. Frank J. Scott, *The Art of Beautifying Suburban Home Grounds* (New York: D. Appleton, 1870), 14.

24. Goldstein and Goldstein, *Art in Every Day Life,* 4, 505.

25. Walter R. Houghton, *Rules of Etiquette and Home Culture* (Chicago: Rand-McNally, 1884), 37; Hale, *Manners,* 81.

26. Graham R. Taylor, *Satellite Cities: A Study of Industrial Suburbs* (New York: D. Appleton, 1915), 194. For commentary on the relation of worker and suburban housing, see Gwendolyn Wright, *Building the Dream: A Social History of Housing in America* (Cambridge: MIT Press, 1983). For the democratizing character of suburban housing, see the introduction by Clinton Rogers Woodruff to

Taylor's *Satellite Cities*. This argument is also implicit in Daniel Boorstin's *The Americans: The Democratic Experience* (New York: Random House, Vintage Books, 1974), 281-91, 346-58.

27. See Alan Gowans, *Images of American Living* (1964; reprint, New York: Harper & Row, 1976), 429-44; Tom Wolfe, *From Bauhaus to Our House* (New York: Farrar, Straus & Giroux, 1981); Roger A. Clouser, "The Ranch House in America" (Ph.D. diss., University of Kansas, 1984).

28. See Roger L. Welsch, "Front Door, Back Door," *Natural History* 8 (June-July 1979): 76-82; Paul Oliver, Ian Davis, and Ian Bentley, *Dunroamin: The Suburban Semi and Its Enemies* (London: Barrie & Jenkins, 1981).

29. William Hubbard, "The Meaning of Buildings," *New Republic* 185 (18 Nov. 1981): 29. Generational relations are also briefly discussed in Boorstin, *Americans,* 290-91; Dennis P. Sobin, *The Future of the American Suburbs* (Port Washington, N.Y.: Kennikat Press, 1971), 79-82; Ernest R. Mowrer, "The Family in Suburbia," in *The Suburban Community,* ed. William N. Dobriner (New York: G.P. Putnam's Sons, 1958), 147-64.

30. These comments were made to me in December 1981 in Great Neck, New York. For further discussion of alteration in modern housing and its relation to folk art and folk studies, see Michael Owen Jones, "L.A. Add-ons and Re-dos: Renovation in Folk Art and Architectural Design," in *Perspectives on American Folk Art,* ed. Ian M.G. Quimby and Scott T. Swank (New York: W.W. Norton, 1980), 325-63; Sara Selene Faulds, " 'The Spaces in Which We Live': The Role of Folkloristics in the Urban Design Process," *Folklore and Mythology Studies* 5 (1981): 48-59.

31. See Cynthia Golomb Dettelbach, *In the Driver's Seat: The Automobile in American Literature and Popular Culture* (Westport, Conn.: Greenwood Press, 1976); James J. Flink, *The Car Culture* (Cambridge: MIT Press, 1975); John A. Kouwenhoven, *The Beer Can by the Highway* (Garden City, N.Y.: Doubleday, 1961); Priscilla Denby, "Self Discovered: The Car as Symbol in American Folklore and Literature" (Ph.D. diss., Indiana University, 1981); Stewart Sanderson, "Folklore of the Motor-Car," *Folklore* 80 (1969): 241-52; Michael Licht, "Some Automotive Play Activities of Suburban Teenagers," *New York Folklore Quarterly* 30 (1974): 44-65.

32. See Mary Shaw Ryan, *Clothing: A Study in Human Behavior* (New York: Holt, Rinehart & Winston, 1966), 57-80; William H. Form and Gregory P. Stone, *The Social Significance of Clothing in Occupational Life* (East Lansing: Michigan State College, 1955); Marilyn J. Horn, *The Second Skin: An Interdisciplinary Study of*

Clothing (Boston: Houghton Mifflin, 1975); J.C. Flugel, *The Psychology of Clothes* (London: Hogarth Press, 1930); Stewart Culin, "Creation in Art: An Introductory Lecture in a Course on Costume Design," *Brooklyn Museum Quarterly* 11 (1924): 91-100; Don Yoder, "Folk Costume" in *Folklore and Folklife: An Introduction,* ed. Richard M. Dorson (Chicago: Univ. of Chicago Press, 1972), 295-324.

33. See Yi-Fu Tuan, *Space and Place: The Perspective of Experience* (Minneapolis: Univ. of Minnesota Press, 1977), 169-78; "Certain New York Houses," *Harper's New Monthly Magazine* 65 (1882): 680-90.

34. Examples from England and Sweden are found in Oliver, Davis, and Bentley, *Dunroamin* (England); John Burnett, *A Social History of Housing, 1815-1970* (Newton Abott, England: David & Charles, 1978); and Orvar Lofgren, "On the Anatomy of Culture," *Ethnologia Europaea* 13 (1981): 26-46 (Sweden). The case for America is made in Wright, *Building the Dream,* 240-61.

35. Peter O. Muller, "Everyday Life in Suburbia: A Review of Changing Social and Economic Forces that Shape Daily Rhythms within the Outer City," *American Quarterly* 34 (1982): 262-77.

36. Constance Y. Bramson, "Urban Renaissance: Penn Street Rowhomes Exemplify the Fine Art of Recycling Houses," Harrisburg, Pa., *Patriot-News* (15 May 1983), G1.

37. Names for residents in this chapter are fictitious.

38. Ira Katznelson, *City Trenches* (New York: Pantheon Books, 1981). For further discussion of armature in material culture, see John R. Stilgoe, *Common Landscape of America, 1580 to 1845* (New Haven: Yale Univ. Press, 1982), 256-62.

39. See Clarence Cook, *The House Beautiful* (1878; reprint, Croton-on-Hudson, N.Y.: North River Press, 1980); Elizabeth Stillinger, *The Antiquers* (New York: Alfred A. Knopf, 1980), 56-60; Christopher Tunnard and Henry Hope Reed, *American Skyline: The Growth and Form of Our Cities and Towns* (Boston: Houghton Mifflin, 1956).

40. Historical information taken from Michael Barton, *Life by the Moving Road: An Illustrated History of Harrisburg* (Woodland Hills, Calif.: Windsor Publications, 1983); William H. Wilson, " 'More Almost than the Men': Mira Lloyd Dock and the Beautification of Harrisburg," *Pennsylvania Magazine of History and Biography* 99 (1975): 490-99; idem, "Harrisburg's Successful City Beautiful Movement, 1900-1915," *Pennsylvania History* 47 (1980): 213-33.

41. Barton, *Life By the Moving Road,* 128.

42. Claude Lévi-Strauss, *The Savage Mind* (Chicago: Univ. of Chicago Press, 1966); Glassie, *Folk Housing in Middle Virginia,* 73.

43. "Foreword," in *Back to the City: Issues in Neighborhood Renovation,* ed. Shirley Bradway Laska and Daphne Spain (New York: Pergamon Press, 1980, ix.

44. See Laska and Spain, *Back to the City,* 95-219; J.E. Vance, Jr., "Institutional Forces that Shape the City," in *Social Areas in Cities: Processes, Patterns and Problems,* ed. D.T. Herbert and R.J. Johnston (New York: John Wiley & Sons, 1978), 97-126.

45. Marissa Piesman and Marilee Hartley, *The Yuppie Handbook: The State-of-the-Art Manual for Young Urban Professionals* (New York: Pocket Books, 1984).

46. Barton, *Life by the Moving Road,* 127.

47. For more discussion of antimodernist behavior, see Jackson Lears, *No Place of Grace: Antimodernism and the Transformation of American Culture, 1880-1920* (New York: Pantheon Books, 1984).

48. Alice Gray Read, "Making a House a Home: Renovation in a Philadelphia Neighborhood" (Paper delivered at the Vernacular Architecture Forum Annual Meeting, Newark, Del., 1984). The back-to-the-city movement in Philadelphia is covered in Paul R. Levy and Roman A. Cybriwsky, "The Hidden Dimensions of Culture and Class: Philadelphia," in *Back to the City,* ed. Laska and Spain, 138-55. Similarities can also be drawn between Cal's work on his house and "environments" illustrated in Seymour Rosen, *In Celebration of Ourselves* (San Francisco: California Living Books, 1979).

49. Lewis Mumford, *The Culture of Cities* (New York: Harcourt, Brace & World, 1938), 403. A significant standpoint for my argument for the symbolic communication of housing from the perspective of an ethnologist is that of Ann Louis Gjesdal Christensen, "Dwellings as Communication," *Ethnologia Scandinavica* 9 (1979): 68-88. See also Henry Glassie, "Artifact and Culture, Architecture and Society," in *American Material Culture and Folklife,* ed. Simon J. Bronner (Ann Arbor, Mich.: UMI Research Press, 1985), 47-62; Paul Oliver, ed., *Shelter, Sign and Symbol* (London: Barrie & Jenkins, 1975); idem, *Shelter and Society* (London: Barrie & Rockliff, 1969); Amos Rapoport, *House Form and Culture* (Englewood Cliffs, N.J.: Prentice-Hall, 1969).

50. Tuan, "Moral Ambiguity in Architecture," 12. The concept of housing classes is covered in John Rex and Robert Moore, *Race, Community and Conflict* (Oxford: Oxford Univ. Press, 1967); Colin Belland Howard Newby, "Community, Communion, Class and Community Action: The Social Sources of the New Urban Politics,"

in *Social Areas in Cities: Processes, Patterns, and Problems,* ed. D.T. Herbert and R.J. Johnston (New York: John Wiley & Sons, 1978), 283-302.

51. Tuan, "Moral Ambiguity in Architecture," 12.

52. Elizabeth Collins Cromley, "Modernizing; or, 'You Never See a Screen Door on Affluent Homes,' " *Journal of American Culture* 5 (1982): 71-79.

Chapter 3: Making Things

1. See Kathleen Neils Conzen, "Community Studies, Urban History, and American Local History," in *The Past Before Us: Contemporary Historical Writing in the United States,* ed. Michael Kammen (Ithaca, N.Y.: Cornell Univ. Press, 1980), 270-91; Barbara Allen and William Lynwood Montell, *From Memory to History: Using Oral Sources in Local Historical Research* (Nashville: American Association for State and Local History, 1981); Thomas E. Felt, *Researching, Writing, and Publishing Local History* (Nashville: American Association for State and Local History, 1976); Michael Kammen, "The American Revolution Bicentennial and the Writing of Local History," *History News* 30 (1975): 179-90; Thomas Schlereth, *Artifacts and the American Past* (Nashville: American Association for State and Local History, 1980).

2. David Russo, *Families and Communities: A New View of American History* (Nashville: American Association for State and Local History, 1974); Carl N. Degler, "Women and the Family," in *The Past Before Us,* ed. Kammen, 308-26; Daniel T. Rodgers, *The Work Ethic in Industrial America, 1850-1920* (Chicago: Univ. of Chicago Press, 1974).

3. Russo, 299-300; Alan Trachtenberg, *The Incorporation of America: Culture and Society in the Gilded Age* (New York: Hill & Wang, 1982); Richard D. Brown, "Modernization: A Victorian Climax," in *Victorian America,* ed. Daniel Walker Howe (Philadelphia: Univ. of Pennsylvania Press, 1976), 29-44; Robert H. Wiebe, *The Search for Order, 1877-1920* (New York: Hill & Wang, 1967); Samuel P. Hays, *The Response to Industrialism, 1885-1914* (Chicago: Univ. of Chicago Press, 1957).

4. Roger Abrahams, "Toward a Sociological Theory of Folklore: Performing Services," in *Working Americans: Contemporary Approaches to Occupational Folklife,* ed. Robert H. Byington (Los Angeles: California Folklore Society, 1978), 19-42; Michael Owen Jones, "A Feeling for Form, as Illustrated by People at Work," in *Folklore on Two Continents,* ed. Nikolai Burlakoff and Carl Lindahl (Bloomington, Ind.: Trickster Press, 1980), 260-69; Stanley H. Udy,

Jr., *Work in Traditional and Modern Society* (Englewood Cliffs, N.J.: Prentice-Hall, 1970); Herbert Gutman, "Work, Culture, and Society in Industrializing America, 1815-1919," *American Historical Review* 78 (1973): 531-88.

5. Lawrence Chenoweth, *The American Dream of Success: The Search for the Self in the Twentieth Century* (North Scituate, Mass.: Duxbury Press, 1974).

6. Trachtenberg, *The Incorporation of America,* 216.

7. William I. Knapp, "Address of Welcome on Behalf of the Chicago Folk-Lore Society," in *The International Folk-Lore Congress of the World's Columbian Exposition,* ed. Helen Wheeler Bassett and Frederick Starr (Chicago: Charles H. Sergel Co., 1898), 24.

8. "German Emigration," *Chamber's Edinburgh Journal,* 20 June 1846, 387-89.

9. Louise Sonderman, ed., *This, Our Town: Jasper, Indiana (Jasper: Jasper Centennial Corp., 1966).*

10. Kenneth L. Ames, "Ideologies in Stone: Meanings in Victorian Gravestones," *Journal of Popular Culture* 14 (1981): 641-50.

11. Sonderman, *This, Our Town,* 83.

12. Rhys Isaac, *The Transformation of Virginia, 1740-1790* (Chapel Hill: Univ. of North Carolina Press, 1982), 122.

13. Maud C. Cooke, *Social Culture; or, Our Manners, Conversation and Dress* (Philadelphia: World Bible House, 1896), 323.

14. See Karen Halttunen, *Confidence Men and Painted Women: A Study of Middle-Class Culture in America, 1830-1870* (New Haven: Yale Univ. Press, 1982), 124-52; Ann Douglas, *The Feminization of American Culture* (New York: Avon Books, 1978), 240-72; Harvey Green, *The Light of Home: An Intimate View of the Lives of Women in Victorian America* (New York: Pantheon, 1983), 165-79; Martha Pike, "In Memory Of: Artifacts Relating to Mourning in Nineteenth Century America," *Journal of American Culture* 3 (1980): 642-59.

15. Harold R. Shurtleff, *The Log Cabin Myth: A Study of the Early Dwellings of the English Colonists in North America* (1939; reprint, Gloucester, Mass.: Peter Smith, 1967); Robert Gray Gunderson, *The Log-Cabin Campaign* (Lexington: Univ. of Kentucky Press, 1957).

16. Warren Roberts, "Traditional Tools as Symbols: Some Examples from Indiana Tombstones," *Pioneer America: The Journal of Historic American Material Culture* 12 (1980): 54-63; idem, "Folklife Research and Fieldwork: The Tree-Stump Tombstone as Exemplar," in *American Material Culture and Folklife,* ed. Simon J. Bronner (Ann Arbor: UMI Research Press, 1985), 135-44.

17. Francis J. Grund, *The Americans in Their Moral, Social and*

Political Relations, 2 vols. (London: Longman, Rees, Orme, Brown, Green, & Longman, 1837), 2:1-2; *The Complete Works of Ralph Waldo Emerson,* centenary ed., 12 vols. (Boston: Houghton Mifflin, n.d.), 11:297.

18. Henry Mercer, "The Tools of the Nation Maker," *A Collection of Papers Read before the Bucks County Historical Society,* 3 (Riegelsville, Penn.: B.F. Fackenthal, Jr., 1909): 469-81.

19. Ken Fones-Wolf, "Employer Unity and the Crisis of the Craftsman," *Pennsylvania Magazine of History and Biography* 107 (1983): 449-55.

20. E.B. Dewing, *Other People's Houses* (New York: Macmillan, 1909), 335; E.V. Smalley, "The German Element in the United States," *Lippincott's Magazine,* April 1883, 359-63; Ernest Poole, "A Mixing Bowl for Nations," *Everybody's Magazine,* Oct. 1910, 554-55, 562-64; Stanley Feldstein and Lawrence Costello, *The Ordeal of Assimilation: A Documentary History of the White Working Class* (Garden City, N.Y.: Anchor Books, 1974), 143-201; Mercer, "Tools of the Nation-Maker," 476.

21. For examples of active use of such tools, see Hettie Wright Graham, "The Fireside Industries of Kentucky," *Craftsman* 1 (1902): 33-40; Sylvester Baxter, "The Movement for Village Industries," *Handicraft* 1 (1902): 145-68; Allen H. Eaton, *Handicrafts of the Southern Highlands* (1937; reprint, New York: Dover Publications, 1973); John Solomon Otto and Augustus Marion Burns III, "Traditional Agricultural Practices in the Arkansas Highlands," *Journal of American Folklore* 94 (1981): 166-87; Jeannette Lasansky, *Willow, Oak and Rye: Basket Traditions in Pennsylvania* (University Park, Penn.: Keystone Books, 1979).

22. Alice Kessler-Harris, *Out to Work: A History of Wage-Earning Women in the United States* (New York: Oxford Univ. Press, 1982); Rodgers, *The Work Ethic,* 182-209.

23. U.S. Senate, Committee on Education and Labor, *Report upon the Relations between Labor and Capital,* 4 vols. (Washington, D.C., 1885), 2: 549.

24. Thorstein Veblen, *The Instinct of Workmanship, and the State of the Industrial Arts* (1914; reprint, New York: Augustus M. Kelley, 1964), 329.

25. See Edward P. Alexander, *Museums in Motion: An Introduction to the History and Functions of Museums* (Nashville: American Association for State and Local History, 1979), 30-32, 61-76; Jay E. Cantor, "Art and Industry: Reflections on the Role of the American Museum in Encouraging Innovation in the Decorative Arts," in *Technological Innovation and the Decorative Arts,* ed. Ian M. G.

Quimby and Polly Anne Earl (Charlottesville: Univ. Press of Virginia, 1974), 331-54; John Cotton Dana, "The Industrialist Is an Artist," *Museum* 1 (1927): 129-31; Brook Hindle, "Museum Treatment of Industrialization: History, Problems, Opportunities," *Curator* 15 (1972): 206-19; Lord Amulree, "The Museum as an Aid to the Encouragement of Arts, Manufactures, and Commerce," *Museums Journal* 39 (1939): 350-56; C. Howard Walker, "The Museum and the School," *Handicraft* 2 (1903): 29-42.

26. David Dempsey, *The Way We Die: An Investigation of Death and Dying in America Today* (New York: McGraw-Hill, 1975), 193.

27. Anna Bock is a fictitious name used at the artist's request.

28. Quoted in Alan Gowans, *Images of American Living: Four Centuries of Architecture and Furniture as Cultural Expression* (1964; reprint, New York: Harper & Row, 1976), 320.

29. T.F. Crane, "Plantation Folk-lore," *Popular Science Monthly* 18 (1881): 824.

30. Peter C. Welsh, *American Folk Art: The Art and Spirit of a People* (Washington, D.C.: Smithsonian Institution, 1965), 14 (on the familiarity of rural America); Agnes Halsey Jones and Louis C. Jones, *Queena Stovall: Artist of the Blue Ridge Piedmont* (Cooperstown: New York State Historical Association, 1974); William Ferris, *Local Color: A Sense of Place in Folk Art* (New York: McGraw-Hill, 1982), 69-100 (on Theora Hamblett); Otto Kallir, ed., *Grandma Moses* (New York: Harry N. Abrams, 1973).

31. Rebecca D. Rickoff, "The Hand-Work of Children," *Popular Science Monthly* 28 (1886): 812-17.

32. Otis T. Mason, *Woman's Share in Primitive Culture* (New York: D. Appleton, 1894), 2-3.

33. Allen Eaton and Lucinda Crile, *Rural Handicrafts in the United States* (Washington, D.C.: Department of Agriculture, 1946); Eaton, *Handicrafts of the Southern Highlands;* idem, *Handicrafts of New England* (New York: Bonanza Books, 1949).

34. See Harvey Cox, *The Secular City: Secularization and Urbanization in Theological Perspective* (New York: Macmillan, 1965); Henry May, *Protestant Churches and Industrial America* (New York: Harper, 1967); Herbert Gutman, "Protestantism and the American Labor Movement: The Christian Spirit in the Gilded Age," *American Historical Review* 72 (1966): 74-101. Roots of the secular city can be found in nineteenth-century essays such as "The Moral Drift of Our Time," *Christian Union* 27 (31 May 1883): 428-29; "The Decay of the New England Churches," *Nation* 43 (4 Nov. 1886): 367-68; Charles Cuthbert Hale, "The Church: Is it a Social Club— or a Divine Foundation?" *Christian Union* 27 (10 May 1888): 370.

35. John Michael Vlach, *Charleston Blacksmith: The Work of Philip Simmons* (Athens: Univ. of Georgia Press, 1981), 113.

36. Edward Taylor, "Upon What Base?" in *The United States in Literature,* ed. Walter Blair et al. (Glenview, Ill.: Scott, Foresman & Co., 1963), 126.

37. Henry W. Bellows, "Influence of the Trading Spirit upon the Social and Moral Life of America," *American Review* 1 (1845): 96.

38. Edward Lucie-Smith, *The Story of Craft: The Craftsman's Role in Society* (Ithaca, N.Y.: Cornell Univ. Press, 1981),232; Ralph Radcliffe-Whitehead, "A Plea for Manual Work," *Handicraft* 2 (1903): 58-73; George Wharton James, "Indian Handicrafts," *Handicraft* 1 (1903): 269-87; Arthur Spencer, "The Relation of the Arts and Crafts to Progress," *Craftsman* 6 (1904): 570-80.

39. "Religious Statistics," *Nation* 43 (16 Dec. 1886): 494-95.

40. Stewart Culin, "The International Jew" (typescript in Stewart Culin Papers, Brooklyn Museum, Brooklyn, N.Y.). For more discussion of Gaster and Jacobs and the battle between diffusionists and evolutionists, see Richard M. Dorson, *The British Folklorists: A History* (Chicago: Univ. of Chicago Press, 1968); Gary Alan Fine, "Joseph Jacobs: Sociological Folklorist" (Paper delivered at the American Folklore Society Annual Meeting, Minneapolis, 1982).

41. Joseph Le Conte, "The Relation of Evolution to Materialism," *Popular Science Monthly* 33 (1888): 79-86.

42. Edward Clodd, *The Childhood of Religion* (New York: D. Appleton, 1876).

43. Frank Riale, "Why So Many Definitions of Religion?" *Popular Science Monthly* 37 (1890): 348-51.

44. See Dickson D. Bruce, Jr., *And They All Sang Hallelujah: Plain-Folk Camp-Meeting Religion, 1800-1845* (Knoxville: Univ. of Tennessee Press, 1974); David Edwin Harrell, Jr., *All Things Are Possible: The Healing and Charismatic Revivals in Modern America* (Bloomington: Indiana Univ. Press, 1975).

45. Dario Sabbatucci, "Devotional Objects and Images, Popular," *Encyclopedia of World Art* (New York: McGraw-Hill, 1961), col. 364.

46. Geddes MacGregor, *Aesthetic Experience in Religion* (London: MacMillan, 1947), 212.

47. Ibid., 218.

48. Betty MacDowell, "Religion on the Road: Highway Evangelism and Worship Environments for the Traveler in America," *Journal of American Culture* 5 (1982): 70.

49. Hilda Adam Kring, "Religious Symbols in a Symbol-less Society," *Pennsylvania Folklife* 33 (Winter 1983-84), 60.

50. C. Kurt Dewhurst, Betty MacDowell, and Marsha MacDowell,

Religious Folk Art in America: Reflections of Faith (New York: E.P. Dutton, 1983), 100-101.

51. Ibid., 86-87.

52. F. David Martin, *Art and the Religious Experience: The "Language" of the Sacred* (Lewisburg: Bucknell Univ. Press, 1972), 50.

53. Rev. John Baer Stoudt, *The Folklore of the Pennsylvania-German* (Lancaster, Penn.: The Pennsylvania-German Society, 1915).

54. John Joseph Stoudt, *Pennsylvania German Folk Art: An Interpretation* (Allentown, Penn.: Schlechter's, 1966), 124.

55. Isaac, *The Transformation of Virginia,* 320.

Chapter 4: Consuming Things

1. Thomas P. Kettell, "Commerce and Trade," in *Eighty Years' Progress of the United States: A Family Record of American Industry, Energy and Enterprise* (Hartford, Conn.: L. Stebbins, 1868), 159.

2. Thorstein Veblen, *The Theory of the Leisure Class* (1899; reprint, New York: Penguin Books, 1979), 73.

3. Theodore Dreiser, *Sister Carrie* (1900; reprint, Cambridge, Mass.: Riverside Press, 1959), 269.

3. Richard Osborn Cummings, *The American and His Food* (1940; reprint, New York: Arno Press, 1970), 23.

5. Waverly Root and Richard de Rochemont, *Eating in America: A History* (New York: William Morrow and Co. 1976), 21.

6. Richard M. Dorson, ed., *America Begins: Early American Writing* (Bloomington: Indiana Univ. Press, 1971), 89-91.

7. Jane Carson, *Colonial Virginia Cookery* (Charlottesville: Univ. Press of Virginia for Colonial Williamsburg, 1968), 60.

8. Ibid., 60-62.

9. Sam Hilliard, "Hog Meat and Cornpone: Food Habits in the Antebellum South," *Proceedings of the American Philosophical Society* 113 (20 Feb. 1969): 12. For more discussion of Southern diet, see Sam Hilliard, *Hog Meat and Hoecake: Food Supply in the Old South, 1840-1860* (Carbondale: Southern Illinois Univ. Press, 1972).

10. Cummings, *The American and His Food,* 22; Root and Rochemont, *Eating in America,* 83-84.

11. Root and Rochemont, *Eating in America,* 136.

12. Ambrose Heath, *Madame Prunier's Fish Cookery Book* (New York: Julian Messner, 1939), 239.

13. Hennig Cohen and William B. Dillingham, *Humor of the Old Southwest* (Boston: Houghton Mifflin, 1964), 162-68. The consumption of salamanders by a men's fraternity is the subject of a film

produced by folklorist Kenneth Thigpen, *Salamanders* (University Park, Penn.: Documentary Resource Center, 1982).

14. John and Marie Roberson, *The Famous American Recipes Cookbook* (Englewood Cliffs, N.J.: Prentice-Hall, 1957), 16-17.

15. Ruth Berolzeimer, ed., *The American Woman's Cookbook* (Garden City, N.Y.: Doubleday & Co., 1972), 226-27; H. Walton Clark and John B. Southall, "Fresh Water Turtles: A Source of Meat Supply," United States Bureau of Fisheries Document 889, *Report of the United States Commissioner of Fish and Fisheries for 1919* (Washington, D.C.: Government Printing Office, 1920). App. 7, 1-29; Frederick W. True, "Useful Aquatic Reptiles and Batrachians of the United States," United States Commission for Fish and Fisheries Report, *Fisheries and Fishery Industries of the United States* (Washington, D.C.: Government Printing Office, 1893), 141-62. Regional market assessments are reported in Robert J. Schoffman, "Turtling for the Market at Reelfoot Lake," *Journal of the Tennessee Academy of Science* 24 (1949): 243-45; Karl F. Lagler, "Economic Relations and Utilization of Turtles," *Investigations of Indiana Lakes and Streams* 3 (1945): 139-65.

16. Marjorie Kinnan Rawlings, *Cross Creek Cookery* (New York: Charles Scribner's Sons, 1942), 126-29; Eliot Wigginton, ed., *The Foxfire Book* (Garden City, N.Y.: Anchor Books, 1972), 273: Jack and Olivia Solomon, *Cracklin Bread and Asfidity: Folk Recipes and Remedies* (University: Univ. of Alabama Press, 1979), 80; Roberson, *The Famous American Recipes Cookbook*, 17 (Maryland); *Food for Thought: An Ethnic Cookbook* (Lexington, Ky.: Fayette Urban County Human Rights Commission, 1976), 72-73; Leonard Roberts, "The Big Turtle," *Kentucky Folklore Record* 8 (1962): 9-14.

17. Thomas A. Adler, *"Sunday Breakfast Was Always Special With Us": A Report on Foodways in South Central Georgia* (Bloomington, Ind.: Folklore Publications Group, Folklore Preprint Series, 1979), 48.

18. Ibid., 54.

19. Thomas A. Adler, "Making Pancakes on Sunday: The Male Cook in Family Tradition," in *Foodways and Eating Habits: Directions for Research*, ed. Michael Owen Jones, Bruce Giuliano, Roberta Krell (Los Angeles: California Folklore Society, 1981), 45-54.

20. Root and Rochemont, *Eating in America*, 200.

21. C. Paige Gutierrez, "The Social and Symbolic Uses of Ethnic/ Regional Foodways: Cajuns and Crawfish in South Louisiana," in *Ethnic and Regional Foodways in the United States: The Performance of Group Identity*, ed. Linda Keller Brown and Kay Mussell (Knoxville: Univ. of Tennessee Press, 1984), 180.

22. Mrs. John Sherwood, *Manners and Social Usages* (New York: Harper & Brothers, 1900), 270.

23. Walter A. Dyer, *The Lure of the Antique* (New York: Century Co., 1910), 8.

24. Harold Donaldson Eberlein and Abbot McClure, *The Practical Book of American Antiques* (1916; reprint, New York: Da Capo Press, 1977), 261; Roger Hinks, "The Superstition of the Antique," *Museum* 2 (Sept. 1928), 10.

25. Alan Axelrod, ed., *The Colonial Revival in America* (New York: W.W. Norton, 1985); Virgil Barker, "Notes on the Exhibition," *Arts* (March 1924), 161.

26. Catherine E. Beecher and Harriet Beecher Stowe, *American Woman's Home* (1869; reprint, Hartford, Conn.: Stowe-Day Foundation, 1975), 91-92; Ella Shannon Bowles, *Homespun Handicrafts* (Philadelphia: J.B. Lippincott, 1931); Harvey Green, *The Light of Home: An Intimate View of the Lives of Women in Victorian America* (New York: Pantheon Books, 1983), 93-111; Francis Lichten, *Decorative Art of Victoria's Era* (New York: Charles Scribner's Sons, 1950), 151-66.

27. Dyer, *The Lure of the Antique*, 4; Eberlein and McClure, *The Practical Book of American Antiques*, i.

28. R.T.H. Halsey and Elizabeth Tower, *The Homes of Our Ancestors: As Shown in the American Wing of the Metropolitan Museum of Art of New York* (Garden City, N.Y.: Doubleday, Doran & Co., 1924), xxii.

29. See Otis Mason, "The Natural History of Folk-Lore," *Journal of American Folklore* 4 (1891): 103; Alfred C. Haddon, *Evolution in Art: As Illustrated by the Life-Histories of Designs* (New York: Charles Scribner's Sons, 1895); Stewart Culin, "Primitive American Art," *University Bulletin* 4 (1900): 191-96; idem, "The Origins of Ornament," *Free Museum of Science and Art Bulletin* 2 (1900): 235-43; A.D.F. Hamlin, *A History of Ornament* (New York: Century Co. 1916); Franz Boas, *Primitive Art* (1927); reprint, New York: Dover Publications, 1955).

30. See Edwin Atlee Barber, *Tulip Ware of the Pennsylvania German Potters: An Historical Sketch of Slip Decoration in the United States* (1903; reprint, New York: Dover Publications, 1970); Henry C. Mercer, *The Decorated Stove Plates of the Pennsylvania Germans* (Doylestown, Penn.: Bucks County Historical Society, 1899); idem, "The Survival of the Mediaeval Art of Illuminative Writing among Pennsylvania Germans," *Proceedings of the American Philosophical Society* 26 (Dec. 1897): 424-33; Earl F. Robacker, "The Rise of Interest in Folk Art," *Pennsylvania Folklife* 10 (Spring 1959):

20-29; Scott T. Swank, *Arts of the Pennsylvania Germans* (New York: W.W. Norton for the Henry Francis du Pont Winterthur Museum, 1983).

31. Albert Hastings Pitkin, *Early American Folk Pottery* (Hartford, Conn.: Mrs. Albert Hastings Pitkin, 1918), 88.

32. Allen H. Eaton, *Immigrant Gifts to American Life* (New York: Russell Sage Foundation, 1932); idem, "American Folk Arts," *Studio* 27 (June 1944): 201-203; Allen H. Eaton and Shelby M. Harrison, *A Bibliography of Social Surveys* (New York: Russell Sage Foundation, 1930); John Glenn, Lillian Brandt, F. Emerson Andrews, "Arts and Social Work: 1932-1946," in *Russell Sage Foundation, 1907-1946*, 2 vols. (New York: Russell Sage Foundation, 1947), 2: 584-97. For accounts of the Homeland exhibit, see "Exhibition of the Arts and Crafts of the Homelands at the Albright Art Gallery," *Academy Notes* 15 (1920): 18-28; "Homeland Art Exhibit Welds Racial Spirit," *Buffalo News*, 18 Oct. 1919; "An Exhibition That was Vital," *Christian Science Monitor*, 17 Nov. 1919. Differences between the "folk" of folklore and "folk" of folk art are discussed in Howard S. Becker, *Art Worlds* (Berkeley: Univ. of California Press, 1982), 246-71.

33. Examples of guides are Alice Morse Earle, *China Collecting in America* (New York: Charles Scribner's Sons, 1892); N. Hudson Moore, *The Old China Book* (New York: Frederick A. Stokes, 1903); idem, *The Old Furniture Book* (New York: Frederick A. Stokes, 1903); Robert and Elizabeth Shackleton, *The Charm of the Antique* (New York: Hearst's International Library Co. 1913); Francis Hill Bigelow, *Historic Silver of the Colonies and Its Makers* (New York: Macmillan, 1917); Arthur H. Hayward, *Colonial Lighting* (Boston: Little, Brown & Co., 1923); Nancy McClelland, *The Practical Book of Decorative Wall-Treatments* (Philadelphia: J.B. Lippincott, 1926); Henry H. Saylor, ed., *Collecting Antiques for the Home* (New York: Robert M. McBride & Co., 1938); for histories of antiques collecting, see Elizabeth Stillinger, *The Antiquers* (New York: Alfred A. Knopf, 1980), 165-70; Marshall B. Davidson, "Those American Things," *Metropolitan Museum Journal* 3 (1970): 219-33; Douglas and Elizabeth Rigby, *Lock, Stock and Barrel: The Story of Collecting* (Philadelphia: J.B. Lippincott, 1944). Francis Lichten, *Folk Art of Rural Pennsylvania* (New York: Charles Scribner's Sons, 1946), v.

34. Stewart Culin, "The Perfect Collector" (typescript, Stewart Culin papers, Brooklyn Museum). Committee of Graduates at Robinson Hall, School of Architecture, Harvard University, *Harvard Tercentenary Exhibition: Furniture and Decorative Arts of the Period,*

1636-1836 (Catalogue of Furniture, Silver, Pewter, Glass, Ceramics, Paintings, Prints, Together with Allied Arts and Crafts of the Period, 1636-1836) (Cambridge, Mass.: Harvard Univ. Press, 1936); Stillinger, *The Antiquers*, 188-89; Wendy Kaplan, "R.T.H. Halsey: An Ideology of Collecting American Decorative Arts," *Winterthur Portfolio* 17 (1982): 43-53.

35. W.D. MacColl, "The International Exhibition of Modern Art"; Kenyon Cox, "The 'Modern' Spirit in Art"; Royal Cortissoz, "The Post-Impressionist Illusion" reprinted in *The Call of the Wild (1900-1916)*, ed. Roderick Nash (New York: George Braziller, 1970), 171-84.

36. Charles Messer Stow, "Primitive Art in America," *Antiquarian* 8 (May 1927), 20-24.

37. Paradoxes of the Victorian Protestant middle-class woman are discussed in Kenneth L. Ames, "Material Culture as Non-Verbal Communication: A Historical Case Study," *Journal of American Culture* 3 (1980): 619-41; Green, *The Light of Home*, 112-43. Edith Gregor Halpert, "Folk Art in America Now Has a Gallery of Its Own," *Art Digest* 6 (1 Oct. 1931), 3.

38. Marion Nicholl Rawson, *Candleday Art* (New York: E.P. Dutton, 1938), 24.

39. Preston A. Barba, *Pennsylvania German Tombstones: A Study in Folk Art* (Allentown, Penn.: Schlecter's for the Pennsylvania German Folklore Society, 1954), 4.

40. Holger Cahill, *American Primitives: An Exhibit of the Paintings of Nineteenth-Century Folk Artists* (Newark, N.J.: Newark Museum, 1931); idem, *American Folk Sculpture: The Work of Eighteenth- and Nineteenth-Century Craftsmen* (Newark, N.J.: Newark Museum, 1931).

41. Holger Cahill, *American Folk Art: The Art of the Common Man in America, 1750-1900* (1932; reprint, New York: Arno Press for the Museum of Modern Art, 1969), 6. For background see John Michael Vlach, "Holger Cahill as Folklorist," *Journal of American Folklore* 98 (1985): 148-62.

42. Beatrix T. Rumford, "Uncommon Art of the Common People: A Review of Trends in the Collecting and Exhibiting of American Folk Art," in *Perspectives on American Folk Art*, ed. Ian M.G. Quimby and Scott T. Swank (New York: W.W. Norton, 1980), 36.

43. William C. Ketchum, "American Folk Art: The View from New York," *Clarion* (Fall 1980), 40-42.

44. Jean Lipman and Alice Winchester, *The Flowering of American Folk Art, 1776-1876* (New York: Viking Press for the Whitney Museum of American Art, 1974), 9. Examples of the criticism are

Eric de Jonge, "The Thing About Folk Art," *National Antiques Review* 4 (Feb. 1972), 10-13; Kenneth L. Ames, *Beyond Necessity: Art in the Folk Tradition* (New York: W.W. Norton for the Henry Francis du Pont Winterthur Museum, 1977); Simon J. Bronner, "Recent Folk Art Publications: A Review Essay," *Mid-South Folklore* 6 (1978): 27-30; John Michael Vlach, "American Folk Art: Questions and Quandaries," *Winterthur Portfolio* 15 (1980): 345-55.

45. "Letter from the Director," *Clarion* (Winter 1983-84), 13.

46. Robert Bishop, "Foreword," *American Folk Art of the Twentieth Century* by Jay Johnson and William C. Ketchum, Jr. (New York: Rizzoli, 1983), ix.

47. Ibid.

48. Robert Bishop, Judith Reiter Weissman, Michael McManus, and Henry Niemann, *Folk Art: Paintings, Sculpture and Country Objects* (New York: Alfred A. Knopf, 1983), 8.

49. Cahill, *American Folk Art*, 27; Bishop et al., *Folk Art*, 11.

50. Ketchum, "The View from New York," 42.

51. Roger Fry, "Culture and Snobbism," in *Transformations: Critical and Speculative Essays on Art* (Garden City, N.Y.: Doubleday, 1956), 81. For further discussion of the Western proclivity for tripartite social stratification represented by "good, better, and best," see Louis Dunmont, "Caste, Racism, and 'Stratification': Reflections of a Social Anthropologist," in *Symbolic Anthropology*, ed. Janet L. Dolgin, David S. Kemnitzer, and David M. Schneider (New York: Columbia Univ. Press, 1977), 72-88; C. Wright Mills, "The Sociology of Stratification," *Power, Politics and People,* ed. Irving Louis Horowitz (London: Oxford Univ. Press, 1974), 305-23; Russell Lynes, "Highbrow, Lowbrow, Middlebrow," in *The Tastemakers: The Shaping of American Popular Taste* (New York: Dover Publications, 1980), 310-33; Alan Dundes, "The Number Three in American Culture," *Interpreting Folklore* (Bloomington: Indiana Univ. Press, 1980), 134-59; Jacques Barzun, "The Arts, The Snobs, and the Democrat," in *Aesthetics Today*, ed. Morris Philipson (New York: World Publishing, 1961), 15-26.

52. Culin, "The Origin of Ornament," 235.

53. Arnold Hauser, "Popular Art and Folk Art," *Dissent* 5 (1958): 237.

55. Alice Winchester, "American Folk Art," *Encyclopedia Americana* (Danbury, Conn.: American Corp. 1979), 11: 495.

56. Louis C. Jones, "Introduction," in *How to Know American Folk Art*, ed. Ruth Andrews (New York: E.P. Dutton, 1977), 13.

57. "Preface," in *Masterpieces of American Folk Art* (Linecroft, N.J.: Monmouth Museum and Monmouth County Historical Association, 1975).

58. Cahill, *American Folk Art*, 3.

59. Jane Kallir, *The Folk Art Tradition: Naive Painting in Europe and the United States* (New York: Galerie St. Etienne and Viking Press, 1981), 8.

60. Ketchum, "The View from New York," 45; Bishop, "Foreword," in *American Folk Art of the Twentieth Century*, x.

61. Eugene W. Metcalf, Jr., "Black Art, Folk Art, and Social Control," *Winterthur Portfolio* 18 (1983): 288.

62. Daniel Robbins, "Folk Sculpture without Folk," in *Folk Sculpture USA*, ed. Herbert W. Hemphill, Jr. (Brooklyn, N.Y.: Brooklyn Museum, 1976), 29-30.

63. Karl E. Myer, *The Art Museum: Power, Money, Ethics* (New York: William Morrow, 1979), 181. The reference to "country chic" was made in a letter of 3 Aug. 1984 from Constance Stapleton, author of *Crafts in America: A Guide to Traditional Crafts . . . . Who Makes Them, Where to Find Them* (New York: Pantheon Books, forthcoming).

64. Ketchum, "The View from New York," 43.

65. Mary Douglas and Baron Isherwood, *The World of Goods: Towards an Anthropology of Consumption* (New York: W.W. Norton, 1979), 75.

66. Robert T. Teske, "What is Folk Art? An Opinion on the Controversy," *El Palacio* 88 (1983): 34-38.

67. Louis C. Jones, "Introduction," in *How to Know American Folk Art*, 6.

68. Aline B. Saarinen, *The Proud Possessors* (New York: Random House, 1958), 288-89. Folk art as a collectible alternative to expensive fine arts is discussed in Robert Bishop, "The Affects and Effects of Collecting: Artists and Objects," *Ohio Antique Review* 10 (Jan. 1984), 13-14.

69. Louis C. Jones, "Introduction," in *How to Know'American Folk Art*, 5.

70. Alice Winchester, "Antiques for the Avant Garde," *Art in America* 51 (Aug. 1963), 53-59; "Living with Antiques: The Cannondale, Connecticut, Home of Mr. and Mrs. Howard Lipman," *Antiques* 72 (June 1957): 542-46; Swank, *Arts of the Pennsylvania Germans*, 79.

71. Louis C. Jones, "Introduction," in *How to Know American Folk Art*, 5. The concept of material accumulation as a status-gaining technique is discussed in Louis Dupré, *Marx's Social Critique of Culture* (New Haven: Yale Univ. Press, 1983), 279-84; Gerald Reitlinger, *The Economics of Taste: The Rise and Fall of the Objects d'Art Market since 1750* (New York: Holt, Rinehart & Winston, 1963); Rigby, *Lock, Stock and Barrel;* Stillinger, *The Antiquers;* Veblen, *Theory of the Leisure Class.*

72. The Rosenaks were lenders to *Black Folk Art in America, 1930-1980* by Jane Livingston and John Beardsley (Jackson: Univ. Press of Mississippi for the Corcoran Gallery of Art, 1982) and *Religious Folk Art in America* by C. Kurt Dewhurst, Betty MacDowell, Marsha MacDowell (New York: E.P. Dutton, 1983). On the metaphor of trade catalogues in American culture, see Fred E.H. Schroeder, "The Wishbook as Popular Icon," in *Outlaw Aesthetics: Arts and the Public Mind* (Bowling Green, Ohio: Bowling Green Univ. Popular Press, 1977), 50-61; idem, "Semi-Annual Installment on the American Dream: The Wishbook as Popular Icon," in *Icons of Popular Culture*, ed. Marshall Fishwick and Ray B. Browne (Bowling Green, Ohio: Bowling Green Univ. Popular Press, 1970), 73-86; Thomas Schlereth, "Mail-Order Catalogs as Resources in Material Culture Studies," in *Artifacts and the American Past* (Nashville: American Association for State and Local History, 1980), 48-65. The metaphor is one of conventionalizing taste for consumption; see Becker, "Conventions," *Art Worlds*, 40-67; Christopher P. Wilson, "The Rhetoric of Consumption: Mass-Market Magazines and the Demise of the Gentle Reader, 1880-1920," in *The Culture of Consumption: Critical Essays in American History, 1880-1980* (New York: Pantheon, 1983), 39-64.
73. Alan Trachtenberg, *The Incorporation of America: Culture and Society in the Gilded Age* (New York: Hill & Wang, 1982), 8.
74. Metcalf, "Black Art, Folk Art, and Social Control," 271.
75. Meyer, *The Art Museum;* Reitlinger, *The Economics of Taste*; Becker, *Art Worlds*, 108-30; Harrison C. White and Cynthia A. White, *Canvases and Careers* (New York: John Wiley, 1965).
76. Marilynn Karp, "The Scholarly Pursuit of American Folk Art," *Clarion* (Winter 1982-83), 23; "Letter from the Director," *Clarion* (Winter 1982-83); Bishop, "Foreword," in *American Folk Art of the Twentieth Century*, vii.
77. Michael Owen Jones, "Folk Art Production and the Folklorist's Obligation," *Journal of Popular Culture* 4 (1970): 207.
78. Maurice Rheims, *The Strange Life of Objects: 35 Centuries of Art Collecting and Collectors* (New York: Atheneum, 1961), 3.

Epilogue

1. "Step-Gables and Clinkers: Birth of the Historic Preservation Idea," *Heritage* 1 (Nov.-Dec. 1984), 1-5.
2. Samuel L. Hynes and Frank D. McConnell, "*The Time Machine* and *The War of the Worlds:* Parable and Possibility in H.G. Wells," in H.G. Wells, *The Time Machine/The War of the Worlds: A Critical*

Edition, ed. Frank D. McConnell (New York: Oxford Univ. Press, 1977), 345-66.

3. See, respectively, Alan Dundes and Carl R. Pagter, *Work Hard and You Shall Be Rewarded* (Bloomington: Indiana Univ. Press, 1978); Gary Alan Fine, "The Goliath Effect: Corporate Dominance and Mercantile Legends," *Journal of American Folklore* 98 (1985): 63-84; Warren Roberts, "Turpin Chairs and the Turpin Family: Chairmaking in Southern Indiana," *Midwestern Journal of Language and Folklore* 7 (1981): 57-106.

4. Maurice Bloch, *Marxism and Anthropology* (Oxford: Clarendon Press, 1983), 155.

5. H.L. Nieburg, "Structure of the American Public," *Journal of American Culture* 7 (1984): 49-56.

6. "Program for Artisans Losing Out to 'Rat Race,'" *Chronicle of Higher Education,* 30 Jan., 1985, 2.

7. Richard Hofstadter, "The Myth of the Happy Yeoman," in *American Vistas: 1877 to the Present,* ed. Leonard Dinnerstein and Kenneth T. Jackson, (New York: Oxford Univ. Press, 1971), 20-32; Marvin Harris, *America Now: The Anthropology of a Changing Culture* (New York: Simon & Schuster, 1981).

Index